THE KINGFISHER
STUDENT ATLAS

KINGFISHER

KINGFISHER
a Houghton Mifflin Company imprint
222 Berkeley Street
Boston, Massachusetts 02116
www.houghtonmifflinbooks.com

Project Management: Picthall & Gunzi Ltd.

For Picthall & Gunzi:
Editor: Margaret Hynes
Designer: Dominic Zwemmer
Place Name Consultant: Roger Bullen
Editorial Assistant: Carmen Hansen
Indexers: Jan Clark, Gill Cooling, Deborah Murrell

For Kingfisher:
Managing Editor: Russell Mclean
Consultant: Dr. Deryck W. Holdsworth, Pennsylvania State University
Coordinating Editor: Stephanie Pliakas
Art Director: Mike Davis
Designer: Carol Ann Davis
DTP Manager: Nicky Studdart
DTP Operator: Primrose Burton
Senior Production Controller: Nancy Roberts
Picture Research Manager: Cee Weston-Baker

Maps designed and produced by Anderson Geographics Limited, Warfield, Berkshire, England

First published by Kingfisher in 2003
1 3 5 7 9 10 8 6 4 2
1TR/0703/TWP/CLSN(CLSN)/130ENSOMA

The publisher would like to thank the following for permission to reproduce their material. Every care has been taken to trace copyright holders. However, if there have been unintentional omissions or failure to trace copyright holders, we apologize and will, if informed, endeavor to make corrections in any future edition.

Key: b = bottom, c = center, l = left, r = right, t = top

6bl Corbis; 8t Lloyd Cuff/Corbis; 8b Lloyd Cuff/Corbis; 9t James A. Sugar/Corbis; 9b Jeff Vanuga/Corbis; 10bc Imagebank/ Getty Images; 10br Imagebank/Getty Images; 11tr Annie Griffiths Belt/National Geographic Image Collection; 12tr Darrell Gulin/Corbis; 12b Laurence Fordyce/Eye Ubiquitous/ Corbis; 13tr Gary Braash/Corbis; 13bl Wolfgang Kaehler/Corbis; 13bc Wolfgang Kaehler/Corbis; 13br DiMaggio/Kalish/Corbis; 14-15 Bill Ross/Corbis; 14bl Adrian Arbib/Corbis; 14br Richard Bickel/Corbis; 15tc Robert Essel NYC/Corbis; 15tr Paul Almasy/Corbis

The publisher would also like to thank the following illustrators for their contribution to this book:
Richard Bonson 11b; Chris Forsey 7tr, 9tr; Jeremy Gower 10bl; Maltings Partnership 8bl; Janos Marphy 6–7

LIBRARY OF CONGRESS CATALOGING-IN-PUBLICATION DATA
Wilkinson, Philip, 1955-
The Kingfisher student atlas / Philip Wilkinson.—1st ed.
p. cm.
Includes index.
Summary: An atlas of physical and political maps of the world, organized by continent.
1. Atlases. [1. Atlases.] I. Title.

G1021.W42 2003
912—dc21
2003055002

ISBN 0-7534-5589-7

Printed in Singapore

THE KINGFISHER
STUDENT
ATLAS

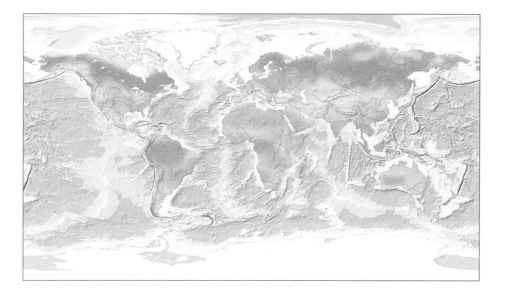

KINGFISHER

BOSTON

CONTENTS

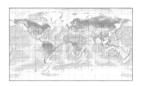

ASIA

AUSTRALASIA AND OCEANIA

KEY TO MAPS

Settlements

■ PARIS	Capital city
● Halifax	Administrative region capital
○ São Paulo	Major town
○ Galway	Other town

Political and cultural regions

MEXICO	Country
Corsica (to France)	Dependent territory
ARIZONA	Internal administrative region
TUSCANY	Cultural region

Boundaries

	International border
	Disputed border
	Internal administrative boundary

Drainage features

Congo	River
Warrego	Seasonal river
Albert Canal	Canal
Angel Falls	Waterfall
Lake Taupo	Lake
Lake Mackay	Seasonal lake

Topographic features

Mont Blanc 15,777 ft.	Spot height of mountain
–28,224 ft.	Spot depth below sea level
Balearic Islands	Island/island group
Thar Desert	Landscape feature/region

Seas and oceans

INDIAN OCEAN	Ocean
North Sea	Sea
Guinea Basin	Sea feature

Ice features

	Limit of summer pack ice
	Limit of winter pack ice

Land height

	4,000m 13,124 ft.
	2,000m 6,562 ft.
	1,000m 3,281 ft.
	500m 1,640 ft.
	200m 656 ft.
	Sea level

6. PLANET EARTH

THE HOME PLANET

Planet Earth is roughly spherical in shape and measures 24,847 mi. around the equator. As far as we know it is the only planet that can support life. There are two main reasons for this. First, Earth has an atmosphere that contains oxygen. Second, the planet is the just the right distance from the Sun. Planets closer to the Sun, such as Mercury, are too hot for life. Those farther away, such as Mars, are too cold.

The solar system

The Sun, our closest star, has powerful gravity that attracts nine major planets, including Earth, and countless minor planets called asteroids. These and other bodies, such as moons and comets, circle the Sun and form its family, or solar system. The planets of the solar system were probably created around 4.5 billion years ago from a cloud of gas and dust thrown out by the Sun when it was formed. The smaller planets closer to the Sun are made up of minerals and metals. The outer planets were formed at lower temperatures and consist of swirling clouds of gases.

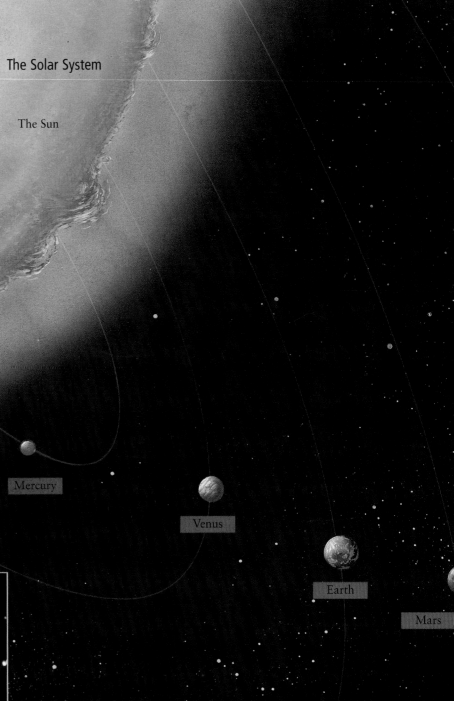

The Solar System

The Sun

Mercury

Venus

Earth

Mars

The Milky Way is an enormous, spiral-shaped galaxy of which our Solar System forms a tiny part. The galaxy contains at least 200 billion stars.

Earth is the third planet from the Sun (above). It takes 365.25 days for Earth to complete one full circle around the Sun.

The Sun and Moon

With a diameter of around 868,000 mi., the Sun is more than 100 times wider than Earth. Like other stars, the Sun is a giant ball of gases. Although it lies around 93 million miles from Earth, the Sun provides the light and warmth needed to make our planet suitable for life. The Moon lies around 238,000 mi. away from Earth and is our planet's closest neighbor in space. Its gravity is weaker than Earth's, so it cannot hang onto any gases to create an atmosphere. However, the Moon's gravity pulls at our oceans to create tides.

Pluto

Neptune

Uranus

Saturn

Jupiter

Inside Earth

Rocky crust

Outer mantle

Inner mantle. It is richer in iron than the outer mantle.

Outer core of molten iron and nickel

Inner core of solid iron and nickel

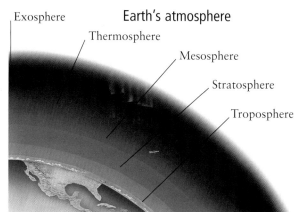

Earth's atmosphere

Exosphere

Thermosphere

Mesosphere

Stratosphere

Troposphere

Earth's outer structure

Earth is surrounded by a layer of air around 1,240 mi. thick called the atmosphere. It contains the air that we breathe, together with water vapor and tiny pieces of dust. Held by the pull of Earth's gravity, the atmosphere protects us from the dangerous rays of the Sun and the cold of outer space. The atmosphere is made up of layers. The layer closest to Earth is the troposphere. It contains most of the gas in the atmosphere and is the narrowest layer. Above the troposphere is the stratosphere. It extends from 6.8 mi. to 31 mi. above Earth. The mesosphere lies between 31 mi. and 50 mi. above Earth. If meteors fall into this layer, they burn up, causing shooting stars. A very thick layer of air, called the thermosphere, extends from around 50 mi. to 298 mi. above the ground. Above this is the exosphere, which has no definite upper limit.

Earth's inner structure

At the center of Earth lies a solid core made of iron and a small amount of nickel. Its temperature is around 8,132°F. Around the core is the outer core, formed of liquid iron and nickel at a temperature of around 5,972°F. Outside the core is the mantle, a layer of rock around 1,718 mi. thick. The temperature reaches around 6,692°F at the bottom of the mantle, but high pressure there keeps the rock solid. There is less pressure on the top part of the mantle, which is fairly soft and can move. We live on Earth's rocky outer layer called the crust.

THE CHANGING EARTH

Earth's crust, which covers the planet's surface, is made up of several sections called tectonic plates. These plates interlock with each other like the pieces of an enormous jigsaw puzzle. They are not fixed in position, however, but move slowly. As a result, the world's continents have shifted their positions over millions of years. More than 200 million years ago the continents made up one single landmass, which gradually split up and moved apart to produce the continent shapes that we see today. The boundaries of the plates are places of huge stress. Sometimes, if plates are drifting apart, new crust is created as hot, liquid rock from the mantle below fills the gap. If the plates are pushing toward each other, the land on one side can be pushed upward, creating mountain ranges.

Earthquakes

Earthquakes occur when two tectonic plates slide past each other, and friction is created along the line that lies between them. The friction causes violent vibrations, called tremors, that spread across the ground from the source. Sometimes the crust of Earth cracks, or is faulted, and the land on one side of the fault line is raised, while the land on the other side of it is lowered.

Sliding plates

The San Andreas Fault extends for more than 620 mi. across California. This area is the site of frequent minor earthquakes.

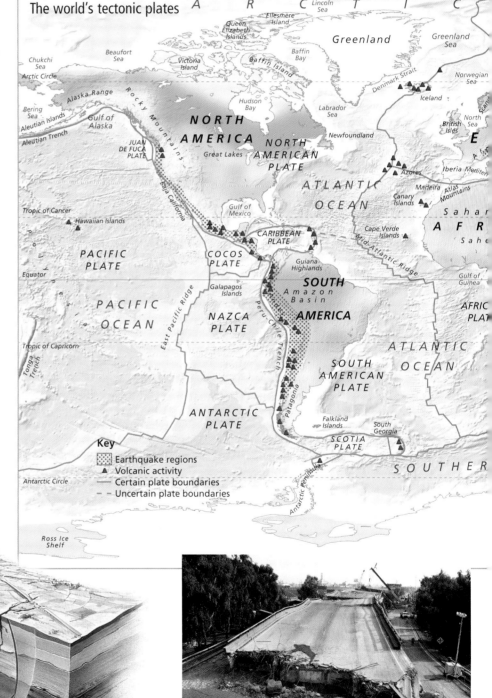

The world's tectonic plates

Key
- Earthquake regions
- ▲ Volcanic activity
- Certain plate boundaries
- - - Uncertain plate boundaries

Fault line

Area of friction

Vibrations spreading away from the source

The enormous power of an earthquake can pull down buildings and rip apart roads, sometimes causing death and injury in the process.

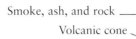

Lava flowing from volcanoes can reach temperatures of more than 1,832°F and reach speeds of 37 mph.

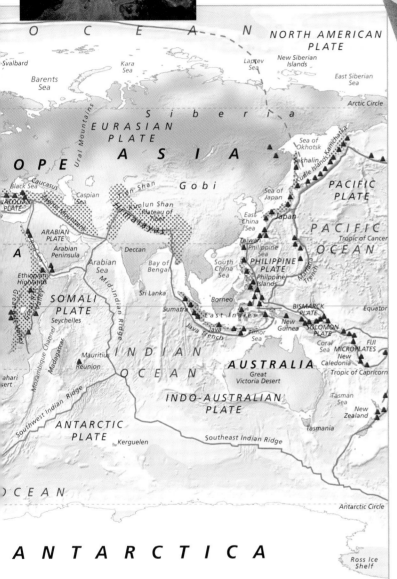

Smoke, ash, and rock
Volcanic cone
Geyser
Layers of cooled lava
Side vent
Lava flow
Magma chamber
Central vent

An erupting volcano

Volcanoes

When hot liquid rock, or magma, from Earth's mantle escapes to the surface of Earth, a volcano is created. Sometimes the magma collects in a huge underground chamber before it rises through a channel, called the central vent, or smaller side vents. Once the magma breaks through the surface it is called lava. The lava gradually cools to form the shape of the volcano. Some volcanoes are cone-shaped, while others, called shield volcanoes, are more rounded. During a volcanic eruption gases, ash, and rocks are often thrown high up into the air.

Geysers

Geysers are found in the volcanic regions of New Zealand, Iceland, Chile, the eastern Russian Federation, and the western U.S. Pools of water in underground caverns made of watertight volcanic rock, such as rhyolite, are heated by scorching hot magma. The water boils, and some of it turns to steam. Eventually the pressure in the cavern builds up, and the water and steam is forced upward through a crevice to Earth's surface. There the water and steam burst out of the ground and spurt up into the air.

There are less than 1,000 geysers in the world. A number of them erupt very often and regularly. Some geysers are known to reach heights of more than 328 ft.

CLIMATE AND WEATHER

Climate is the average sunshine, wind, rainfall, and humidity that an area receives over a long period of time. The major influence on a region's climate is its latitude (the distance it lies north or south of the equator). The equator receives the most direct rays from the Sun, so the climates there are warm. Places close to the poles receive less heat from the Sun, so they have colder climates. Other influences on an area's climate include its distance from an ocean, its height above sea level, ocean currents, and wind patterns.

Earth's climate zones

Earth's climate varies from place to place. Polar and mountainous zones are freezing and dry all year-round. Continental regions are cold in the winter and warmer in the summer. Steppe areas have cold winters and very hot summers, while temperate regions enjoy a milder climate without extremes of temperature. The tropics are mainly hot and wet all year-round. Some subtropical zones have hot, dry summers and warm, wet winters. Arid areas are hot with very little rain at all. Savanna regions are hot throughout the year, but they have a rainy season that lasts around three months.

The greenhouse effect

Certain gases in the atmosphere, such as carbon dioxide, are called greenhouse gases because they act like the glass panes in a greenhouse. These gases let the Sun's rays pass through to Earth, but they restrict the amount of energy that can pass back into space. The heat becomes trapped in the atmosphere, causing Earth to warm up.

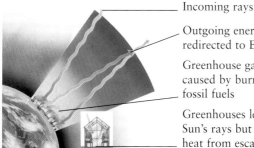

- Incoming rays
- Outgoing energy redirected to Earth
- Greenhouse gases caused by burning fossil fuels
- Greenhouses let in Sun's rays but keep heat from escaping

How the greenhouse effect works

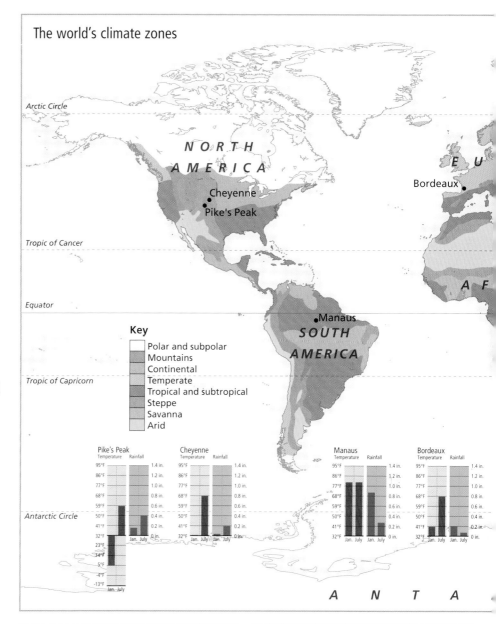

The world's climate zones

Key
- Polar and subpolar
- Mountains
- Continental
- Temperate
- Tropical and subtropical
- Steppe
- Savanna
- Arid

Many deserts are so dry that virtually no plants can grow. The Namib Desert in southern Africa receives an average rainfall of only one inch per year.

Temperatures on Antarctica reach as low as −126.4°F. A few animals, such as penguins, have adapted to the freezing conditions and howling winds.

Tropical areas, such as the coast of Texas, are wet and hot all year-round. During storms the rain falls in torrents, and fierce winds lash trees and houses.

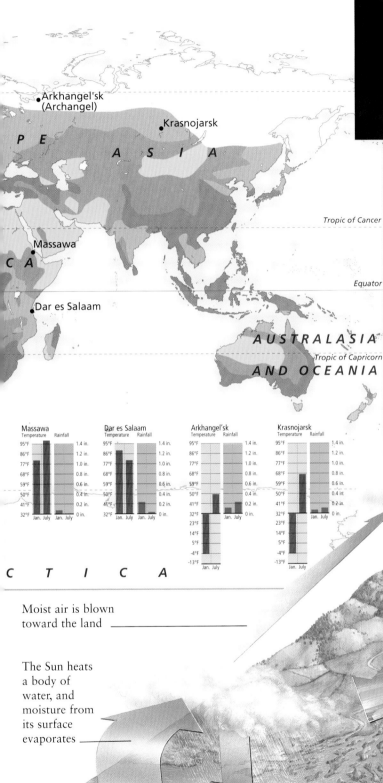

P E

A S I A

Tropic of Cancer

Arkhangel'sk
(Archangel)

Krasnojarsk

Massawa

C A

Equator

Dar es Salaam

AUSTRALASIA

Tropic of Capricorn

AND OCEANIA

Massawa
Temperature Rainfall

		1.4 in.
95°F		1.2 in.
86°F		1.0 in.
77°F		0.8 in.
68°F		0.6 in.
59°F		0.4 in.
50°F		0.2 in.
41°F		0 in.
32°F	Jan. July	Jan. July

Dar es Salaam
Temperature Rainfall

		1.4 in.
95°F		1.2 in.
86°F		1.0 in.
77°F		0.8 in.
68°F		0.6 in.
59°F		0.4 in.
50°F		0.2 in.
41°F		0 in.
32°F	Jan. July	Jan. July

Arkhangel'sk
Temperature Rainfall

		1.4 in.
95°F		1.2 in.
86°F		1.0 in.
77°F		0.8 in.
68°F		0.6 in.
59°F		0.4 in.
50°F		0.2 in.
41°F		0 in.
32°F	Jan. July	Jan. July
23°F		
14°F		
5°F		
-4°F		
-13°F	Jan. July	

Krasnojarsk
Temperature Rainfall

		1.4 in.
95°F		1.2 in.
86°F		1.0 in.
77°F		0.8 in.
68°F		0.6 in.
59°F		0.4 in.
50°F		0.2 in.
41°F		0 in.
32°F	Jan. July	Jan. July
23°F		
14°F		
5°F		
-4°F		
-13°F	Jan. July	

C T I C A

Weather

Short-term events in the atmosphere, from showers to hurricanes, make up the world's daily weather. Changes in weather are mainly caused by the movements of large air masses. The temperature and moisture content of these air masses change as they pass over land and water. They also swirl around to produce depressions—bringing cooler, wetter weather—and anticyclones—tending to bring warmer, drier conditions.

The water vapor forms clouds that produce rain or snow

Rivers carry water to the sea

Water runs below the surface of the land to the sea

The water cycle

The continuous movement of water across Earth and through its atmosphere is called the water cycle. Water in the oceans and the ground evaporates as the Sun heats Earth. The water vapor rises into the sky, where it begins to cool down, forming drops of water within clouds. Eventually the drops of water become heavy enough to fall back to Earth as rain or snow. The water soaks into the ground and feeds lakes and rivers. Then the cycle starts all over again.

Moist air is blown toward the land

The Sun heats a body of water, and moisture from its surface evaporates

Water falls back to the land and sea

How the water cycle works

THE NATURAL WORLD

All living things are connected to one another and rely on each other for food, protection, or even shelter. It is possible to divide the world into a number of broad zones, in which certain species of plants and animals live together within particular climate conditions. These ecological areas are called biomes.

The harshest habitats

The toughest of the world's biomes are those that have low rainfall or experience bitterly cold or scorching hot temperatures. Polar regions are permanently covered in ice, so no plants can live in them. Animals, such as the walrus, have developed insulating fat and stocky limbs in order to survive in the freezing conditions there. With very little soil and large areas of frozen ground, tundra regions are treeless. A few plants, such as lichens and mosses, grow during the summer months. Needle-leaved trees, including spruces and pines, are the only type of vegetation that can survive the long, snowy winters in the northern parts of Scandinavia, the Russian Federation, and Canada. In mountainous regions the lower slopes may be forested, but only ground-hugging shrubs can grow above the tree line. Deserts have very little rain. Certain plants and animals have adapted to the extreme temperatures and the lack of water in these regions.

For 50 to 60 days each year the tundra regions, which are usually frozen, become carpeted with colorful, low-lying plants.

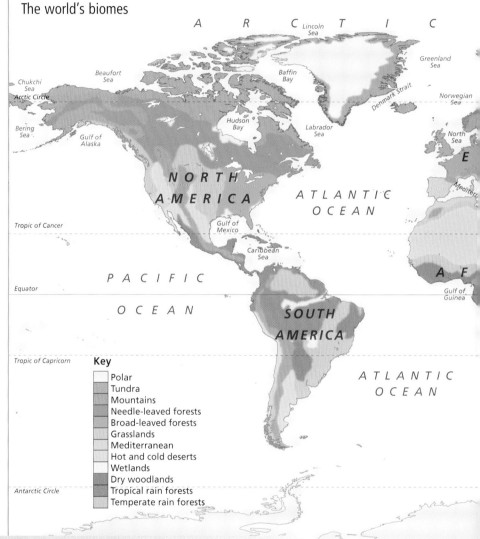

The world's biomes

Key
- Polar
- Tundra
- Mountains
- Needle-leaved forests
- Broad-leaved forests
- Grasslands
- Mediterranean
- Hot and cold deserts
- Wetlands
- Dry woodlands
- Tropical rain forests
- Temperate rain forests

Mountain peaks are hostile environments. The rocky terrain and thin air at high altitudes make it very difficult for plants and animals to survive.

A wealth of species of trees, ferns, and creeping plants are found in tropical rain forests. These regions are also home to various animals, which range from snakes and monkeys to sloths, parrots, and countless insects.

Temperate and tropical zones

Much of the Northern Hemisphere was once covered in broad-leaved, deciduous trees, but most of them have now been cleared for settlements. Trees and evergreen shrubs, adapted to the dry summers, grow in Mediterranean regions and dry woodlands. The world's major grasslands are found in the center of the larger continents. These regions are grazed by herbivores such as bison and zebras. Wetlands are rich feeding grounds for fish and breeding grounds for birds. With plenty of rain and sunshine, the rain forests have the greatest variety of species on Earth.

Biodiversity

The number of plant and animal species—and the variety within each species—make up Earth's biodiversity. Some plants and animals, such as kangaroos in Australia, are endemic (found only in one region). Human-made environments, including cities and farms, ruin natural habitats and threaten plant and animal biodiversity. Increasing efforts are now being made to conserve Earth's wild places.

The grasslands of Africa, with trees dotted here and there, are broad, open habitats where herds of grazing animals range free while watching out for carnivores such as leopards and lions.

Isolated places have the greatest range of endemic species. Lemurs (above) are only found in Madagascar and Comoros.

The planet's oceans have a huge variety of different species, from enormous whales to the tiniest plankton.

THE HUMAN WORLD

There have been people on planet Earth for more than 130,000 years. Humans first evolved in Africa, and they gradually spread across the world. They probably traveled in search of food, either following herds of animals or looking for fruit. By around 10,000 years ago people had reached most parts of the globe, and some had started to settle down. Today there are around six billion people in the world, but they are not distributed evenly. Some areas, including China, India, and Europe, are densely populated, while others are not.

Feeding the world

Humans have developed skills to help them survive, and these have had an impact on Earth. One of the earliest skills developed was farming. In different parts of the world people learned how to raise animals. They also learned how to cultivate crops that grew well in the local environment—from rice in eastern Asia to wheat in North America. Today almost two fifths of the planet's land are farmed. Through fishing we have also changed the oceans. A modern fishing ship can catch entire schools of fish at one time, and some species, such as cod, have suffered badly as a result. Agreements have now been made to reduce the numbers of fish caught in order to allow stocks to recover.

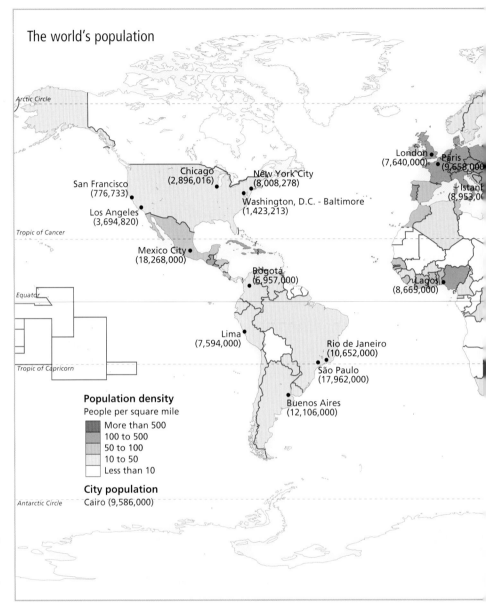

The world's population

London (7,640,000)
Paris (9,658,000)
Istanbul (8,953,000)
Chicago (2,896,016)
New York City (8,008,278)
San Francisco (776,733)
Washington, D.C. - Baltimore (1,423,213)
Los Angeles (3,694,820)
Mexico City (18,268,000)
Bogotá (6,957,000)
Lagos (8,665,000)
Lima (7,594,000)
Rio de Janeiro (10,652,000)
São Paulo (17,962,000)
Buenos Aires (12,106,000)

Arctic Circle
Tropic of Cancer
Equator
Tropic of Capricorn
Antarctic Circle

Population density
People per square mile
- More than 500
- 100 to 500
- 50 to 100
- 10 to 50
- Less than 10

City population
Cairo (9,586,000)

The staple diet of half the world's people, rice has been cultivated for more than 5,000 years. Asia grows 91 percent of the world's rice.

Traditional fishing methods, shown left, catch enough fish for the local market. But in some places modern trawlers bring in large quantities of fish. The catch is usually sold to factories, where it is processed for export.

In 1500 the world's population was around 425 million

In 1600 the world's population was around 545 million

In 1700 the world's population was around 610 million

1500   1600   170

Cities, such as Tokyo in Japan (right), have many luxuries, but some are also home to shantytowns (far right), where the very poor live with little or no services.

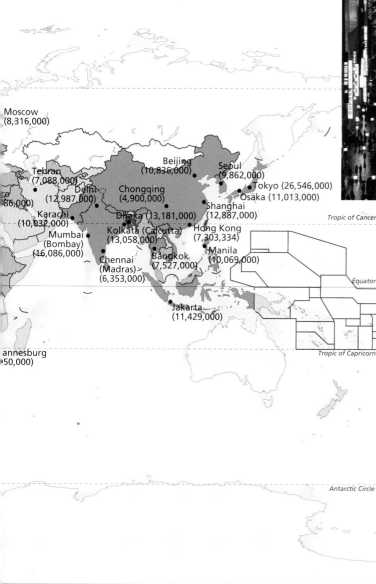

Moscow
(8,316,000)

Tehran
(7,088,000)

Delhi
(12,987,000)

Beijing
(10,836,000)

Seoul
(9,862,000)

Chongqing
(4,900,000)

Tokyo (26,546,000)

Osaka (11,013,000)

86,000)

Karachi
(10,032,000)

Dhaka (13,181,000)

Shanghai
(12,887,000)

Tropic of Cancer

Mumbai
(Bombay)
(16,086,000)

Kolkata (Calcutta)
(13,058,000)

Hong Kong
(7,303,334)

Chennai
(Madras)
(6,353,000)

Bangkok
(7,527,000)

Manila
(10,069,000)

Equator

Jakarta
(11,429,000)

annesburg
50,000)

Tropic of Capricorn

Antarctic Circle

Rushing to the cities

By 2007 half of the world's population will live in urban environments. This figure is expected to rise to 60 percent of the total population by 2030. In many developing countries cities are growing two or three times faster than the overall population. The world's cities are centers of government, education, industry, and trade, but they also have problems, including crime, poverty, and pollution.

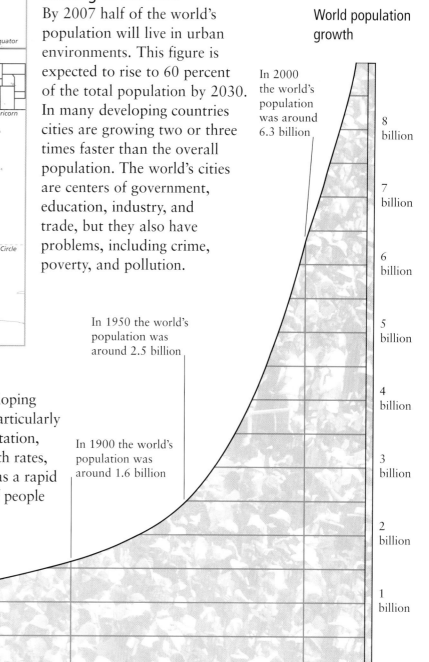

World population growth

In 2000 the world's population was around 6.3 billion

8 billion

7 billion

6 billion

5 billion

In 1950 the world's population was around 2.5 billion

4 billion

The population explosion

In the second half of the 1900s death rates in the developing countries of Africa, Asia, and Latin America halved, particularly among children. This was due to improved public sanitation, better personal hygiene, and advances in medicine. Birth rates, however, did not decrease at the same rate, so there was a rapid rise in the population. By the year 2020 the number of people in the world is likely to reach around 8.6 billion.

In 1900 the world's population was around 1.6 billion

3 billion

2 billion

In 1800 the world's population was around 900 million

1 billion

1800

1900

2000

THE PHYSICAL WORLD

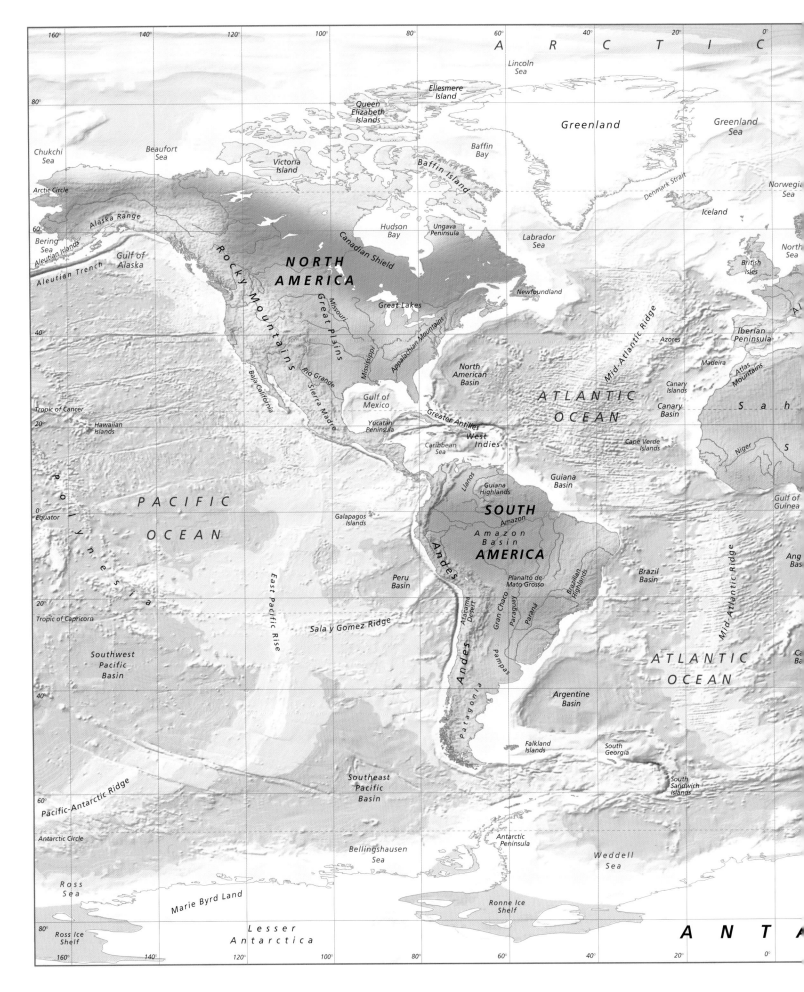

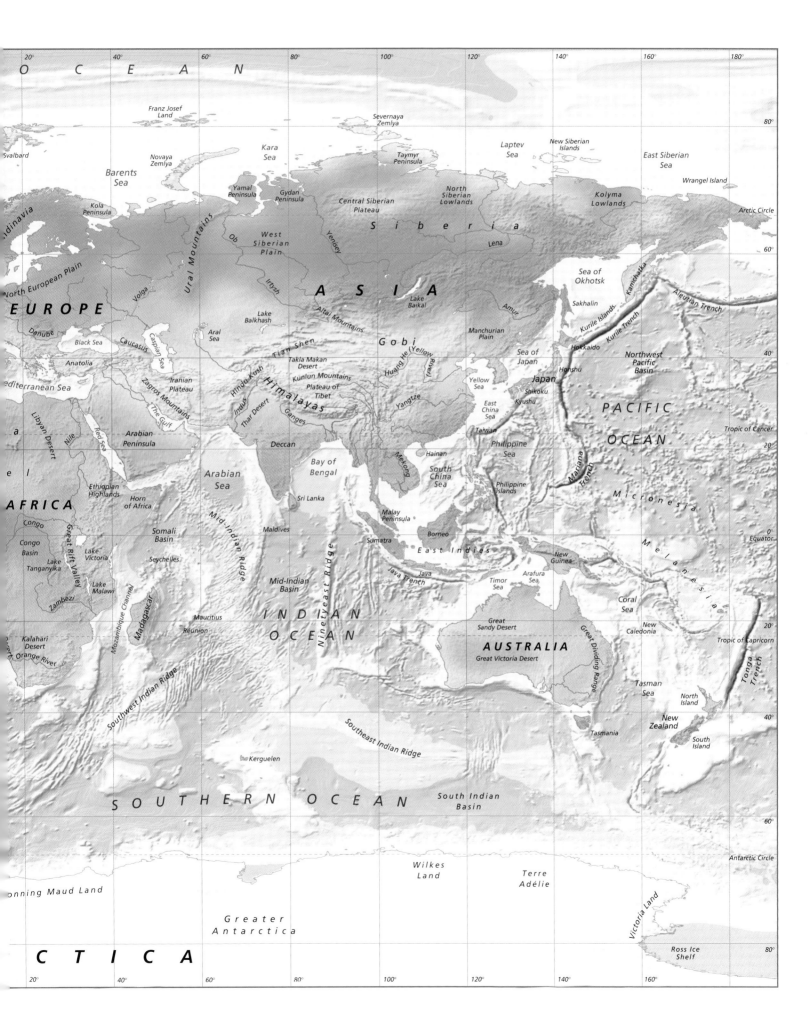

20° 40° 60° 80° 100° 120° 140° 160° 180°

O C E A N

Franz Josef
Land

Svalbard

Severnaya
Zemlya

80°

Barents
Sea

Novaya
Zemlya

Kara
Sea

Taymyr
Peninsula

Laptev
Sea

New Siberian
Islands

East Siberian
Sea

Wrangel Island

dinavia

Kola
Peninsula

Yamal
Peninsula

Gydan
Peninsula

Central Siberian
Plateau

North
Siberian
Lowlands

Kolyma
Lowlands

Arctic Circle

North European Plain

EUROPE

Ural Mountains

Ob

West
Siberian
Plain

S i b e r i a

Yenisey

Lena

Amur

Sea of
Okhotsk

Sakhalin

Kamchatka

Aleutian Trench

60°

Volga

Irtysh

A S I A

Lake
Baikal

Kurile Islands

Kurile Trench

Danube

Black Sea

Caucasus

Caspian Sea

Aral
Sea

Lake
Balkhash

Altai Mountains

Gobi

Manchurian
Plain

Hokkaido

Northwest
Pacific
Basin

40°

Anatolia

Zagros Mountains

Iranian
Plateau

Tian Shen

Takla Makan
Desert

Huang He (Yellow River)

Sea of
Japan

Honshu

Japan

diterranean Sea

The Gulf

Hindu Kush

Kunlun Mountains

Plateau of
Tibet

Yangtze

Shikoku

Kyushu

PACIFIC

a

Libyan Desert

Nile

Red Sea

Arabian
Peninsula

Indus

Himalayas

Thar Desert

Ganges

Yellow
Sea

East
China
Sea

OCEAN

Tropic of Cancer

el

Deccan

Taiwan

20°

AFRICA

Ethiopian
Highlands

Horn
of Africa

Arabian
Sea

Bay of
Bengal

Sri Lanka

Mekong

Hainan

South
China
Sea

Philippine
Sea

Mariana Trench

Micronesia

Congo

Somali
Basin

Mid-Indian Ridge

Maldives

Philippine
Islands

Equator

Congo
Basin

Lake
Victoria

Seychelles

Malay
Peninsula

Borneo

0°

Lake
Tanganyika

Sumatra

East Indies

New
Guinea

Melanesia

Lake
Malawi

Mid-Indian
Basin

Java Trench

Java

Timor
Sea

Arafura
Sea

Zambezi

Ninetyeast Ridge

Coral
Sea

New
Caledonia

20°

Mauritius

INDIAN

Great
Sandy Desert

Great Dividing Range

Tropic of Capricorn

Kalahari
Desert

Madagascar

Reunion

OCEAN

AUSTRALIA

Tonga Trench

Orange River

Mozambique Channel

Great Victoria Desert

Tasman
Sea

New

40°

Southwest Indian Ridge

Southeast Indian Ridge

Tasmania

North
Island

Zealand

South
Island

Kerguelen

S O U T H E R N   O C E A N

South Indian
Basin

60°

Antarctic Circle

onning Maud Land

Wilkes
Land

Terre
Adélie

Victoria Land

G r e a t e r
A n t a r c t i c a

C T I C A

Ross Ice
Shelf

80°

20° 40° 60° 80° 100° 120° 140° 160°

THE POLITICAL WORLD

Abbreviations
B&H   - BOSNIA & HERZEGOVINA
CRO.   - CROATIA
LIE.   - LIECHTENSTEIN
LUX.   - LUXEMBOURG
MAC.   - MACEDONIA
RUSS. FED. - RUSSIAN FEDERATION
SAN.   - SAN MARINO
SWITZ.   - SWITZERLAND
SERB. & MONT. - SERBIA & MONTENEGRO

A R C T I C

Greenland
(to Denmark)

Jan Mayen
(to Norway)

Arctic Circle

UNITED STATES
OF AMERICA
(ALASKA)

C A N A D A

ICELAND

Faroe Islands
(to Denmark)

A T L A N T I C

UNITED
KINGDOM   DENM

REPUBLIC OF
IRELAND   NETHERLAN

Isle
of Man
(to U.K.)   BELGIUM

O C E A N

Channel Islands
(to U.K.)   SW
FRANC

St. Pierre &
Miquelon
(to France)

MON

ANDORRA

PORTUGAL   SPAIN

UNITED STATES
OF AMERICA

Bermuda
(to U.K.)

Azores
(to Portugal)

Madeira
(to Portugal)

Gibraltar
(to U.K.)

MOROCCO

Tropic of Cancer

MEXICO

BAHAMAS

Canary Islands
(to Spain)

WESTERN
SAHARA
(occupied by Morocco)

ALGER

Hawaiian Islands
(to U.S.)

CUBA

Turks & Caicos
Islands (to U.K.)

British
Virgin Islands (to U.K.)

MAURITANIA

MALI

Johnston Atoll
(to U.S.)

Cayman Islands
(to U.K.)

Navassa
Island
(to U.S.)

DOMINICAN
REPUBLIC

Virgin Islands
(to U.S.)

Anguilla (to U.K.)

Montserrat (to U.K.)

CAPE VERDE

BELIZE

HAITI

Puerto Rico
(to U.S.)

ANTIGUA & BARBUDA

Guadeloupe (to France)

SENEGAL

THE GAMBIA

JAMAICA

ST. KITTS
& NEVIS

DOMINICA

Martinique (to France)

BURKINA
FASO

GUATEMALA

HONDURAS

Netherlands
Antilles (to Neth.)

ST. LUCIA

ST. VINCENT & THE GRENADINES

GUINEA-BISSAU   GUINEA

EL SALVADOR

NICARAGUA

Aruba
(to Neth.)

BARBADOS

SIERRA LEONE

IVORY
COAST

GHANA

Clipperton Island
(to France)

COSTA
RICA   PANAMA

GRENADA

TRINIDAD & TOBAGO

LIBERIA

TO

P A C I F I C

VENEZUELA

French
Guiana
(to France)

EQUATORIAL GUI

Kingman Reef (to U.S.)
Palmyra Atoll (to U.S.)

COLOMBIA

GUYANA

SURINAME

Equator

Jarvis Island
(to U.S.)

Galapagos Islands
(to Ecuador)

ECUADOR

SÃO TO
& PRÍN

KIRIBATI

O C E A N

BRAZIL

Ascension
Island
(to St. Helena)

American
Samoa
(to U.S.)

Cook
Islands
(to N.Z.)

PERU

St. Helena
(to U.K.)

Niue
(to N.Z.)

BOLIVIA

French Polynesia
(to France)

PARAGUAY

Tropic of Capricorn

Pitcairn Islands
(to U.K.)

A T L A N T I C

Easter Island
(to Chile)

URUGUAY

O C E A N

Juan
Fernández Islands
(to Chile)

CHILE

ARGENTINA

Tristan da Cunha
(to St. Helena)

Gough Island
(to Tristan da Cunha)

Falkland Islands
(to U.K.)

Bouvet Island
(to Norway)

South Georgia
(to U.K.)

South Sandwich Islands
(to U.K.)

S O U T H

Antarctic Circle

Peter I
Island
(to Norway)

A N T A R C T I C A

O C E A N

Franz Josef Land

Novaya
Zemlya

Severnaya Zemlya

New Siberian Islands

Arctic Circle

KWAY

SWEDEN

FINLAND

ESTONIA
LATVIA
LITHUANIA
RUSS. FED.
BELARUS
POLAND
UKRAINE

RUSSIAN FEDERATION

CZECH
REP.
SLOVAKIA
TRIA
HUNGARY
MOLDOVA
SLOVENIA
ROMANIA
B&H
SERB. &
MONT.
BULGARIA
ALBANIA
MAC.
GREECE

KAZAKHSTAN

MONGOLIA

TY
CRO.

TURKEY

GEORGIA
ARMENIA
AZERBAIJAN

UZBEKISTAN

KYRGYZSTAN

MALTA
CYPRUS
SYRIA
UNISIA
LEBANON
ISRAEL

IRAQ

TURKMENISTAN

TAJIKISTAN

CHINA

NORTH
KOREA
SOUTH
KOREA

JAPAN

JORDAN

IRAN

AFGHANISTAN

LIBYA

EGYPT

KUWAIT
BAHRAIN
QATAR
UNITED ARAB
EMIRATES

SAUDI
ARABIA

OMAN

PAKISTAN

NEPAL

BHUTAN

INDIA

BANGLADESH

TAIWAN

P A C I F I C

Midway Islands
(to U.S.)

Tropic of Cancer

CHAD

SUDAN

ERITREA

YEMEN

OMAN

MYANMAR
(BURMA)

LAOS

VIETNAM

THAILAND

Paracel
Islands
(disputed)

Wake Island
(to U.S.)

O C E A N

Northern
Mariana Islands
(to U.S.)

MARSHALL
ISLANDS

DJIBOUTI

CENTRAL
AFRICAN
REPUBLIC

ETHIOPIA

Laccadive
Islands
(to India)

Andaman
Islands
(to India)

CAMBODIA

Spratly
Islands
(disputed)

PHILIPPINES

Guam
(to U.S.)

MICRONESIA

SRI
LANKA

Nicobar
Islands
(to India)

PALAU

SON
CONGO

UGANDA

KENYA

DEMOCRATIC
REPUBLIC

RWANDA
BURUNDI

MALDIVES

MALAYSIA

BRUNEI

SINGAPORE

NAURU

KIRIBATI

Equator

OF THE CONGO

TANZANIA

SEYCHELLES

British
Indian Ocean
Territory
(to U.K.)

I N D O N E S I A

EAST TIMOR

PAPUA
NEW
GUINEA

SOLOMON
ISLANDS

TUVALU

Tokelau
(to N.Z.)

COMOROS

Mayotte
(to France)

Christmas Island
(to Australia)

Wallis
& Futuna
(to France)

SAMOA

ANGOLA

MALAWI

ZAMBIA

MADAGASCAR

Réunion
(to France)

MAURITIUS

I N D I A N

Cocos Islands
(to Australia)

Ashmore &
Cartier Islands
(to Australia)

Coral Sea
Islands
(to Australia)

VANUATU

New
Caledonia
(to France)

FIJI

TONGA

NAMIBIA

ZIMBABWE

MOZAMBIQUE

BOTSWANA

SWAZILAND

O C E A N

Tropic of Capricorn

SOUTH
AFRICA

LESOTHO

AUSTRALIA

Norfolk Island
(to Australia)

Prince Edward Islands
(to S. Africa)

Crozet Islands
(to France)

Kerguelen
(to France)

NEW
ZEALAND

Heard & McDonald Islands
(to Australia)

E R N   O C E A N

Antarctic Circle

A N T A R C T I C A

THE ARCTIC OCEAN

The poles, at Earth's northern and southern tips, are the planet's coldest places, where temperatures can fall as low as –112°F in the winter. At the North Pole is the Arctic Ocean. With an area of 5,105,700 sq. mi., it is the smallest ocean on the planet. The Arctic is made up of two large basins divided by three underwater ridges, the greatest of which is the Lomonosov Ridge. Its waters are mainly covered with pack ice. When this ice breaks up, it forms enormous blocks of floating ice called icebergs. The Arctic is fringed by the northernmost parts of North America, Russia, Europe, and Greenland.

Despite the region's harsh climate, it has been inhabited for thousands of years by people such as the European Lapps (Sami), Russian Nenet, and North American Inuit.

These peoples make their living by herding, hunting, and fishing. There are stocks of cod, plaice, and haddock in the unfrozen Arctic waters, but numbers have fallen over the years. Now there are restrictions on the amount of fish that people can take from the ocean. The peoples of the Arctic region must import foods, such as grains and vegetables, from elsewhere.

The Arctic is rich in oil, gas, and coal, but because of the bitterly cold climate and severe landscape, extracting these resources is difficult and expensive. There are mines and wells in the coastal regions, but these cause pollution and threaten the area's unique wildlife. These industries have also damaged the traditional lifestyles of many of the Arctic region's native peoples.

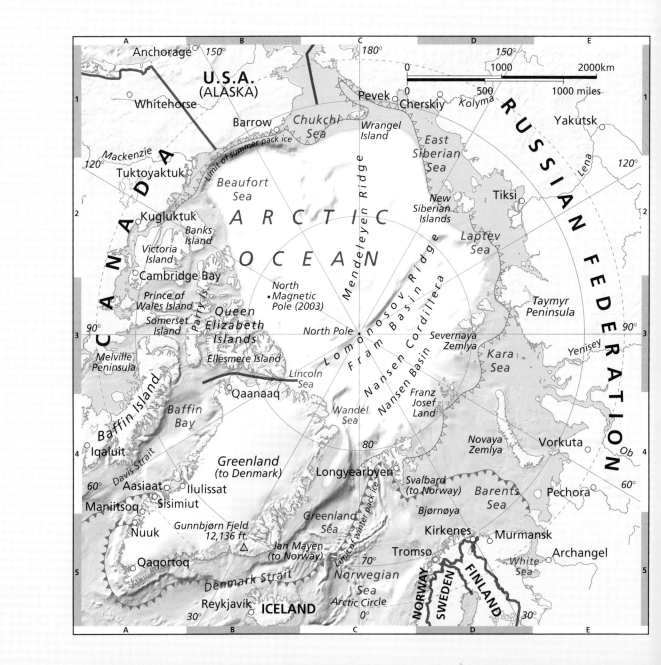

ANTARCTICA

Antarctica, at Earth's southern tip, is the planet's coldest and smallest continent. It is a frozen world where the land lies beneath a thick layer of ice. Almost half of the Antarctic coastline is surrounded by ice shelves, which float on the sea. There are two distinct parts of Antarctica. Lesser Antarctica is a series of ice-covered, mountainous islands that are joined together by ice. Greater Antarctica is a high plateau.

No people live permanently in Antarctica, but teams of scientists visit this important environmental region and live in research stations for months at a time. These scientists observe the region's wildlife and even study the ice itself. By analyzing chemicals in the ice they can find out how Earth's atmosphere has changed over the years.

Antarctica is governed by Argentina, Brazil, Chile, the United Kingdom, Norway, France, Australia, and New Zealand. All of these countries have agreed that the continent should only be used for peaceful work.

Colonies of penguins breed along the continent's coastal regions, and there are whales, seals, and many fish species living in the surrounding waters. Antarctica has rich mineral reserves, such as gold, iron, and coal, and there is natural gas in the seas. The harsh conditions in the region mean that the mining of these resources is too expenisve and difficult. Each year between 2,000 and 3,000 tourists visit the Antarctic region. They come to view the unique wildlife and dramatic landscape from the decks of cruise ships.

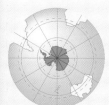

NORTH AMERICA

The continent of North America is shaped like a huge triangle, stretching from the frozen Arctic in the north to the tropics in the south. In the north there are two enormous countries, Canada and the U.S. Smaller countries lie in the south and in the Caribbean Sea. The northern part of the continent has many different types of landscapes. The towering Rocky Mountains to the west give way to the Great Plains, where fertile soils help farmers grow millions of acres of crops. To the east are the vast Great Lakes, major rivers such as the Mississippi, and the lower mountains of the

Appalachians. Farther south the Rocky Mountains continue into Mexico and southern North America, where they are called the Sierra Madre. This region also contains high plateaus and low-lying tropical forests, lagoons, and mangrove swamps.

North America has a variety of climates, from the frozen wastes and pine forests of northern Canada to the baking deserts of Arizona and Mexico. Areas like these can support few people, but the northeast and west coasts are more densely populated, and North America is home

to some of the world's biggest cities—New York City, Los Angeles, Chicago, and sprawling Mexico City.

Politically there is a marked difference between northern and southern North America. The U.S. and Canada have stable administrations in which the central government shares power with the individual states and provinces. The nations of southern North America have been less peaceful, and dictators ruled some countries, such as Nicaragua and Haiti, for many years.

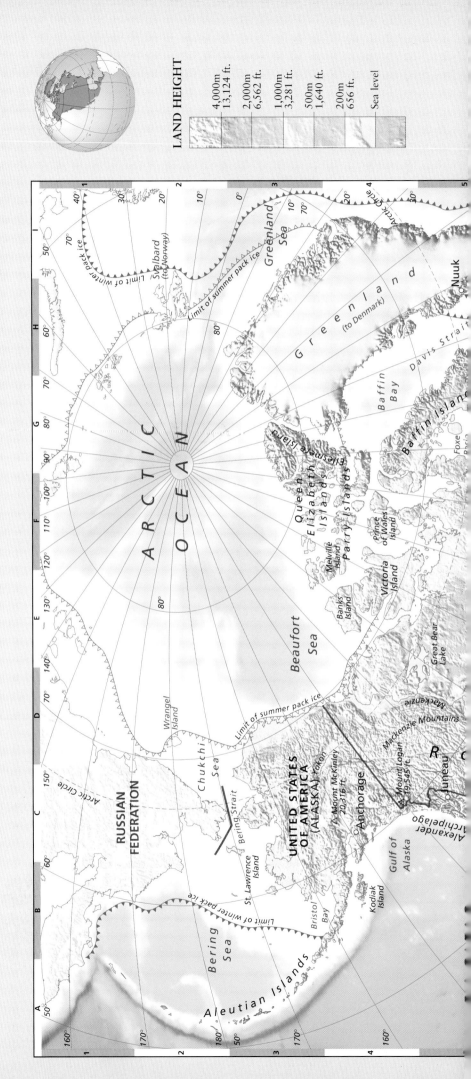

LAND HEIGHT

4,000m	13,124 ft.
2,000m	6,562 ft.
1,000m	3,281 ft.
500m	1,640 ft.
200m	656 ft.
	Sea level

PACIFIC OCEAN

ATLANTIC OCEAN

SOUTH AMERICA

CANADA

UNITED STATES OF AMERICA

MEXICO

Cape Farewell

Labrador Sea

limit of winter pack ice

Cape Chidley

Ungava Peninsula

Labrador

St. Pierre & Miquelon (to France)

Newfoundland

Cape Breton Island

Gulf of St. Lawrence

Halifax

Laurentian Highlands

Smallwood Reservoir

Hudson Strait

Hudson Bay

Belcher Islands

James Bay

St. Lawrence

Québec

Montréal

OTTAWA

Boston

Cape Cod

New York

Long Island

Philadelphia

Baltimore

WASHINGTON, D.C.

Bermuda (to U.K.)

Charlotte Islands

Charlotte

Cape Hatteras

Columbia

Jacksonville

Lake Nipigon

Great Lakes

Lake Superior

Toronto

Lake Ontario

Lake Erie

Cleveland

Lake Huron

Lake Michigan

Detroit

Appalachian Mountains

Columbus

Indianapolis

St. Louis

Nashville

Atlanta

Tampa

The Everglades

Miami

Straits of Florida

NASSAU

BAHAMAS

Turks & Caicos Islands (to U.K.)

DOMINICAN REPUBLIC

Puerto Rico (to U.S.)

SANTO DOMINGO

West Indies

HAITI

PORT-AU-PRINCE

Lesser Antilles

Netherlands Antilles (to Netherlands)

Aruba (to Netherlands)

TRINIDAD & TOBAGO

Winnipeg

Lake Winnipeg

Reindeer Lake

Lake Athabasca

Edmonton

Calgary

Saskatoon

Saskatchewan

Peace

Great Plains

Minneapolis

St. Paul

Milwaukee

Chicago

Missouri

Kansas City

Arkansas

Memphis

Jackson

Baton Rouge

New Orleans

Mississippi Delta

Mississippi

Gulf of Mexico

HAVANA

CUBA

Cayman Islands (to U.K.)

Greater Antilles

Caribbean Sea

KINGSTON

JAMAICA

Denver

Oklahoma City

Fort Worth

Dallas

Austin

San Antonio

Houston

Monterrey

Sierra Madre Oriental

Yucatan Peninsula

BELIZE

BELMOPAN

GUATEMALA CITY

GUATEMALA

San Salvador

EL SALVADOR

HONDURAS

TEGUCIGALPA

MANAGUA

NICARAGUA

Lake Nicaragua

SAN JOSÉ

COSTA RICA

PANAMA CITY

PANAMA

Rocky Mountains

Great Basin

Great Salt Lake

Las Vegas

Mount Whitney 14,491 ft.

Death Valley 282 ft.

Colorado

Grand Canyon

Colorado Plateau

Phoenix

El Paso

Ciudad Juárez

Hermosillo

Rio Grande

MEXICO CITY

Popocatépetl 17,883 ft.

Pico de Orizaba 18,696 ft.

León

Guadalajara

Acapulco

Sierra Madre del Sur

Sierra Madre Occidental

Gulf of California

Baja California

Coast Mountains

East Mountains

Mount Rainier 14,406 ft.

Columbia

Vancouver

Vancouver Island

Seattle

Portland

San Francisco

San Jose

Los Angeles

San Diego

Coast Ranges

Tropic of Cancer

Equator

1. ST. KITTS & NEVIS
2. ANTIGUA & BARBUDA
3. DOMINICA
4. ST. LUCIA
5. BARBADOS
6. ST. VINCENT & THE GRENADINES
7. GRENADA

2000km

1000 miles

1000

500

CANADA

The second-largest country in the world, Canada covers a vast area just north of the U.S. This nation has quite a small population of just over 30 million, most of whom live in the south. Some of the people are Native Americans, members of tribes such as the Inuit, Algonquian, and Cree. Others are descendants of the Europeans who settled here from the 1500s onward, especially the French and British.

The landscape of Canada varies greatly. There are mountains in the west and east, and between these two regions is the Canadian Shield. This is a vast area of ancient rocks, low hills, thousands of lakes, and huge tracts of forests. In the north the Arctic regions are cold all year-round, and the areas of tundra experience only a slight rise in temperature during the summer. Farther south, where most of the cities lie, the climate is a bit warmer, although the winter in many places is long, cold, and snowy.

Canadians work in all types of businesses—from mining and farming to high-tech industries. The country is rich in minerals such as zinc and iron ore, and it has huge reserves of oil, coal, and natural gas. There are good fishing waters off the east and west coasts, and large areas of forest make Canada the world's biggest exporter of timber products. Wheat, which grows well on fertile plains just west of the Canadian Shield, is exported to many countries.

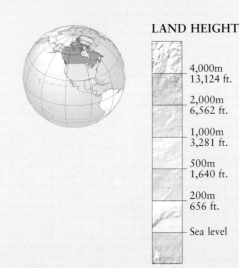

LAND HEIGHT

4,000m
13,124 ft.

2,000m
6,562 ft.

1,000m
3,281 ft.

500m
1,640 ft.

200m
656 ft.

Sea level

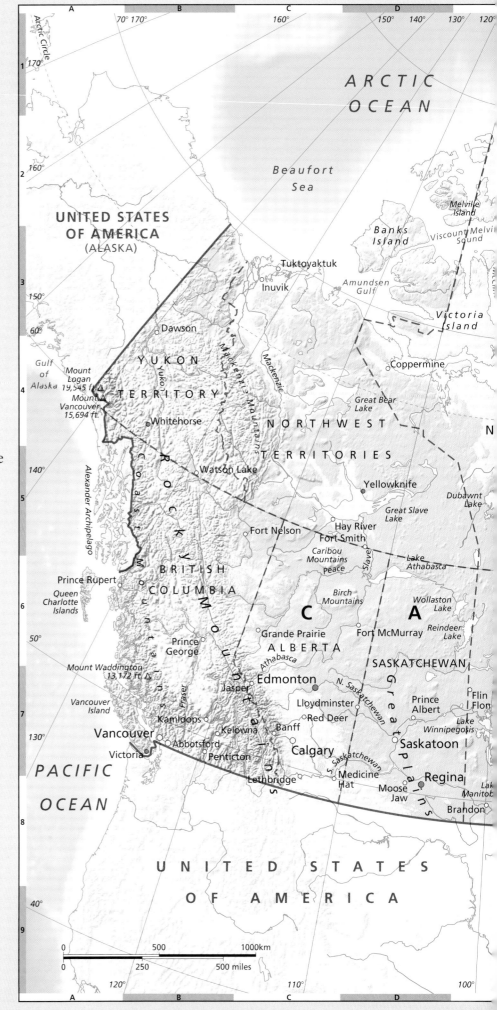

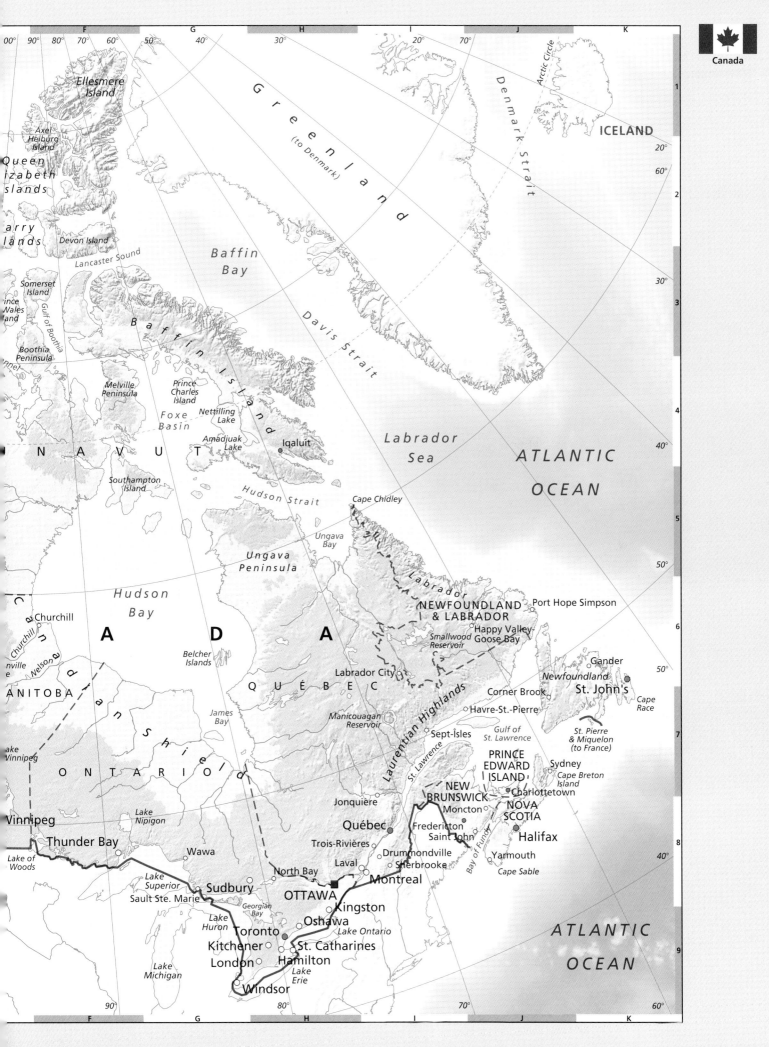

Canada

90° 80° 70° 60° 50° 40° 30° 20° 70°

F G H I J K

Ellesmere Island

Axel Heiburg Island

Queen Elizabeth Islands

Parry Islands

Devon Island

Lancaster Sound

G r e e n l a n d

(to Denmark)

ICELAND

Somerset Island

Prince of Wales Island

Gulf of Boothia

Boothia Peninsula

Baffin Bay

Melville Peninsula

Prince Charles Island

Foxe Basin

Nettilling Lake

Baffin Island

Amadjuak Lake

Davis Strait

Denmark Strait

Arctic Circle

N U N A V U T

Southampton Island

Iqaluit

Labrador Sea

ATLANTIC
OCEAN

Hudson Strait

Cape Chidley

Ungava Bay

C A N A D A

Churchill

Hudson Bay

Churchill

Nelson

Ungava Peninsula

Labrador

NEWFOUNDLAND
& LABRADOR

Port Hope Simpson

Lake Winnipeg

MANITOBA

Belcher Islands

James Bay

Canadian Shield

Q U É B E C

Smallwood Reservoir

Happy Valley-
Goose Bay

Gander

Newfoundland

O N T A R I O

Labrador City

Laurentian Highlands

Corner Brook

St. John's

Cape Race

Manicouagan Reservoir

Havre-St.-Pierre

St. Pierre
& Miquelon
(to France)

Winnipeg

Thunder Bay

Lake Nipigon

Jonquière

Sept-Îsles

Gulf of St. Lawrence

PRINCE
EDWARD
ISLAND

Sydney

Cape Breton Island

Lake of Woods

Wawa

St. Lawrence

NEW
BRUNSWICK

Charlottetown

Lake Superior

North Bay

Québec

Trois-Rivières

Moncton

NOVA
SCOTIA

Sault Ste. Marie

Sudbury

Laval

Drummondville

Montreal

Fredericton

Saint John

Halifax

Georgian Bay

OTTAWA

Sherbrooke

Bay of Fundy

Yarmouth

Lake Huron

Kingston

Cape Sable

ATLANTIC
OCEAN

Oshawa

Toronto

Lake Ontario

Kitchener

St. Catharines

London

Hamilton

Lake Michigan

Lake Erie

Windsor

80° 90° 70° 60°

WESTERN UNITED STATES

The western states have some of the most dramatic scenery in the U.S. All of these states are partly mountainous, and much of the region is arid. In the west the Central Valley separates the Sierra Nevada mountains from California's Coast Ranges. The area east of the Sierra Nevada contains mountain ranges, river basins, deserts, and salt lakes. Off the southwest coast is a chain of volcanoes that emerge from the Pacific Ocean as the Hawaiian islands.

A break in Earth's crust, known as the San Andreas Fault, runs through California. It is the site of frequent earthquakes. Most of the west has dry, hot summers, and to the south of the region the Sonoran Desert and California's Death Valley are two of the hottest places on Earth. In the winter, while the Pacific coast is wet and warm, the temperature inland, in states such as Utah and Idaho, drops dramatically.

With large areas of forest, Oregon and Washington are the U.S.'s major timber-producing states. Alaska is rich in oil and natural gas. In other areas farming is important. There are cattle ranches in Nevada, and the heavily irrigated land of California produces half of the U.S.'s fruit and vegetables.

Manufacturing industries, from aircraft building to clothing, employ many people in this region. The western states' best-known products are the computers and other electronic goods that are made in the famous "Silicon Valley" just south of San Francisco, California. Tourism is another major industry. Some people come to visit the spectacular physical features, such as the Grand Canyon, while others are lured by the sunny beaches of Hawaii and California.

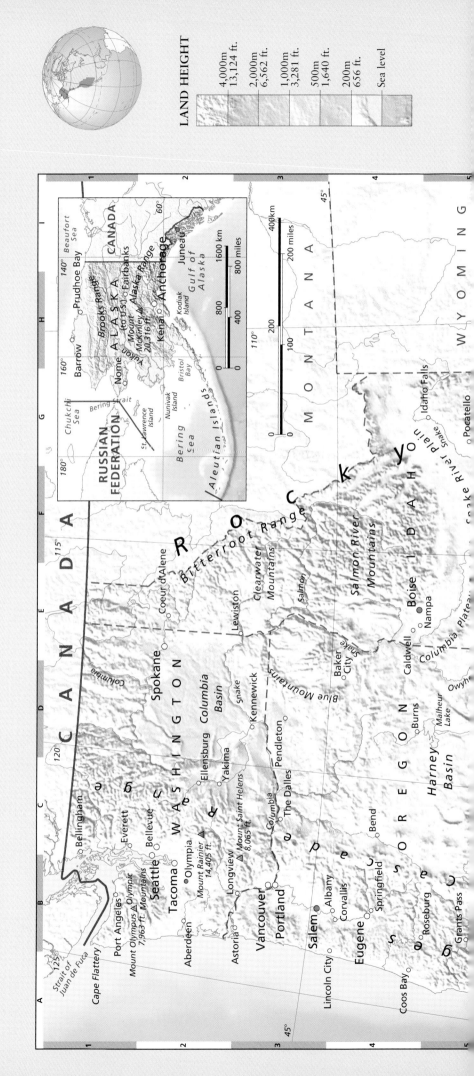

LAND HEIGHT

| 4,000m 13,124 ft. | 2,000m 6,562 ft. | 1,000m 3,281 ft. | 500m 1,640 ft. | 200m 656 ft. | Sea level |

United States
of America

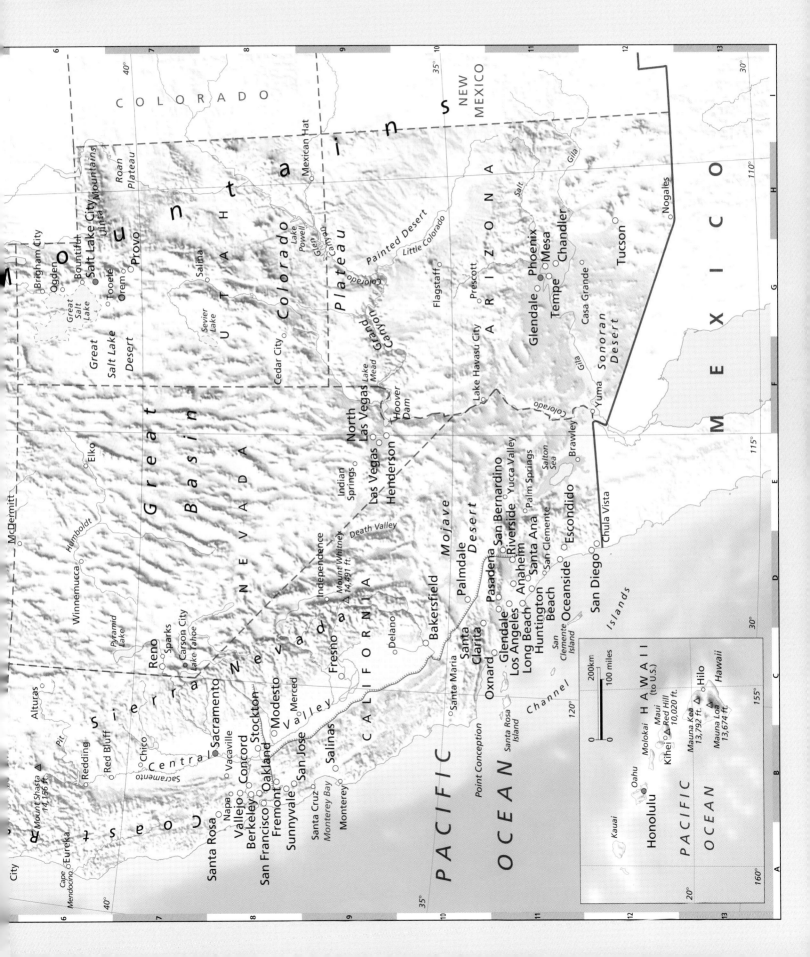

COLORADO

NEW MEXICO

M o u n t a i n s

Mexican Hat

Roan
Plateau

Uinta Mountains

Brigham City
Ogden
Bountiful
Salt Lake City
Tooele
Orem
Provo

Salina

Great
Salt
Lake

Great Salt Lake Desert

Sevier
Lake

U T A H

Cedar City

C o l o r a d o   P l a t e a u

Lake
Powell
Glen
Canyon

Grand
Canyon

Colorado

Painted Desert

Little Colorado

Flagstaff

Prescott

Casa Grande

Nogales

Tucson

A R I Z O N A

Glendale Phoenix
Mesa
Tempe Chandler

Lake Havasu City

Gila

Salt

Gila

Sonoran
Desert

Yuma

Colorado

Brawley

M E X I C O

G r e a t   B a s i n

Elko

McDermitt

Humboldt

Winnemucca

Pyramid
Lake

N E V A D A

Reno
Sparks
Carson City
Lake Tahoe

Indian
Springs

North
Las Vegas

Las Vegas
Henderson

Lake
Mead
Hoover
Dam

Death Valley

Independence

Mount Whitney
14,491 ft.

S i e r r a   N e v a d a

Alturas

Mount Shasta
14,156 ft.

Pit

Redding
Red Bluff
Chico

Eureka

Cape
Mendocino

City

Sacramento

Santa Rosa
Napa
Vallejo
Concord
Berkeley Stockton
San Francisco Oakland
Fremont Modesto
Sunnyvale Merced
San Jose
Santa Cruz
Monterey Bay
Monterey

Vacaville

Central

Sacramento

V a l l e y

Salinas

C A L I F O R N I A

Fresno

Delano

Bakersfield

Mojave
Desert

Palmdale

Santa
Clarita
Oxnard
Glendale
Pasadena
Los Angeles
Long Beach
Huntington
Beach

San Bernardino
Riverside
Anaheim
Santa Ana
San Clemente

Yucca Valley

Palm Springs

Salton
Sea

Escondido
Oceanside

San Diego
Chula Vista

San
Clemente
Island

Point Conception

Santa Maria

Santa Rosa
Island

Channel

Islands

C   o   a   s   t

P A C I F I C

O C E A N

35°

120°

30°

115°

110°

30°

40°

40°

35°

20°

160°

155°

Honolulu
Oahu

Kauai

Molokai
Kihei
Maui
Red Hill
10,020 ft.

H A W A I I
(to U.S.)

Mauna Kea
13,792 ft.
Mauna Loa
13,674 ft.

Hilo

Hawaii

P A C I F I C

O C E A N

200km

0

100 miles

0

A
B
C
D
E
F
G
H
I

6
7
8
9
10
11
12
13

MIDWESTERN UNITED STATES

In the heart of the U.S. is a large area of land known as the Midwest. To the west it is bordered by the Rocky Mountains—a huge chain of peaks running all the way from Alaska to New Mexico. Few people live in this rugged landscape, but many of those who do are involved in the mining industry because the Rockies are rich in coal, natural gas, and many metals.

To the east of the Rocky Mountains much of the Midwest is covered by the Great Plains. These plains were once natural grasslands, where native peoples, such as the Crow and Cheyenne, hunted buffalo. Today the plains contain many large cattle ranches and cereal farms. Food processing is an important industry in the cities. Far inland the plains have low rainfall and are hot in the summer, so the U.S.'s longest river, the Missouri River, is a vital source of water for farming. This river is also used to generate electricity and for transporting heavy goods.

Not all of the plains are covered in lush grasslands. In the north are the Badlands. The land here is dry, and few plants and animals can survive in the arid conditions. Storms have washed away the soil to reveal a harsh, stony landscape covered with multicolored rocks such as shale and limestone. This striking terrain makes parts of the Badlands popular with tourists.

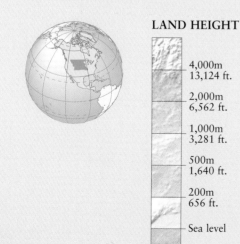

LAND HEIGHT

	4,000m 13,124 ft.
	2,000m 6,562 ft.
	1,000m 3,281 ft.
	500m 1,640 ft.
	200m 656 ft.
	Sea level

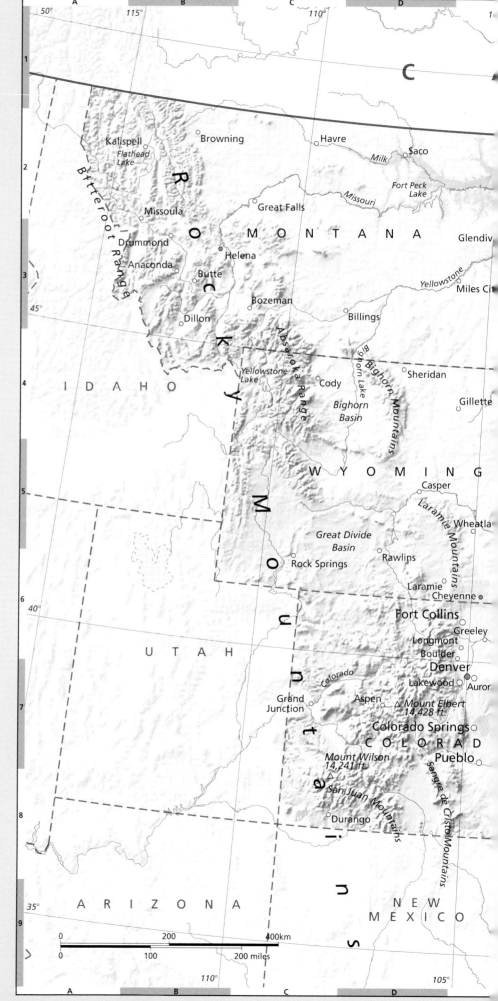

F 100° G 95° H J 90° K

N A D A

50° 1

2 2

45° 50°

Williston
Lake Sakakawea Minot
Sheyenne
Red River
Lake of the Woods
Grand Forks
Bemidji
Hibbing
Lake Superior

NORTH DAKOTA
Dickinson
Jamestown
Missouri
Bismarck
Fergus Falls
Brainerd
Duluth
MINNESOTA
St. Cloud
Mississippi
3

Lake Oahe
Grand River
Aberdeen
James
Willmar
Stillwater
Minneapolis St. Paul
Bloomington
WISCONSIN
45°

SOUTH DAKOTA
Watertown
Minnesota
New Ulm
Faribault
Winona
4

Rapid City
Cheyenne
Pierre
Mitchell
Fairmont
Albert Lea
Rochester
Austin
Mississippi

Badlands
Pine Ridge
Niobrara
Valentine
Sioux Falls
Spencer
Mason City
Cedar Falls
Dubuque
Waterloo
5

Scottsbluff
North Platte
NEBRASKA
Norfolk
Sioux City
Fort Dodge
Des Moines
IOWA
Ames
Cedar
Cedar Rapids
Iowa City
Davenport

Columbus
Council Bluffs
Omaha
Burlington
6

Big Springs
North Platte
Grand Island
Lincoln
ILLINOIS 40°
South Platte
Sterling
Platte
Hastings
Maryville
Kirksville
Republican
Saint Joseph
Mississippi

Colby
Manhattan
Kansas City Kansas City
Columbia
St. Charles
7
Burlington
Hays
Topeka
Independence
Overland Park
Missouri
St. Louis
Cheyenne Wells
Smoky Hill
KANSAS
Ottawa
Jefferson City
Great Bend
Emporia
MISSOURI
Garden City
Arkansas
Hutchinson
Wichita
Pittsburg
Springfield
Poplar Bluff
8
Springfield
Dodge City
Arkansas City
Joplin
Ozark Plateau
Liberal

TENNESSEE

TEXAS
OKLAHOMA
ARKANSAS
35° 9

MISSISSIPPI

F 100° G 95° H J 90° K

SOUTHERN UNITED STATES

This region of the U.S. is the home of many Native American peoples such as the Cherokee, Creek, and Choctaw. To the south of the area is the large Gulf Coastal Plain. It is drained by many rivers, including the Mississippi River, which flows south to a large swampy delta on the coast of Louisiana. Elsewhere the landscape ranges from the deserts and mountains of New Mexico to the Everglades—southern Florida's swamplands. Farther north are uplands, including the Appalachian and Ouachita mountains. The southern states have a warm climate with mild winters. Summer is generally hot, and the southeastern part of the region can be very humid.

Crops, such as peanuts and citrus fruits, grow well in the south, while the west contains large cattle ranches and wheat farms. Another typical crop is cotton, which was grown on plantations worked mainly by slaves until the mid-1800s. Many of this region's cities are industrialized, and the states of Texas and Oklahoma are major sources of oil and natural gas. As well as manufacturing and engineering, this area has high-tech computer and aerospace industries. Florida's unique scenery and warm climate make it a favorite tourist destination. People from all over the world come to visit its attractions, including Everglades National Park.

LAND HEIGHT

4,000m	13,124 ft.
2,000m	6,562 ft.
1,000m	3,281 ft.
500m	1,640 ft.
200m	656 ft.
Sea level	

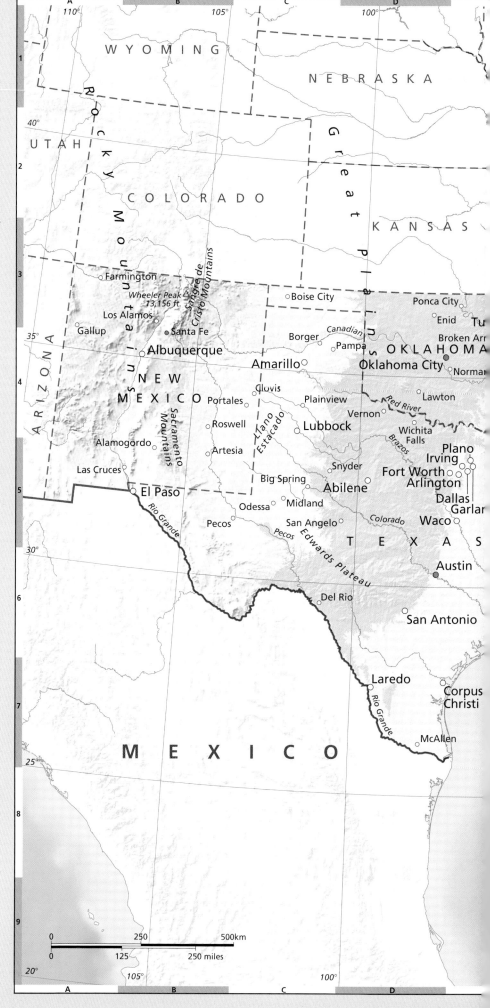

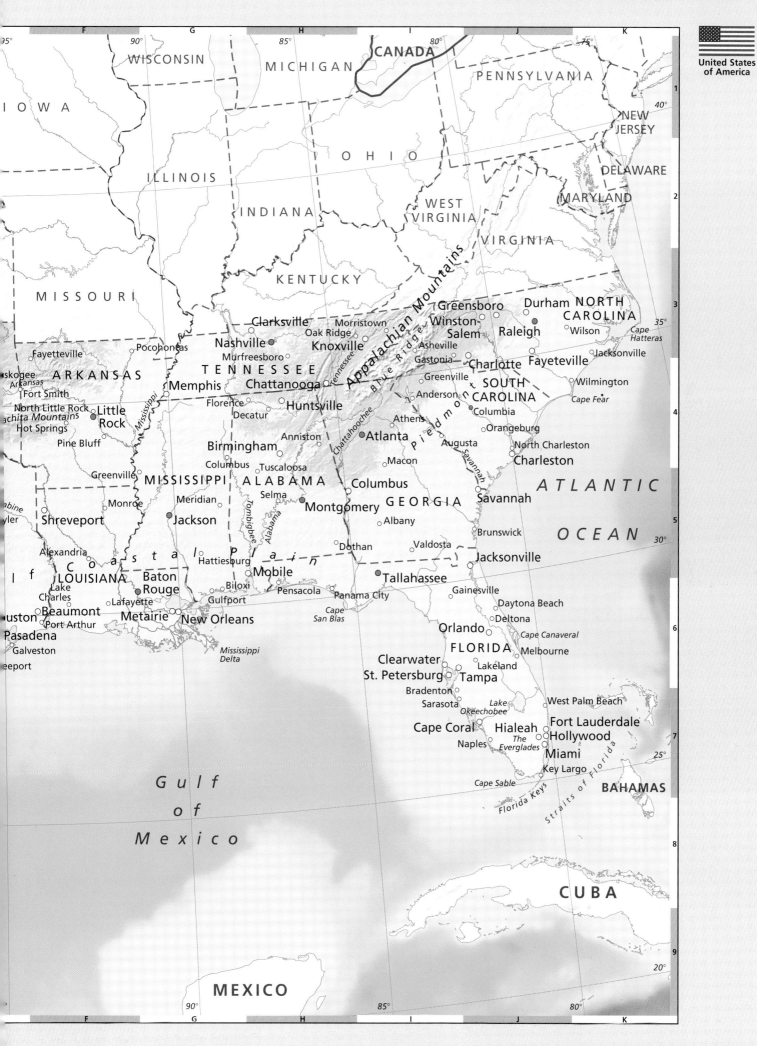

WISCONSIN

MICHIGAN

CANADA

PENNSYLVANIA

IOWA

NEW
JERSEY

ILLINOIS

OHIO

DELAWARE

INDIANA

WEST
VIRGINIA

MARYLAND

MISSOURI

KENTUCKY

VIRGINIA

Appalachian Mountains

Greensboro
Durham
NORTH
CAROLINA

Clarksville
Morristown
Winston-
Salem
Raleigh
Wilson
Cape
Hatteras

Oak Ridge
Nashville
Murfreesboro
Knoxville
Asheville
Jacksonville

Fayetteville
Pocohontas
Gastonia
Charlotte
Fayeteville

skogee
Arkansas
ARKANSAS
Memphis
Chattanooga
Blue Ridge
Greenville
SOUTH
CAROLINA
Wilmington

Fort Smith
TENNESSEE
Tennessee
Anderson
Piedmont

North Little Rock
Little
Rock
Florence
Huntsville
Chattahoochee
Athens
Columbia
Cape Fear

achita Mountains
Decatur
Orangeburg

Hot Springs
Anniston
Atlanta
Augusta
North Charleston

Pine Bluff
Birmingham
Macon
Charleston

Columbus
Tuscaloosa

Greenville
MISSISSIPPI
ALABAMA
Columbus
ATLANTIC

Selma
GEORGIA
Savannah

Monroe
Meridian
Montgomery

abine
Shreveport
Jackson
Albany
Brunswick
OCEAN

yler
Tombigbee
Alabama
Dothan
Valdosta

Alexandria
Coastal
Plain
Jacksonville

LOUISIANA
Hattiesburg
Mobile
Tallahassee
Gainesville

If
Baton
Rouge
Biloxi
Pensacola
Panama City
Daytona Beach

Lake
Charles
Lafayette
Gulfport
Cape
San Blas
Deltona

Beaumont
Metairie
New Orleans
Orlando
Cape Canaveral

uston
Port Arthur
FLORIDA
Melbourne

Pasadena
Mississippi
Delta
Clearwater
Lakeland

Galveston
St. Petersburg
Tampa

eeport
Bradenton
West Palm Beach

Sarasota
Lake
Okeechobee
Fort Lauderdale

Cape Coral
Hialeah
Hollywood

Naples
The
Everglades
Miami

Gulf
Key Largo

of
Cape Sable
BAHAMAS

Mexico
Florida Keys
Straits of Florida

CUBA

MEXICO

NORTHEASTERN UNITED STATES

Along the eastern coast of this area are rocky headlands and sandy beaches with flooded river valleys that make ideal harbors. Inland, beyond the coastal plain, are the Appalachians, an ancient chain of mountains covered in forests. Still farther to the west is the huge Mississippi basin, with the Great Lakes to the north.

For thousands of years the region was home to native peoples such as the Iroquois and Delaware. They were expert farmers and fishers. In the 1600s some of North America's first European settlers arrived there, and the native peoples showed the settlers how to grow local crops. In the 1800s millions of immigrants passed through New York City before settling in the region, and today it is still densely populated. The northeast contains major cities such as New York City, the country's financial center, Chicago, and Washington, D.C., the capital of the U.S.

Many farmers in the northeast grow corn or fruit or raise livestock. Some areas, such as Detroit in Michigan and the state of Pennsylvania, have for many years been centers of heavy industry, from mining and steel production to manufacturing. Although these are still important, newer, high-tech industries that produce electronic goods have been set up in Massachusetts and New Jersey.

LAND HEIGHT

	4,000m 13,124 ft.
	2,000m 6,562 ft.
	1,000m 3,281 ft.
	500m 1,640 ft.
	200m 656 ft.
	Sea level

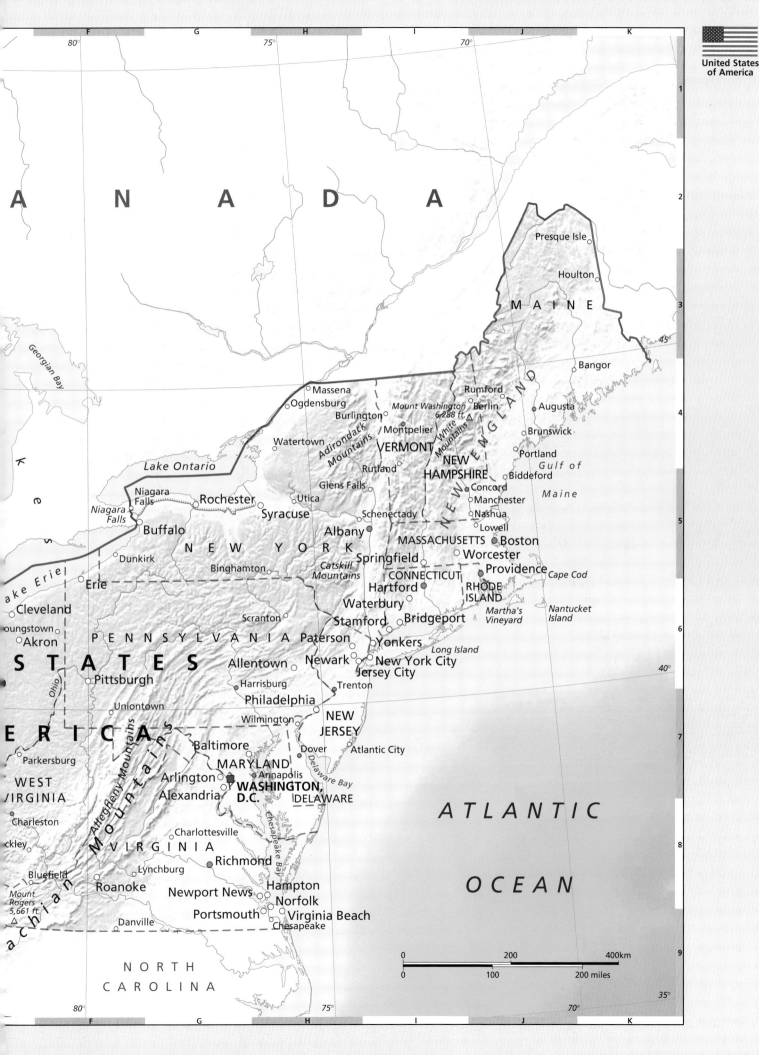

United States
of America

CANADA

Presque Isle

Houlton

MAINE

Georgian Bay

Massena
Ogdensburg
Burlington
Rumford
Berlin
Mount Washington
6,288 ft.
Bangor

Augusta

Watertown
Adirondack
Mountains
Montpelier
White
Mountains
VERMONT
NEW
HAMPSHIRE
Brunswick

Lake Ontario
Rutland
NEW ENGLAND
Portland
Biddeford
Gulf of
Maine

Niagara
Falls
Rochester
Utica
Glens Falls
Schenectady
Concord
Manchester
Nashua
Lowell

Niagara
Falls
Syracuse
Albany
MASSACHUSETTS
Boston
Worcester

Buffalo
NEW YORK
Springfield
Providence
Cape Cod

Dunkirk
Binghamton
Catskill
Mountains
CONNECTICUT
Hartford
RHODE
ISLAND
Martha's
Vineyard
Nantucket
Island

Lake Erie
Erie
Waterbury

Cleveland
Scranton
Stamford
Bridgeport

oungstown
Akron
PENNSYLVANIA
Paterson
Yonkers
Long Island

Ohio
Pittsburgh
Allentown
Newark
New York City
Jersey City

STATES
Harrisburg
Trenton

Uniontown
Philadelphia

Parkersburg
ERICA
Wilmington
NEW
JERSEY
Atlantic City

Baltimore
Dover

WEST
VIRGINIA
Alleghany Mountains
Arlington
MARYLAND
Annapolis
Delaware Bay

Charleston
Alexandria
WASHINGTON,
D.C.
DELAWARE

ckley
Charlottesville
VIRGINIA
Chesapeake Bay
ATLANTIC

Bluefield
Lynchburg
Richmond

Mount
Rogers
5,661 ft.
Roanoke
Newport News
Hampton
Norfolk
OCEAN

achian
Danville
Portsmouth
Virginia Beach
Chesapeake

NORTH
CAROLINA

0   200   400km
0   100   200 miles

MEXICO AND CENTRAL AMERICA

A chain of mountains, broken by fertile river valleys, forms the backbone of Mexico and Central America. Lowlands run along the east coast, widening to form Mexico's Yucatán Peninsula and Nicaragua's Mosquito Coast (Golfo de los Mosquitos). In the south Costa Rica and Panama form a narrow neck of land that measures less than 60 mi. across in some places. The Panama Canal, which was completed in 1914, provides a shipping link between the Atlantic and Pacific oceans.

Most of the inhabitants of this area are descended from native peoples—such as the Maya and Aztec—and Europeans, especially the Spanish, who conquered the region in the 1400s and 1500s. They are mainly farmers, either producing corn and beans for local use or growing crops, such as coffee, cotton, and bananas, for export. The area's major industries include mining, manufacturing, and construction.

The population of this region is rising rapidly. Millions of people, unable to make a living from farming, have moved to the towns. Some cities have grown very quickly and have poor housing, education, and health services. The air quality in these urban areas is often low owing to pollution from cars and factories. As the cities grow large areas of tropical rain forests are being cut down to clear land for building.

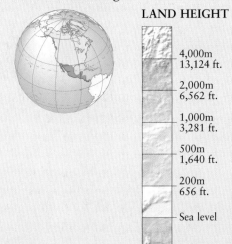

LAND HEIGHT

4,000m
13,124 ft.

2,000m
6,562 ft.

1,000m
3,281 ft.

500m
1,640 ft.

200m
656 ft.

Sea level

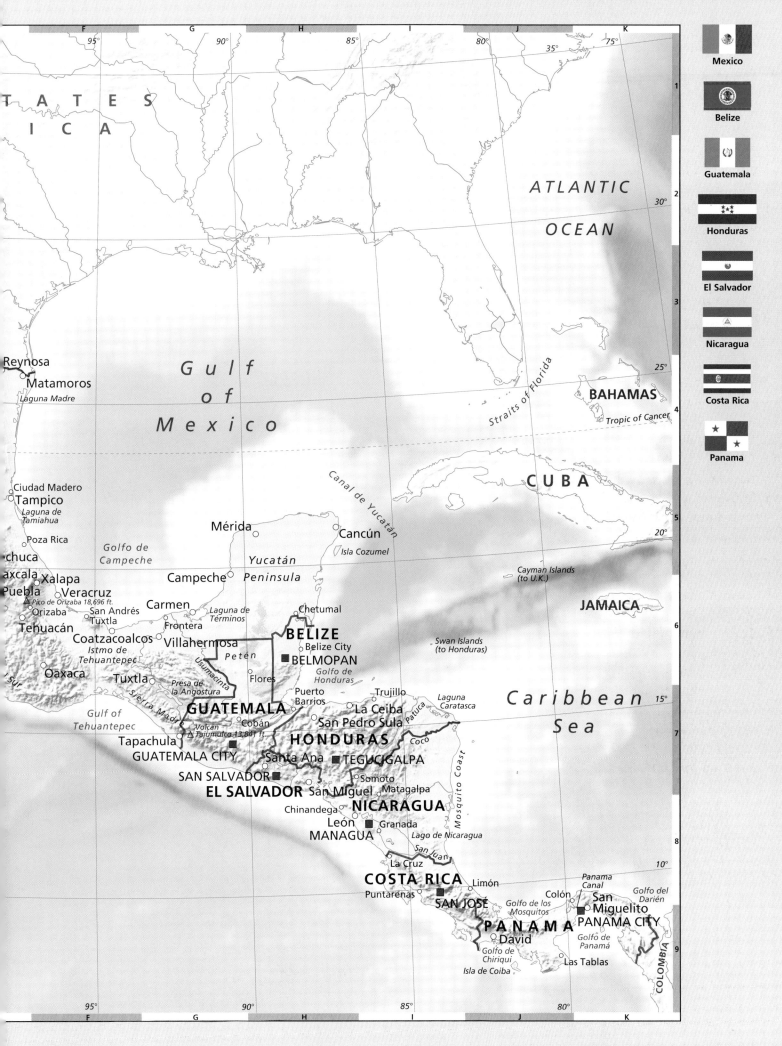

Mexico

Belize

Guatemala

Honduras

El Salvador

Nicaragua

Costa Rica

Panama

F   G   H   I   J   K

95°   90°   85°   80°   35°

ATLANTIC

OCEAN

1

2   30°

3

T A T E S

I C A

Reynosa

Matamoros

Laguna Madre

Gulf

of

Mexico

BAHAMAS   25°

Straits of Florida   Tropic of Cancer   4

Ciudad Madero

Tampico

Laguna de
Tamiahua

Poza Rica

chuca

axcala

Puebla   Xalapa

Veracruz

△Pico de Orizaba 18,696 ft.

Orizaba

San Andrés
Tuxtla

Tehuacán

Oaxaca

Golfo de
Campeche

Mérida

Campeche   Yucatán
Peninsula

Carmen

Laguna de
Términos

Frontera

Villahermosa

Coatzacoalcos
Istmo de
Tehuantepec

Tuxtla

Presa de
la Angostura

Canal de Yucatán

Cancún

Isla Cozumel

CUBA   20°   5

Cayman Islands
(to U.K.)

JAMAICA   6

Chetumal

BELIZE

Belize City

BELMOPAN

Petén   Golfo de
Honduras

Flores

Usumacinta   Swan Islands
(to Honduras)

Caribbean

Sea   15°

Trujillo

GUATEMALA

Sierra Madre   Volcán
△Tajumulco 13,841 ft.

Cobán

Puerto
Barrios

La Ceiba

San Pedro Sula

HONDURAS

Laguna
Caratasca

Patuca

Coco   7

Gulf of
Tehuantepec

Tapachula

GUATEMALA CITY

Santa Ana   TEGUCIGALPA

SAN SALVADOR

EL SALVADOR   San Miguel

Somoto

Matagalpa

Mosquito Coast

Chinandega

NICARAGUA

León   Granada

MANAGUA

Lago de Nicaragua   8

San Juan

La Cruz   10°

COSTA RICA   Limón

Puntarenas   Colón

San
Miguelito

SAN JOSÉ

Golfo de los
Mosquitos

PANAMA   PANAMA CITY

David

Golfo de
Chiriquí   Golfó de
Panamá

Las Tablas

Isla de Coiba

Panama Canal

Golfo del
Darién

COLOMBIA   9

95°   90°   85°   80°

THE CARIBBEAN

In the Caribbean Sea there are two mountain ranges, called the Greater and Lesser Antilles, that run from Florida to Trinidad. For part of their length these mountains are hidden underwater, but where they break the surface they form the islands of the Caribbean. Many of these islands are small and mountainous, but two larger ones, Cuba and Hispaniola (which is divided into Haiti and the Dominican Republic), have a more varied landscape. On Cuba the mountains are broken up by plains, while on Hispaniola valleys divide the uplands.

The Caribbean is well-known for its warm, sunny climate, but during the hottest months, between July and October, violent storms and hurricanes blow in from the Atlantic Ocean and lash the islands. These winds reach up to 155 mph, and they can flatten everything in their path.

The people of the Caribbean are mostly descendants of Africans, Europeans, and Asians who settled here over the years or were brought to the area as slaves. In the past almost everyone lived by farming, and these islands still produce large amounts of crops such as sugarcane and bananas. Today the Caribbean's warm weather and sandy beaches attract millions of visitors from North America and even farther away. Tourism has had a damaging effect on the environment, but it has also brought much needed money into the region.

LAND HEIGHT

- 4,000m 13,124 ft.
- 2,000m 6,562 ft.
- 1,000m 3,281 ft.
- 500m 1,640 ft.
- 200m 656 ft.
- Sea level

Bahamas

Cuba

Haiti

Dominican Republic

Jamaica

Antigua & Barbuda

St. Kitts & Nevis

Dominica

St. Lucia

St. Vincent & the Grenadines

Barbados

Grenada

Trinidad & Tobago

0   250   500km
0   125   250 miles

A T L A N T I C

O C E A N

West   Indies

West

Turks & Caicos Islands
(to U.K.)

Great ragua

ins d

ward Passage

**DOMINICAN
REPUBLIC**

Port-de-Paix

Cap-Haïten

Santiago

La Vega   San Francisco
de Macorís

onaïves

St. Marc

Pico Duarte ▲
10,414 ft

HAITI

Hispaniola

PORT-AU-
PRINCE

ayes

Jacmel

SANTO
DOMINGO

San
Pedros de
Macorís

La
Romana

San Juan

Bayamón

Mayagüez   Caguas

Ponce

Puerto Rico
(to U.S.)

Mona Passage

British
Virgin Islands
(to U.K.)

Anguilla
(to U.K.)

St. Martin
(to France & Netherlands)

St. Barthélémy (to France)

Barbuda

Netherlands
Antilles
(to Netherlands)

Virgin Islands
(to U.S.)

Leeward   Islands

St. Kitts

Nevis

BASSETERRE

**ST. KITTS
& NEVIS**

Montserrat
(to U.K.)

Antilles

ntilles

ANTIGUA & BARBUDA

Antigua

☐ ST. JOHN'S

Guadeloupe Passage

Basse Terre

Grande Terre

Guadeloupe
(to France)

Basse Terre

DOMINICA ROSEAU

Martinique Passage

Martinique
(to France)

Fort-de-France

ST. LUCIA

CASTRIES

St. Vincent Passage

KINGSTOWN

St. Vincent

**ST. VINCENT &
THE GRENADINES**

The Grenadines

BARBADOS

BRIDGETOWN

Windward   Islands

ST. GEORGE'S

GRENADA

Lesser   Antilles

Aruba
(to Netherlands)

Oranjestad

Netherlands Antilles
(to Netherlands)

Willemstad   Bonaire

Curaçao

Tobago

PORT-OF-SPAIN

Arima

**TRINIDAD
& TOBAGO**

Point Fortin   *Trinidad*

V E N E Z U E L A

IA

I A

70°   65°   60°

SOUTH AMERICA

The continent of South America is shaped like a triangle. It tapers from the warm Caribbean coasts of Colombia and Venezuela to the cold waters of the Southern and Pacific oceans at the southern tips of Argentina and Chile. Three very different types of landscapes dominate the continent. In the west the Andes stretch for 4,495 mi. along the entire Pacific coast. These towering mountains reach more than 22,000 ft. in height. In the hot and humid regions of the northeast the world's largest rain forest, the Amazon, covers an area of four million sq. mi. The mighty Amazon river flows through this region. Farther south there are great open plains of grass and scrubland.

Hundreds of years ago the native peoples of South America built powerful civilizations, but later, between the 1500-1800s, much of the continent was ruled by the Spanish and Portuguese. As a result, the official language in Brazil is Portuguese, while Spanish is spoken in most of the other countries. The Spanish and Portuguese also developed South America's cities, building on the Atlantic coast for easy access to Europe. Today most South Americans still live on the coast in places such as Rio de Janeiro, Montevideo, and São Paulo—which is one of the world's largest cities.

South America has rich mineral deposits and fertile farming lands, and most of the countries export goods, including oil and foodstuffs. The wealth is not divided equally. Many people are desperately poor, and large sections of the population cannot read or write. A number of South America's countries have borrowed money from wealthier nations, and they are struggling to repay their debts.

LAND HEIGHT

4,000m	13,124 ft.
2,000m	6,562 ft.
1,000m	3,281 ft.
500m	1,640 ft.
200m	656 ft.
	Sea level

Maceió

Salvador

Represa de Sobradinho

Tocantins

Planalto de Mato Grosso

B r a z i l i a n   H i g h l a n d s

BRASÍLIA

Goiânia

Belo Horizonte

Ribeirão Prêto

Nova Iguaçu

São Gonçalo

Rio de Janeiro

Uberlândia

Rio Grande

Campinas

São Paulo Guarulhos

Curitiba

Campo Grande

Araguaia

Pantanal

Paraná

Serra Geral

Porto Alegre

Lagoa dos Patos

Lagoa Mirim

URUGUAY

MONTEVIDEO

ATLANTIC OCEAN

1000km

500 miles

500

250

South Georgia (to U.K.)

PARAGUAY

ASUNCIÓN

Paraguay

Gran Chaco

Pilcomayo

Mesopotamia

Uruguay

Paraná

Rio de la Plata

La Plata

BUENOS AIRES

Lomas de Zamora

Mar del Plata

Rosario

Córdoba

Pampas

Bahía Blanca

Punta Rasa

Falkland Islands (to U.K.)

Stanley

East Falkland

West Falkland

PERU

Callao

LIMA

Arequipa

BOLIVIA

LA PAZ

Cochabamba

Santa Cruz

SUCRE

Lago Titicaca

Altiplano

Nevado Sajama 21,463 ft.

Desierto Atacama

Ojos del Salado 22,565 ft.

San Miguel de Tucumán

Salado

Laguna Mar Chiquito

Aconcagua 22,828 ft.

SANTIAGO

A   N   D   E   S

C H I L E

A R G E N T I N A

P a t a g o n i a

Rio Negro

Golfo San Matías

Golfo San Jorge

Bahía Grande

Strait of Magellan

Tierra del Fuego

Cape Horn

Isla de Chiloé

Archipiélago de los Chonos

Isla Wellington

Archipiélago Reina Adelaida

Madre de Dios

Beni

Mamoré

Guaporé

Juruena

Islas de los Desventurados

Juan Fernandez Islands

PACIFIC OCEAN

Tropic of Capricorn

Tropic of Capricorn

NORTHERN SOUTH AMERICA

The northern part of South America is fringed by uplands—the Guiana Highlands in the north, the Andes in the west, and the Brazilian Highlands in the south. This region has many amazing physical features. Lake Titicaca, on the border between Peru and Bolivia, is South America's largest lake. It is also the highest navigable lake in the world. Angel Falls in Venezuela is the world's highest waterfall. Across the middle of this region is the basin of the Amazon—a river so large that it carries around one fifth of the world's freshwater.

Few people live in the interior areas. Most of this region's huge population lives in coastal cities, working in the industries that have developed around them. These include oil production and metal refining in Venezuela and chemical and textile industries in Brazil. Mining occurs in most countries. The Amazon region has a thriving timber industry, but loggers are steadily cutting away the rain forest. Large areas of trees have been cleared by farmers for cropland and cattle ranches. Plans to build new oil pipelines and roads across the region will also lead to deforestation. Every year around three million acres of forests disappear from the Amazon, and because around half of the world's known plant and animal species live here, environmentalists are fighting to preserve this important area.

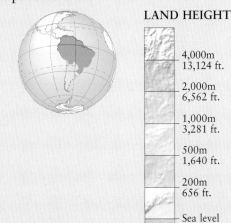

LAND HEIGHT

	4,000m 13,124 ft.
	2,000m 6,562 ft.
	1,000m 3,281 ft.
	500m 1,640 ft.
	200m 656 ft.
	Sea level

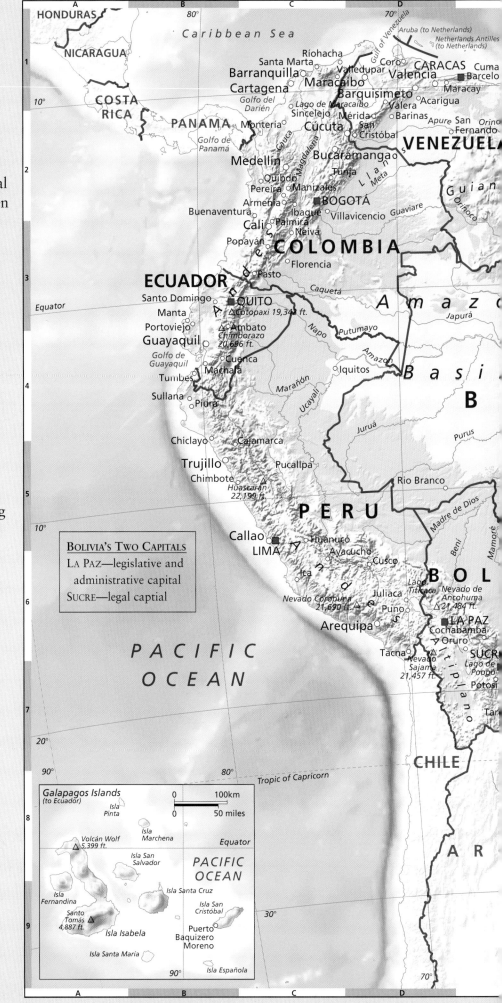

BOLIVIA'S TWO CAPITALS
LA PAZ—legislative and administrative capital
SUCRE—legal captial

ATLANTIC
OCEAN

60°
GRENADA
de
argarita
TRINIDAD
& TOBAGO
Maturin
Ciudad Guayana
Ciudad Bolívar
Embalse
de Guri
GEORGETOWN
GUYANA
PARAMARIBO
SURINAME French
Guiana
(to France)
Cayenne
gel
alls
ighlands
Essequibo
Boa Vista
Branco
ro

Mouths of
the Amazon
Baía de Marajó
Macapá
Represa de
Balbina
Isla de
Marajó
Amazon
Belém
Baía de São Marcos
São Luís
Parnaíba
Manaus
Santarém
Tapajós
Iriri
Sobral
Fortaleza
Amazon
Represa
Tucuruí
Imperatriz
Teresina
Cabo de
São Roque
Madeira
Xingu
A Z I L
Mossoró
Natal
São Manuel
Juazeiro do Norte
Campina
Grande
João Pessoa
orto Velho
Parnaíba
Jaboatão
Olinda
Araguaia
Caruarú
Recife
Juruena
Tocantins
Juàzeiro
Maceió
Rio das Mortes
Represa de
Sobradinho
Arapiraca
Guaporé
Taguatinga
Aracaju
IA
Planalto de
Mato Grosso
São Francisco
Feira de Santana
Alagoinhas
Salvador
Cuiabá
Jequié
Santa Cruz
BRASÍLIA
Vitória da
Conquista
Ilhéus
Corumba
Goiânia
Anápolis
Montes Claros
Pantanal
Brazilian
Uberlândia
Teófilo Otoni
Paranaíba
Highlands
Uberaba
Linhares
Campo
Grande
Franca
Divinópolis
Belo Horizonte
Ribeirão Prêto
Rio Grande
Vitória
Dourados
Marília
Juiz de Fora
Paraná
Campos
PARAGUAY
Campinas
Guarulhos
São Gonçalo
Londrina
Nova
Iguaçu
Rio de Janeiro
Maringá
São Paulo
Santos
Cascavel
Ponta Grossa
Serra Geral
Curitiba
Joinville
Uruguay
Lages
Florianópolis
NTINA
Passo Fundo
ATLANTIC
OCEAN
Santa Maria
Porto Alegre
Bagé
Lagoa
dos Patos
Río Grande
URUGUAY
Lagoa Mirim

0 500 1000km
0 250 500 miles

60°
50°
40°
30°
F G H I J K
10°
1
2
3
Equator
4
5
10°
6
7
20°
8
Tropic of Capricorn
9
30°
60° 50° 40° 30°

Colombia
Venezuela
Guyana
Suriname
Brazil
Ecuador
Peru
Bolivia

SOUTHERN SOUTH AMERICA

The southern part of South America is made up of Paraguay, Uruguay, Argentina, and Chile. The Andes mountains run from the north to the south, forming the backbone of the region. The Atacama Desert, the driest place on Earth, lies in the northwest. To the east are the forests and grasslands of Gran Chaco, the grasslands of the Pampas, and Patagonia, a high, cold plateau in southern Argentina. The southwest has a dramatic landscape of icy fjords, jagged mountain peaks, and frozen glaciers. Farther south are the windy islands of Tierra del Fuego.

Most of the people in southern South America live in cities, especially in the capitals. Buenos Aires, for example, is the home of over one third of Argentina's population. The majority of those who live in this region speak Spanish—the language of the people who ruled the area until the 1800s. In some places small groups of people still speak the native languages.

The big cities in Chile, Argentina, and Uruguay are centers for heavy industries, and some of these have polluted the larger rivers such as the Paraná and its tributaries. Argentina is famous

for raising cattle on its rich grasslands, and beef from its ranches is exported worldwide. Some of this meat is processed into products, such as corned beef, in factories in Córdoba and Buenos Aires. Paraguay grows wheat and other crops for its own use, while cotton, coffee, tobacco, and oilseeds, such as soybeans, are the country's major export crops. Uruguay's main export is wool. The Chilean Andes, with their deposits of copper, are mined heavily. A wide range of fruits and more specialized crops, such as walnuts and grapes for wine, are grown in Chile's fertile Central Valley.

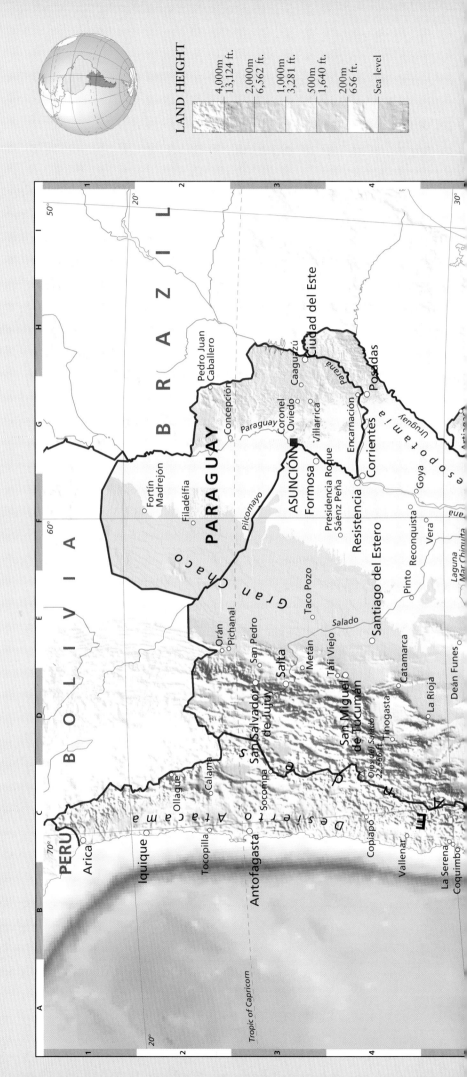

LAND HEIGHT

4,000m 13,124 ft.	2,000m 6,562 ft.	1,000m 3,281 ft.	500m 1,640 ft.	200m 656 ft.	Sea level

Chile
Paraguay
Argentina
Uruguay

SOUTHERN SOUTH AMERICA

ATLANTIC OCEAN

PACIFIC OCEAN

URUGUAY

ARGENTINA

CHILE

Paysandú
Melo
Mercedes
Durazno
Lagoa Mirim
Fray Bentos
Minas
MONTEVIDEO
San José de Mayo
San Nicolás de Los Arroyos
Florida
Las Piedras
Río de la Plata
La Plata
Punta Norte
Mar del Plata
Necochea
Punta Rasa
Punta Alta

Francisco Santa
Fé Paraná
Gualeguaychu
Rosario
Venado Tuerto
Pergamino
Rufino
Junín
BUENOS AIRES
Lomas de Zamora
Azul
Tres Arroyos
Coronel Pringles
Bahía Blanca
Bahía Blanca
Olavarría
Río Colorado
Viedma

San Juan
Villa María
Mendoza Río Cuarto
Godoy Cruz San Luis
San Rafael
Malargüe
Salado
Colorado
General Roca
Neuquén
Zapala
Chos Malal
Río Negro
Golfo San Matías
Península Valdés
Rawson
Golfo San Jorge
Chubut

Aconcagua 22,828 ft.
Viña del Mar Andes
Valparaíso
Rancagua
Pichilemu
Constitución
Talca
Chillán
Talcahuano
Concepción
Lebu
Los Ángeles
Temuco
Valdivia
Osorno
Puerto Montt
Corcovado
Golfo Corcovado
Isla de Chiloé
Archipiélago de los Chonos
Puerto Aisén
Coihaique
Taitao Península
Golfo de Penas
Isla Wellington

San Carlos de Bariloche
Esquel
Nueva Lubecka
Sarmiento
Comodoro Rivadavia
Fitz Roy Cabo Tres Puntas
Puerto Deseado
Deseado
Chico
Gobernador Gregores
Chico
Santa Cruz
El Calafate
Puerto San Julián
Puerto Santa Cruz
Bahía Grande
Río Gallegos
Puerto Natales
Punta Arenas
Archipiélago Reina Adelaida

Strait of Magellan
San Sebastián
Río Grande
Tierra del Fuego
Ushuaia
Isla de los Estados
Cape Horn

Falkland Islands (to U.K.)
Stanley
East Falkland
West Falkland

SANTIAGO
San Bernado

40°
50°
60°
70°
80°

600km
300 miles
300
300
150

THE ATLANTIC OCEAN

Covering around one fifth of the planet's surface, the Atlantic is the world's second-largest ocean. To the west are the Americas, and Europe and Africa lie to the east. Earth's longest mountain chain, the Mid-Atlantic Ridge, dominates the ocean's underwater landscape. In places the ridge rises above the water as volcanic islands such as Iceland and the Azores. The deepest part of the Atlantic, the Puerto Rico Trench, plunges to −28,224 ft.

Since Portuguese and Spanish explorers began to cross the ocean from Europe to America in

the 1400s the Atlantic has been one of the world's major transportation routes. Today ships carry bulk goods, such as oil, grain, and iron, between the ocean's many international ports.

The Atlantic is rich in natural resources. The shallow areas along the coasts have deposits of oil and gas, and in recent years offshore oil and gas reserves have been exploited in the Gulf of Mexico, the Niger Delta, and the North Sea. Sand, gravel, and shell deposits are mined by the U.S. and the United Kingdom for use in the construction industry. The ocean is also a vital

source of food. Most of the Atlantic's coastal countries fish in its waters, but in the north Atlantic stocks of cod, herring, and haddock have been reduced by overfishing. The ocean's environment is also threatened by pollution. Oil is released into the water by ships and drilling rigs. Industrial waste, fertilizers, and sewage enter the Atlantic at the coasts, particularly in the Mediterranean, Baltic, and North Sea regions, as well as off the U.S., southern Brazil, and eastern Argentina. A number of countries are trying to reach agreements to combat some forms of pollution.

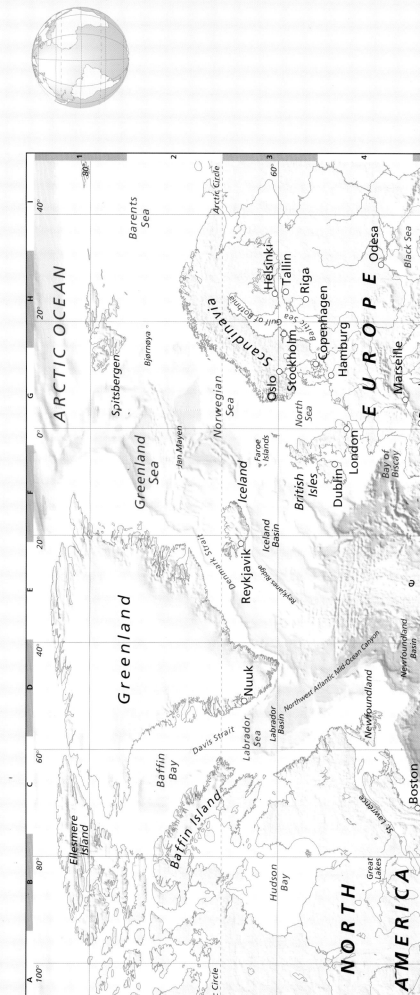

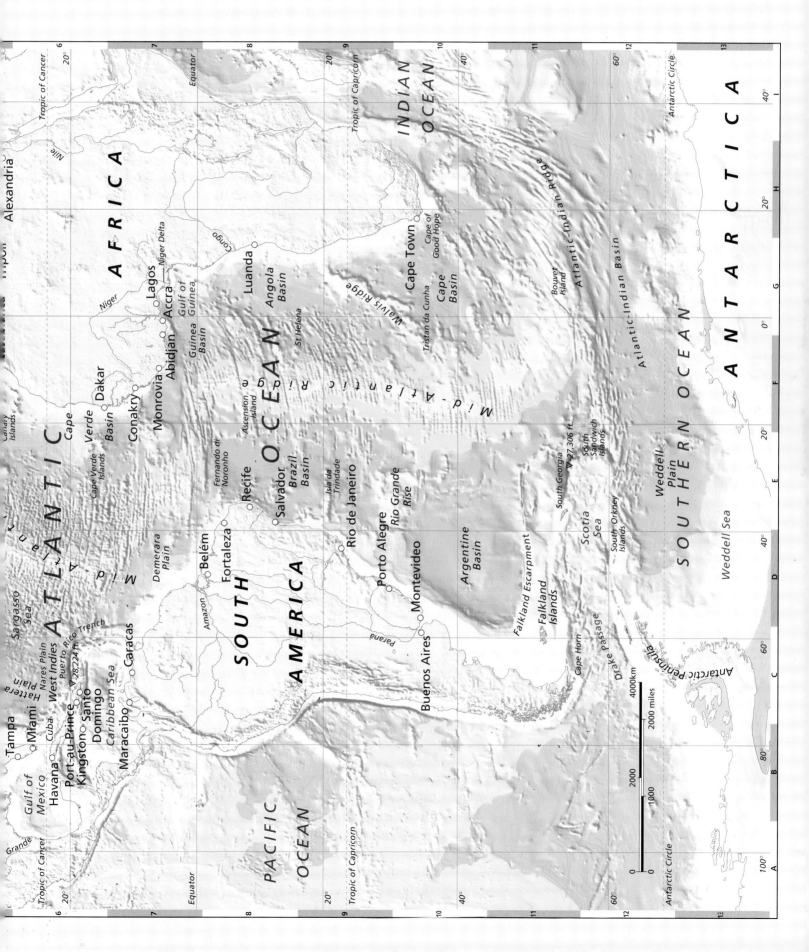

THE ATLANTIC OCEAN

Tropic of Cancer
20°
Equator
20°
Tropic of Capricorn
40°

INDIAN OCEAN

ANTARCTIC CIRCLE

AFRICA

Alexandria
Nile
Niger Delta
Congo
Lagos
Niger
Accra
Gulf of Guinea
Abidjan
Monrovia
Guinea Basin
Conakry
Dakar
Cape Verde
Cape Verde Islands
Basin

Luanda
Angola Basin

Cape Town
Cape of Good Hope
Cape Basin

Walvis Ridge

Tristan da Cunha
Bouvet Island

Atlantic-Indian Ridge
Atlantic-Indian Basin

ANTARCTICA

ATLANTIC
OCEAN

Sargasso Sea
Canary Islands
Cape

Mid-Atlantic Ridge

St Helena
Ascension Island
Fernando di Noronho

Recife
Salvador
Brazil Basin
Fortaleza
Belém
Demerara Plain

SOUTH
AMERICA

Amazon

Isla da Trindade
Rio de Janeiro
Porto Alegre
Rio Grande Rise
Montevideo
Buenos Aires
Paraná

Argentine Basin

South Georgia
V 27,306 ft.
South Sandwich Islands

Scotia Sea
South Orkney Islands

Weddell Plain

Weddell Sea

SOUTHERN OCEAN

Falkland Escarpment
Falkland Islands
Cape Horn
Drake Passage

Antarctic Peninsula

PACIFIC
OCEAN

Tampa
Miami
Havana
Cuba
Port-au-Prince
Kingston
Santo Domingo
West Indies
V 28,224 ft.
Puerto Rico Trench
Caribbean Sea
Maracaibo
Caracas
Nares Plain
Hatteras Plain
Grande
Gulf of Mexico

Tropic of Cancer
20°
Equator
20°
Tropic of Capricorn
40°
60°

4000km
2000 miles
2000
1000
0
0

Antarctic Circle

EUROPE

The continent of Europe extends from the Ural Mountains in the east to the Atlantic Ocean in the west, north to the Arctic Ocean, and south to the Mediterranean Sea. There are a number of mountain ranges, including the Alps, that rise to more than 15,700 ft., as well as lesser ranges such as the Carpathians, Pyrenees, and Apennines. Most of the continent's population lives between these uplands on the North European Plain. The plain's rich, fertile soil and temperate climate help farmers grow a variety of crops, such as wheat, fruit, and vegetables, and raise both dairy and beef cattle.

During the Industrial Revolution of the 1700s and 1800s Europe developed heavy industries such as iron and steelmaking. Today, in Western Europe, these businesses are being replaced by high-tech industries and financial services. In the east, however, many old-fashioned factories remain. These cause terrible environmental pollution in some places.

Many European countries have existed for hundreds of years, and some, such as the United Kingdom and France, had large empires. Although these empires no longer exist, the countries that ran them still play a major role in world affairs. In the 1900s many of Western Europe's countries came together to form the European Union. The union is working toward bringing its members closer politically and economically.

LAND HEIGHT

4,000m
13,124 ft.

2,000m
6,562 ft.

1,000m
3,281 ft.

500m
1,640 ft.

200m
656 ft.

Sea level

ASIA

Barents
Sea

North Cape

Novaya
Zemlya

Murmansk

Kola
Peninsula

Pechora

Ural Mountains

Arctic Circle

ØVesterålen
Øten

White
Sea

Archangel

Perm

Oulu

Northern Dvina

Kirov

Izhevsk

Ufa

FINLAND

Lake
Onega

R U S S I A N

Tampere

Lake
Ladoga

F E D E R A T I O N

Naberezhnyye Chelny

Gulf of Bothnia

Turku
(Abo)

HELSINKI

St. Petersburg

Yaroslavl

Kazan

Kama

Gulf of Finland

Ivanovo

ØCKHOLM

TALLINN

ESTONIA

Tver

Nizhniy Novgorod

Tolyatti

Orenburg

Gotland

Volga

MOSCOW

Simbirsk

Samara

Ural

LATVIA

RIGA

Western Dvina

Ryazan

Volga

ØItand

LITHUANIA

Vitsyebsk

Tula

Penza

Baltic
Sea

RUSS. FED.

Øsk

VILNIUS

Smolensk

Saratov

Kaliningrad

Bryansk

Lipetsk

Volga

Øznan

MINSK

Kursk

Voronezh

BELARUS

WARSAW

Homyel

Don

Volgograd

Vistula

Øodz

POLAND

Rivne

KIEV

Kharkiv

Astrakhan

Øroclaw

Krakow

UKRAINE

Dnipropetrovsk

Caspian Sea

ØLVIA

Lviv

Dniester

Krivyy Rih

Donetsk

Rostov-na-Donu

ØSLOVAKIA

Carpathian Mountains

MOLDOVA

Stavropol

ØRATISLAVA

Cluj-
Napoca

Iasi

CHISINAU

Dnieper

Sea of
Azov

ØBUDAPEST

Tisza

Odesa

Crimean
Peninsula

Krasnodar

Grozlyy

ØNGARY

Timisoara

ROMANIA

Elbrus
18,505 ft.

ØATIA

BELGRADE

BUCHAREST

Sevastopol

Caucasus

Ø&

Danube

Constanta

 ØVINA

SERBIA &
MONTENEGRO

BULGARIA

Black Sea

ØSARAJEVO

Pristina

SOFIA

Burgas

ØSKOPJE

Plovdiv

Istanbul

ØIRANA

MACEDONIA

Thessaloniki

ØBANIA

GREECE

Aegean
Sea

ØPatra

ATHENS

ASIA

Rhodes

Irakleio

Crete

ØMediterranean
Sea

0   500   1000km
0   250   500 miles

NORTHWESTERN EUROPE

Denmark, Norway, and Sweden, in the far northwest of Europe, are together known as Scandinavia. These countries have similar languages, and for part of their history they shared the same rulers. Out at sea to the west lies Iceland. Finland is in the east. Until 1917 Finland was a province of the Russian Empire, so it has a very different language and culture to Scandinavia. All of these countries are highly industrialized and have a high standard of living.

Iceland has a unique landscape. Icy and rocky, it is dotted with volcanoes and dramatic hot springs, some of which are tapped to heat buildings. Much of the rest of northwestern Europe is rugged, mountainous, and wooded. The landscape is harsh, and most of the population live in the flatter southern areas where lakes were scraped out by glaciers thousands of years ago. The soil in the south is more fertile than in the north, allowing farmers to grow crops and lush grass for dairy farming. The western coasts have been eroded by the sea and ice into deep inlets known as fjords. The climate in this part of the region is wet but mild, and many of the people who live here

work in fishing and fish processing. Farther east the climate is much colder and drier. A large number of those who live inland are employed in the timber industry.

The countries of northwestern Europe produce very little pollution. Most of the region's power is generated from clean hydroelectric stations that harness the fast-flowing mountain streams to produce electricity. However, pollution from elsewhere in Europe blows north and falls as acid rain. This rain poisons forests and lakes, killing the plants and animals living in them.

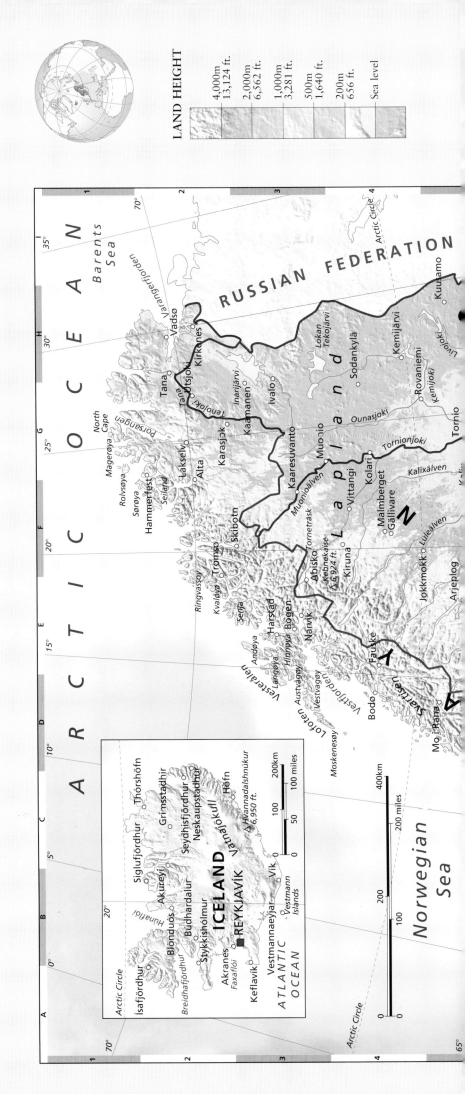

LAND HEIGHT

| 4,000m 13,124 ft. | 2,000m 6,562 ft. | 1,000m 3,281 ft. | 500m 1,640 ft. | 200m 656 ft. | Sea level |

Iceland Norway Sweden Finland Denmark

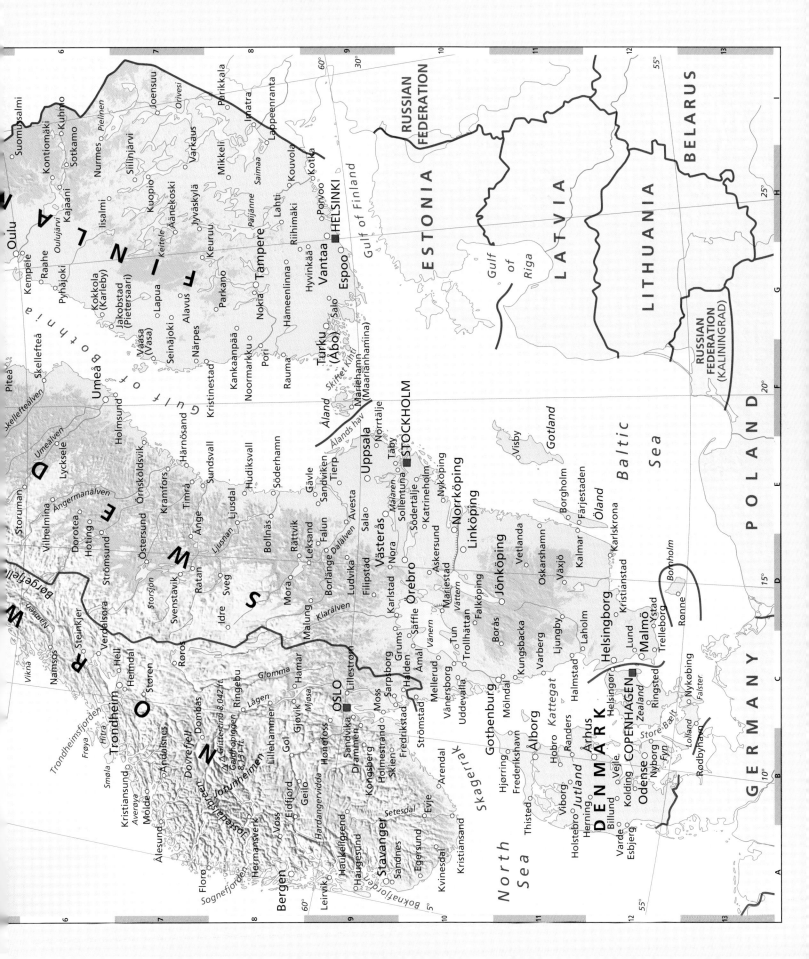

THE BRITISH ISLES

Located in the northwest of Europe, this group of islands contains two countries: the United Kingdom and the Republic of Ireland. The United Kingdom includes the national regions of England, Wales, and Scotland, plus the province of Northern Ireland. Great Britain and Ireland are the British Isles' largest islands.

In the north and west of Great Britain are uplands fringed by rocky, jagged coasts. To the south and east of the island are lowlands. They range from the flat fens of the east to the rolling hills of the southeast. Ireland has a low-lying plain in its center, which is covered by numerous lakes, peat bogs, and grassy hills. The plain is surrounded by low coastal mountains.

Sheep and cattle are raised in Great Britain's uplands, and cereal crops are grown in the east. The flatter areas of the island, such as central England, produce fruit and vegetables. Dairy products and beef are important sources of income for the Republic of Ireland.

In the late 1700s the United Kingdom began to develop heavy industries, and by the early 1900s the country was a world leader in mining, steel production, and textiles. Recently many of these heavy industries have been replaced by high-tech businesses and financial services. Computer hardware and software companies employ a large number of people in Ireland, Scotland, and southern England, while tourism is an important industry throughout the islands. The move away from heavy industry has helped reduce pollution in the area, but the British Isles is a small, densely populated region with high numbers of cars, so poor air quality is a big problem in large cities.

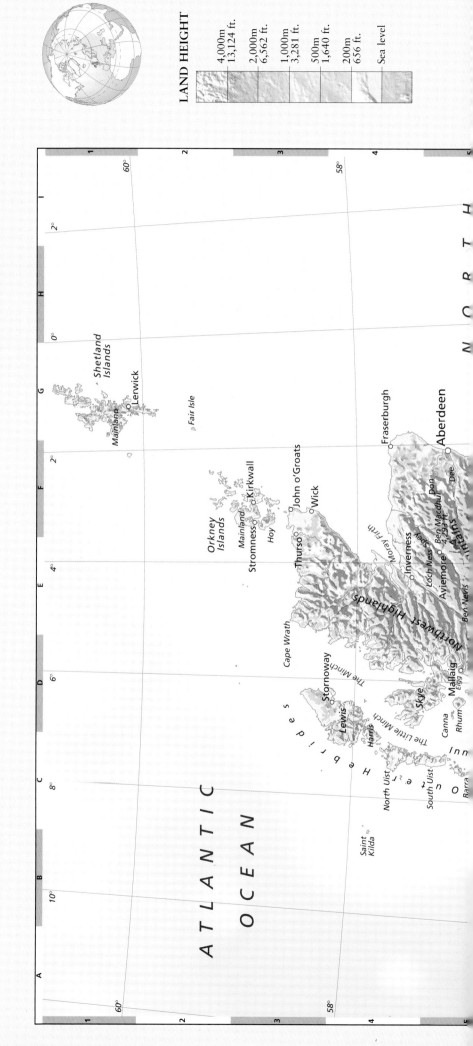

LAND HEIGHT

4,000m	13,124 ft.
2,000m	6,562 ft.
1,000m	3,281 ft.
500m	1,640 ft.
200m	656 ft.
Sea level	

Republic of Ireland

United Kingdom

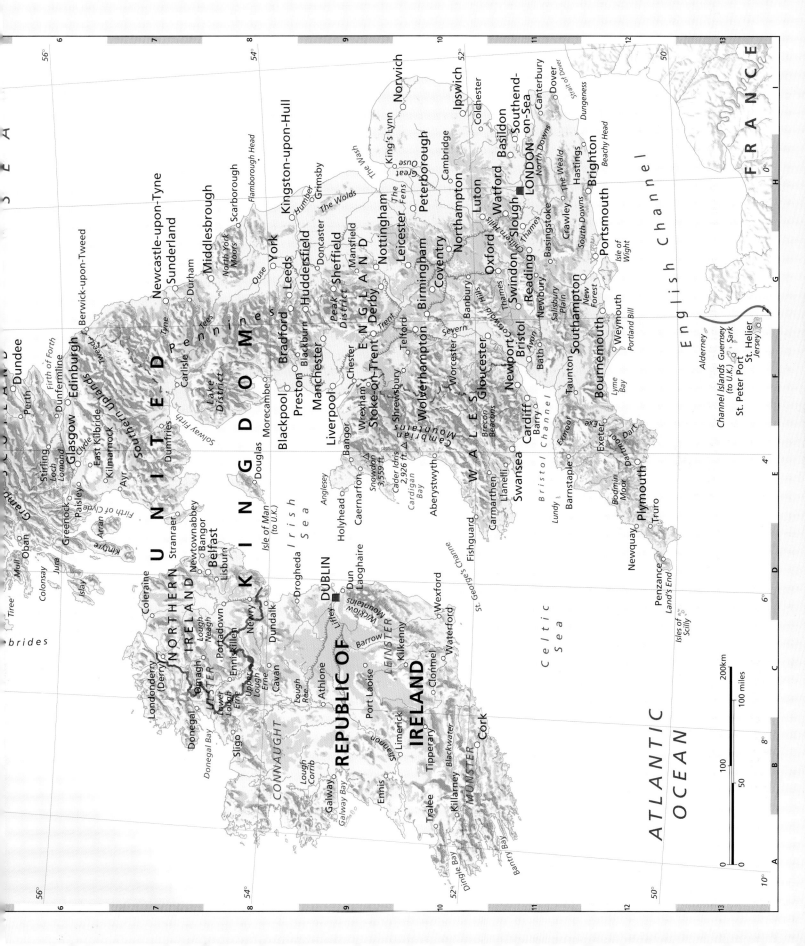

FRANCE

THE BRITISH ISLES

NORTH SEA

ATLANTIC OCEAN

Celtic Sea

Irish Sea

English Channel

Bristol Channel

UNITED KINGDOM

ENGLAND

WALES

NORTHERN IRELAND

REPUBLIC OF IRELAND

IRELAND

LEINSTER

MUNSTER

CONNAUGHT

ULSTER

Dundee
Perth
Stirling
Glasgow
Greenock
Paisley
Kilmarnock
East Kilbride
Edinburgh
Dunfermline
Ayr
Oban
Mull
Colonsay
Jura
Islay
Arran
Tiree
Kintyre
Firth of Clyde
Firth of Forth
Loch Lomond
Southern Uplands
Grampian

Berwick-upon-Tweed
Newcastle-upon-Tyne
Sunderland
Durham
Middlesbrough
Carlisle
Stranraer
Dumfries
Solway Firth
Lake District
Pennines
Tweed
Tyne
Tees

Londonderry (Derry)
Coleraine
Ballymena
Omagh
Enniskillen
Newtownabbey
Bangor
Belfast
Lisburn
Portadown
Newry
Dundalk
Donegal
Donegal Bay
Sligo
Lough Neagh
Lower Lough Erne
Upper Lough Erne
Cavan
Lough Ree
Lough Corrib
Athlone
Galway
Galway Bay
Dingle Bay
Tralee
Killarney
Ennis
Limerick
Tipperary
Cork
Bantry Bay
Shannon
Blackwater

Drogheda
Dún Laoghaire
DUBLIN
Port Laoise
Kilkenny
Clonmel
Waterford
Wexford
Wicklow Mountains
Liffey
Barrow
Nore

Isle of Man (to U.K.)
Douglas
Holyhead
Anglesey
Caernarfon
Bangor
Snowdon 3,559 ft.
Cader Idris 2,926 ft.
Cardigan Bay
Aberystwyth
Fishguard
St. George's Channel
Cambrian Mountains
Brecon Beacons
Carmarthen
Llanelli
Swansea
Cardiff
Barry
Newport
Llangollen

Blackpool
Morecambe
Preston
Blackburn
Manchester
Liverpool
Chester
Wrexham
Stoke-on-Trent
Shrewsbury
Telford
Wolverhampton
Birmingham
Coventry
Worcester
Gloucester
Bristol
Bath
Severn
Avon
Wye
Trent

Leeds
Bradford
Huddersfield
Sheffield
Doncaster
York
Scarborough
Flamborough Head
Kingston-upon-Hull
Grimsby
Humber
North York Moors
The Wolds
Ouse
Peak District

Derby
Nottingham
Mansfield
Leicester
Northampton
Banbury
Oxford
Swindon
Reading
Newbury
Basingstoke
Salisbury Plain
Chiltern Hills
Cotswold Hills

Mansfield
Peterborough
Cambridge
King's Lynn
Norwich
Ipswich
Colchester
The Fens
The Wash
Great Ouse

Luton
Watford
Slough
Chiltern Hills
LONDON
Basildon
Southend-on-Sea
Canterbury
Dover
Strait of Dover
Dungeness
North Downs
The Weald
Hastings
Beachy Head
Brighton
Crawley
South Downs
Thames

Bournemouth
Southampton
Portsmouth
Isle of Wight
Weymouth
Portland Bill
Lyme Bay
New Forest

Exeter
Exe
Dartmoor
Dart
Bodmin Moor
Plymouth
Truro
Penzance
Land's End
Isles of Scilly
Newquay
Barnstaple
Lundy
Exmoor

Channel Islands (to U.K.)
Alderney
Guernsey
St. Peter Port
Sark
Jersey
St. Helier

56°
54°
52°
50°
56°
54°
52°
50°

6° 7° 8° 9° 10° 11° 12° 13°
10° 8° 6° 4° 2° 0° 2°

A B C D E F G H I

200km
100 miles
100
50
100
0
0

THE LOW COUNTRIES

Luxembourg, Belgium, and the Netherlands are known as the "Low Countries" because most of their land is flat and low-lying. Almost one third of the Netherlands lies below sea level. The Dutch reclaimed this land from the sea by building dikes to enclose areas of shallow water, which were then drained into canals by pumps. Regions such as these are called polders, and they need constant care to stop them from flooding. Rising to heights of 1,640 ft., the forested hills of the Ardennes, in southern Belgium and Luxembourg, are the Low Countries' only uplands. Two major rivers—the Meuse and the Rhine—flow through the region on their way to the North Sea.

The reclaimed areas, plus flat plains, such as Flanders in northern Belgium, have fertile soils and provide good conditions for agriculture. Barley, potatoes, and flax are the main crops. The Netherlands also produces cut flowers and bulbs, which are exported all over the world. Beef, dairy, and pig farming take place in the higher inland parts of this region. Luxembourg is a major center for banking, and Belgium has a large number of factories.

Brussels, the capital of Belgium, is also the administrative capital of the European Union.

Many people work in chemical companies, engineering, the textile industry, and in the new high-tech businesses that are springing up in this region. The majority of people live in towns or cities, and the largest urban area is known as *Randstad Holland*. This is a densely populated, built-up region between Amsterdam and Rotterdam. Most people have a comfortable lifestyle in the cities, but large numbers of cars and factories cause serious air pollution.

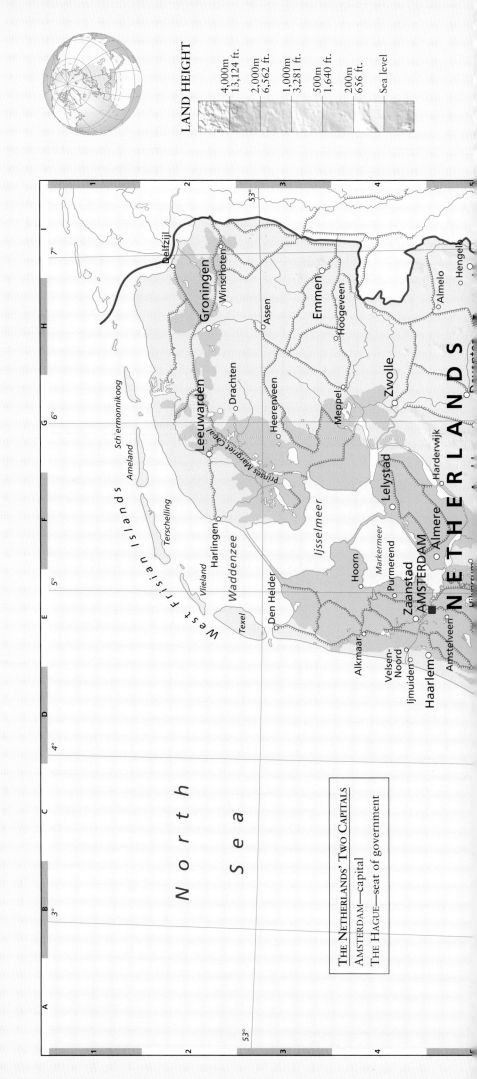

LAND HEIGHT

4,000m	13,124 ft.
2,000m	6,562 ft.
1,000m	3,281 ft.
500m	1,640 ft.
200m	656 ft.
	Sea level

THE NETHERLANDS' TWO CAPITALS
AMSTERDAM—capital
THE HAGUE—seat of government

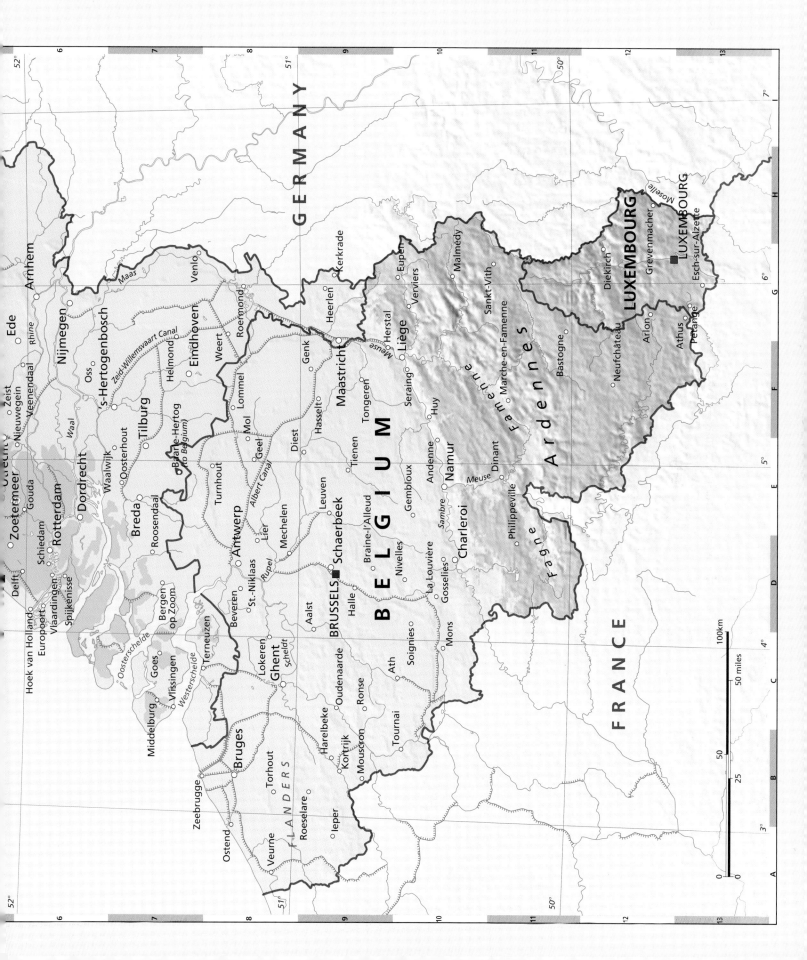

Netherlands
Belgium
Luxembourg

GERMANY

FRANCE

LUXEMBOURG

BELGIUM

FLANDERS

ARDENNES

Fagne

Famenne

Arnhem
Ede
Zeist
Nieuwegein
Veenendaal
Zoetermeer
Gouda
Nijmegen
Oss
Schiedam
Vlaardingen
Rotterdam
Spijkenisse
Delft
Dordrecht
Waalwijk
Oosterhout
's-Hertogenbosch
Tilburg
Helmond
Eindhoven
Weert
Venlo
Roermond
Hoek van Holland
Europoort
Breda
Roosendaal
Bergen op Zoom
Goes
Middelburg
Vlissingen
Terneuzen
Lokeren
Ghent
Zeebrugge
Bruges
Ostend
Torhout
Veurne
Roeselare
Ieper
Harelbeke
Kortrijk
Mouscron
Oudenaarde
Ronse
Tournai
Ath
Soignies
Mons
Gosselies
La Louvière
Nivelles
Charleroi
Braine-l'Alleud
Halle
Aalst
Braine-Hertog (to Belgium)
Mechelen
Lier
Rupel
St.-Niklaas
Beveren
Antwerp
Turnhout
Geel
Mol
Lommel
Diest
Hasselt
Genk
Maastricht
Tongeren
Tienen
Leuven
Schaerbeek
BRUSSELS
Gembloux
Andenne
Namur
Dinant
Philippeville
Huy
Seraing
Liège
Herstal
Heerlen
Kerkrade
Eupen
Verviers
Malmédy
Sankt-Vith
Marche-en-Famenne
Bastogne
Neufchâteau
Diekirch
Grevenmacher
LUXEMBOURG
Arlon
Athus
Pétange
Esch-sur-Alzette

Maas
Rhine
Waal
Zeid-Willemsvaart Canal
Albert Canal
Scheldt
Westerschelde
Oosterschelde
Meuse
Sambre
Moselle

100km
50 miles
0 25 50

52°
51°
50°
6° 7° 8° 9° 10° 11° 12° 13°

FRANCE

One of the largest countries in Western Europe, France has a variety of landscape types, which fall into two main areas. In the north and west are flat plains and low hills. The plains are drained by three great rivers, the Seine, Loire, and Garonne. These rivers form basins with rich soils. To the south and east are the uplands —the high plateau of the Massif Central and two mountain ranges, the Pyrenees and the Alps. The Pyrenees form a natural border with Spain. The Alps are crossed by high passes that lead into Italy and Switzerland.

Fertile soils and a temperate climate make France a successful food producer. Wheat and vegetables are grown in the north, and corn and fruit are produced in the south. The lowlands make good dairy pastureland, and grapes for wine are grown in many areas. France is also highly industrialized. It exports a vast range of products, from cars to clothing. Both the northern and southern coasts suffer from industrial pollution, but because France generates around 75 percent of its electricity in nuclear power plants, the country is less polluted by the use of fossil fuels than other industrialized nations.

From the 1700s–1900s France was a colonial power, with an empire in Africa, Asia, and North America. Almost all of its colonies are now independent. Today France plays a leading role in the European Union.

LAND HEIGHT

4,000m
13,124 ft.

2,000m
6,562 ft.

1,000m
3,281 ft.

500m
1,640 ft.

200m
656 ft.

Sea level

France

Monaco

Strait of Dover
2°
Dunkerque
Calais
Boulogne-
sur-Mer
Lille
Béthune
Lens
Arras
Tourcoing
Roubaix
Valenciennes
4°
6°
BELGIUM
8°
10°
1
50°

Abbeville

Dieppe
Somme
Amiens
St.-Quentin
Oise
LUXEMBOURG
GERMANY
2

Rouen
Beauvais
Laon
Charleville-
Mézières
Thionville
Metz
Forbach
Haguenau
Compiègne
Reims
Meuse
Creil
Pontoise
Évreux
Argenteuil
Versailles
PARIS
Créteil
Seine
Châlons-en-Champagne
Bar-le-Duc
Nancy
Strasbourg
St.-Dié
Épinal
Colmar
Marne
CHAMPAGNE
Moselle
Vosges
Rhine
3
48°

Chartres
Melun
Seine
Troyes
Chaumont
Yonne
Sens
Langres
Mulhouse
Belfort
Vesoul
Montbéliard
LIECHTENSTEIN
AUSTRIA

Orléans
Olivet
Blois
Auxerre
Clamecy
Dijon
Besançon
BURGUNDY
Morvan
Cher
ours
AUSTRIA
4

Bourges
Nevers
Loire
Jura
SWITZERLAND
Creuse
Châteauroux
Montceau-les-Mines
Chalon-sur-
Saône
Saône
A
l
p
s
Moulins
Montluçon
Mâcon
Lake
Geneva
Thonon-les-Bains
5
46°

Vichy
Bourg-en-Bresse
Annemasse
Roanne
Chamonix
Clermont-Ferrand
Lyon
Villeurbanne
Annecy
Mont Blanc
15,777 ft.
Limoges
Puy de Sancy
6,183 ft.
St.-Étienne
St.-Chamond
Chambéry
ITALY

rigueux
Brive-la-
Gaillarde
Massif
Isère
Grenoble
6
Dordogne
Le Puy
Valence
Les Ecrins
13,454 ft.
A
l
Central
Lot
Mende
Gap
Cahors
Rhône
Montélimar
Digne
Maritime Alps
44°
en
Rodez
Tarn
Orange
7
Montauban
Cévennes
Alès
Avignon
Durance
MONACO
MONACO
Albi
Nîmes
Tarascon
Nice
Antibes
Toulouse
Castres
Montpellier
Arles
Camargue
Aix-en-Provence
Cannes
Fréjus
Canal du Midi
Béziers
Sète
PROVENCE
St.-Tropez
Cap Corse
Carcassonne
Narbonne
Marseille
Toulon
Îles Côte d'Azur
Bastia
8
Foix
La Seyne-sur-Mer
d'Hyères
Strait of Bonifacio
Perpignan
Gulf
du Lion

ANDORRA
e
e
s
Corsica
Aléria
42°

*Mediterranean
Sea*
Ajaccio
Sartène
Bonifacio
Strait of Bonifacio
9
2°
4°
6°
8°
10°

THE IBERIAN PENINSULA

The Iberian Peninsula is separated from the rest of Europe by the Pyrenees mountains. To the west is the Atlantic Ocean, while the Mediterranean Sea lies in the east. Spain and Portugal occupy most of this large landmass, together with the tiny mountainous state of Andorra and Gibraltar, a small British territory. The center of the peninsula is dominated by a vast plateau, which is enclosed by the Cordillera Cantábrica to the north and the Sierra Morena to the south.

Wheat and barley are Iberia's main crops, but in the south farmers irrigate the dry land to grow citrus fruits, especially oranges and lemons. Both Spain and Portugal make wines, and these two countries also produce two thirds of the world's cork.

Spain's industries, which are concentrated in the north of the country, make cars, machinery, steel, and chemicals. Portugal exports textiles, clothing, shoes, and processed fish, and tourism is an important source of income for this entire region.

Soil erosion, which is caused when forests are cleared for farmland, has affected much of the peninsula. High-rise hotels along the Mediterranean coast have spoiled the character of this area, and popular beaches there are extremely overcrowded.

LAND HEIGHT

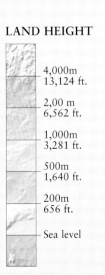

4,000m
13,124 ft.

2,00 m
6,562 ft.

1,000m
3,281 ft.

500m
1,640 ft.

200m
656 ft.

Sea level

Spain

Andorra

Portugal

FRANCE

Gulf of Gascony

Golfe du Lion

ntander
San Vicente de Barakaldo
Bilbao
Donostia-San Sebastián
Irún
PAIS VASCO
toria-Gasteiz
Pamplona
NAVARRA
Jaca
Aneto 11,165 ft. △
ANDORRA LA VELLA
ANDORRA
Llívia (to Spain)
Segre
Figueres
Roses
Burgos
Logroño
LA RIOJA
Huesca
Ripoll
Girona
Costa Brava
Aranda de Duero
Soria
Sistema Ibérico
Ebro
Monzón
CATALONIA
Manresa
Mataró
Terrassa
Duero
Zaragoza
Lleida
Sabadell
Badalona
Calatayud
ARAGÓN
L'Hospitalet de
Barcelona
Daroca
Embalse de Mequinenza
Llobregat
Reus
Alcañiz
Tarragona
Guadalajara
Tortosa
Alcobendas
Amposta
Alcalá de Henares
Vinaròs
MADRID
etafe
Teruel
Costa del Azahar
Ciutadella de Menorca
Aranjuez
Castelló de la Plana
Balearic Islands
Mahón
Cuenca
Menorca (Minorca)
A   I   N
Alcúdia
Palma de Mallorca
Alcázar de San Juan
Sagunto
Andratx
Manacor
Villarrobledo
Paterna
Utiel
Torrente
Valencia
Mallorca (Majorca)
Santanyí
La Roda
Júcar
Alzira
Gulf of Valencia
LA MANCHA
Manzanares
Gandía
San Antonio
Abad
Eivissa (Ibiza)
Valdepeñas
Albacete
Denia
Cabo de la Nao
Eivissa (Ibiza)
Alcoy
Formentera
Hellín
Elda
Benidorm
Elche (Elx)
Alicante
Segura
Orihuela
Linares
Murcia
Torrevieja
Costa Blanca
Mediterranean Sea
én
Huéscar
Lorca
Cabo de Palos
Cartagena
éticos
Baza
Aguilas
Granada
Huércal-Overa
Nevada
Mulhacén 11,408 ft.
Almería
Motril
Adra
Cabo de Gata
el Sol

ALGERIA

Melilla (to Spain)

GERMANY

Germany lies in the heart of Europe. There are flat plains in the northern part of the country, and in the south are forests and the Alps. Two of Europe's greatest rivers flow through Germany. The Rhine runs from the south, where it forms a natural border with France, to the north. It is an important transportation link between many industrial centers. To the south the Danube rises in the Black Forest and flows east on its course to the Black Sea.

Germany's northern plains make good farmland—cattle and pigs are raised here, and cereal crops are grown. Livestock farms are located in the south, but the uplands there are often more suited to growing vegetables. Grapes for Germany's successful wine industry also grow well in the mountainous regions, and vineyards cover the slopes surrounding the Rhine and its tributaries. The chemicals industry, car manufacturing, and engineering employ many people in and around major cities, especially in Berlin and in the Ruhr, Rhine, and Main valleys. Germany also has strong high-tech industries, producing goods such as computers and telecommunications equipment.

In 1945 Germany was defeated in World War II, and the country was divided. East Germany became part of communist Europe. Many people worked in old-fashioned heavy industries, and salaries and working conditions were poor for most. West Germany made a rapid recovery following the war and became one of Europe's richest and most powerful countries. In 1990 the two states joined again, and since then the German government has been trying to unite the country economically and politically. Germany is also an important member of the European Union.

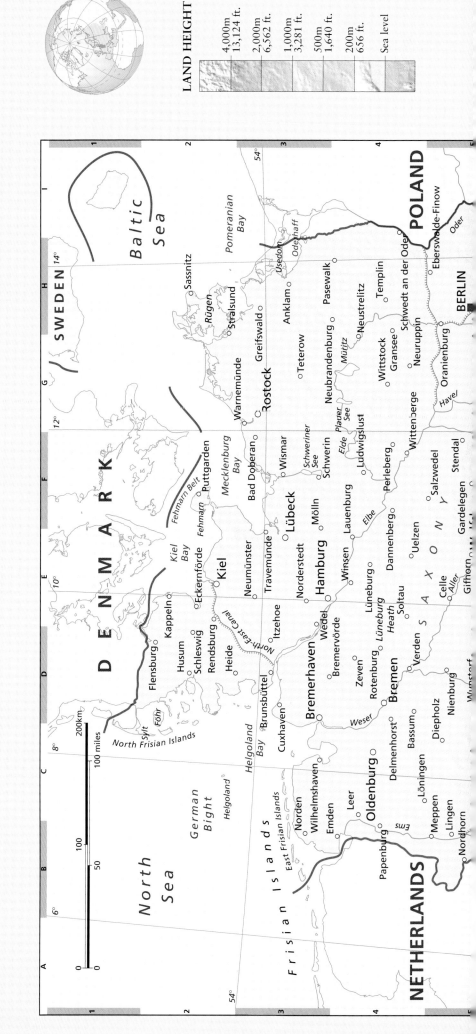

LAND HEIGHT

4,000m	13,124 ft.
2,000m	6,562 ft.
1,000m	3,281 ft.
500m	1,640 ft.
200m	656 ft.
	Sea level

Germany

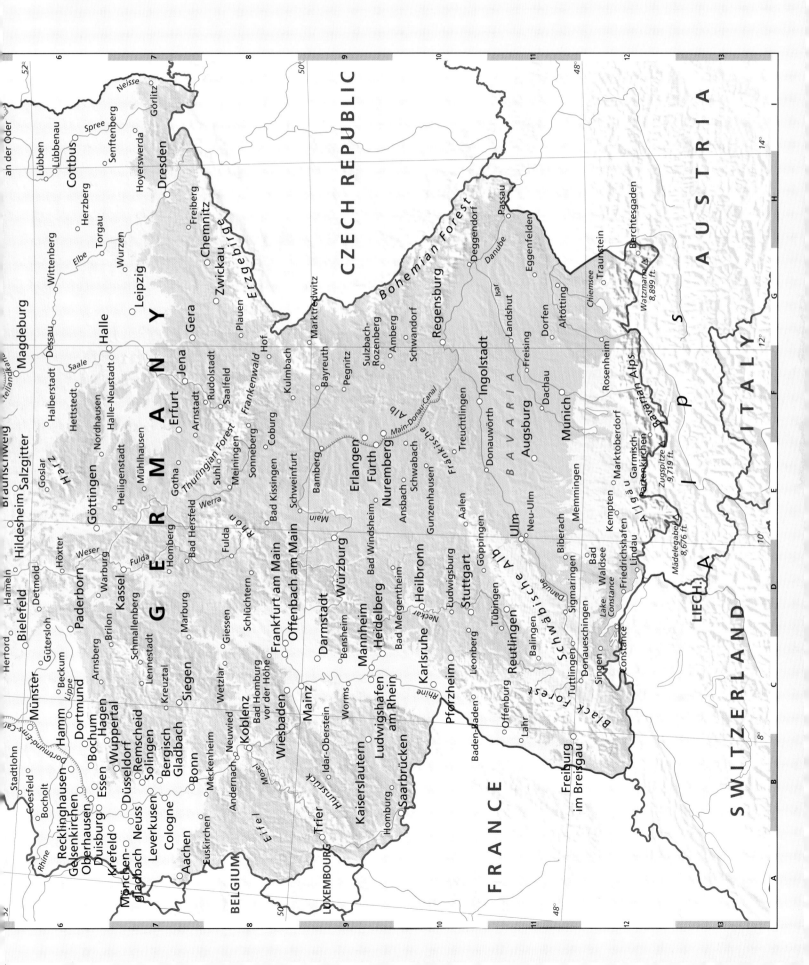

AUSTRIA

CZECH REPUBLIC

GERMANY

BAVARIA

FRANCE

BELGIUM

LUXEMBOURG

SWITZERLAND

ITALY

LIECH.

Neisse
Spree
Senftenberg
Görlitz
Hoyerswerda
Dresden
Freiberg
Chemnitz
Zwickau
Gera
Plauen
Hof
Erzgebirge
Marktredwitz
Bayreuth
Pegnitz
Sulzbach-
Rozenberg
Amberg
Schwandorf
Regensburg
Bohemian Forest
Passau
Deggendorf
Danube
Isar
Eggenfelden
Dorfen
Altötting
Landshut
Freising
Dachau
Munich
Rosenheim
Chiemsee
Traunstein
Berchtesgaden
Watzmann △ 8,899 ft.
Bavarian Alps
Garmisch-
Partenkirchen
Zugspitze △ 9,719 ft.
A l p s

an der Oder
Lübben
Lübbenau
Cottbus
Herzberg
Torgau
Wurzen
Leipzig
Wittenberg
Dessau
Elbe
Halle
Halle-Neustadt
Saale
Magdeburg
Tangermünde
Halberstadt
Hettstedt
Nordhausen
Mühlhausen
Jena
Erfurt
Arnstadt
Rudolstadt
Saalfeld
Gotha
Suhl
Meiningen
Sonneberg
Coburg
Bad Kissingen
Schweinfurt
Bamberg
Schwabach
Erlangen
Fürth
Nuremberg
Ansbach
Gunzenhausen
Treuchtlingen
Donauwörth
Ingolstadt
Aalen
Augsburg
Neu-Ulm
Ulm
Memmingen
Kempten
Marktoberdorf
Lindau
Friedrichshafen
Lake Constance
Bad Waldsee
Biberach
Sigmaringen
Danube
Mädelegabel △ 8,676 ft.

Harz
Goslar
Halle
Göttingen
Heiligenstadt
Braunschweig
Hildesheim
Salzgitter
Höxter
Weser
Warburg
Kassel
Fulda
Homberg
Bad Hersfeld
Fulda
Marburg
Giessen
Wetzlar
Frankenwald
Thuringian Forest
Rhön
Werra
Main
Bad Windsheim
Würzburg
Bad Mergentheim
Heilbronn
Ludwigsburg
Stuttgart
Göppingen
Tübingen
Reutlingen
Balingen
Leonberg
Pforzheim
Schwäbische Alb
Tuttlingen
Singen
Donaueschingen
Constance

Hertford
Hameln
Detmold
Bielefeld
Detmold
Paderborn
Brilon
Arnsberg
Lennestadt
Schmallenberg
Siegen
Kreuztal
Marburg
Schlüchtern
Bad Homburg
vor der Höhe
Frankfurt am Main
Offenbach am Main
Darmstadt
Bensheim
Mannheim
Heidelberg
Weinheim
Worms
Bad Bergzabern
Karlsruhe
Baden-Baden
Offenburg
Lahr
Freiburg
im Breisgau
Black Forest

Stadtlohn
Coesfeld
Bocholt
Recklinghausen
Gelsenkirchen
Oberhausen
Duisburg
Mönchen-
gladbach
Neuss
Krefeld
Essen
Bochum
Hagen
Wuppertal
Remscheid
Solingen
Bergisch
Gladbach
Leverkusen
Cologne
Bonn
Aachen
Euskirchen
Meckenheim
Andernach
Neuwied
Koblenz
Mainz
Wiesbaden
Bad Homburg
Eifel
Mosel
Hunsrück
Idar-Oberstein
Kaiserslautern
Ludwigshafen
am Rhein
Homburg
Saarbrücken
Trier
Rhine
Münster
Hamm
Beckum
Lippe
Dortmund
Gütersloh
Beckum
Dortmund-Ems-Canal

Münster
Düsseldorf

Rhine

52°
50°
48°
14°
12°
10°
8°
6 7 8 9 10 11 12 13

THE ALPINE STATES

The Alps, Europe's tallest range of mountains, stretch across the Alpine states—Austria, Liechtenstein, Switzerland, and Slovenia. This region in central Europe has a landscape of jagged, snow-topped peaks, deep valleys, and lakes that were scooped out by glaciers more than 20,000 years ago. The mountainous terrain of the Alpine states limits the amount of land that can be cultivated by farmers, although the rich pastures of the lower slopes are used to graze both beef and dairy cattle.

Switzerland and Liechtenstein have few raw materials, so these countries concentrate on producing high-quality goods, including pharmaceuticals and watches. They also act as international centers for banking. Austria is heavily industrialized, and all four countries have strong tourist industries. People from many parts of the world come to the Alpine states to ski and to admire the mountain scenery. The large numbers of visitors and the buildings needed to house them put a strain on the environment. This region lies on the main trading routes across the Alps, so air pollution caused by passing trucks is another environmental problem.

Switzerland takes a neutral position in wars and other conflicts. This policy makes the country an ideal base for a number of important international organizations, including the Red Cross and various agencies of the United Nations.

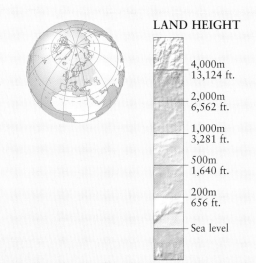

LAND HEIGHT

4,000m
13,124 ft.

2,000m
6,562 ft.

1,000m
3,281 ft.

500m
1,640 ft.

200m
656 ft.

Sea level

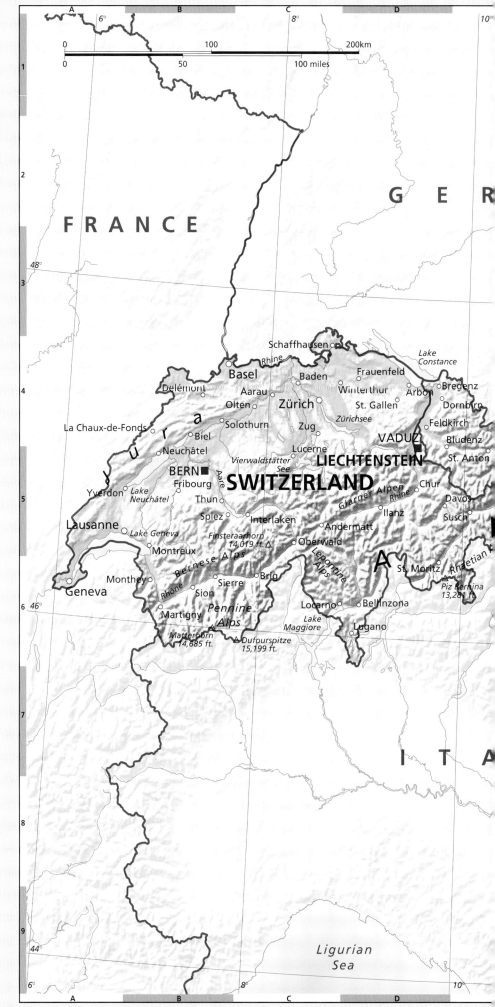

Austria

Switzerland

Liechtenstein

Slovenia

C Z E C H
R E P U B L I C

M A N Y

SLOVAKIA

Gmünd

Mistelbach

Hollabrunn

Krems an
der Donau

Danube

Tulln

■ VIENNA

Linz

St. Pölten

Mödling

48°

Wels

Amstetten

Salzach

Vocklabruck

Steyr

Baden

*Neusiedler
See*

Waidhofen
an der Ybbs

Wiener
Neustadt

Eisenstadt

Attersee

Gmunden

A U S T R I A

Salzburg

Traunsee

Neunkirchen

Hallein

Bad Ischl

Enns

Mürzzuschlag

Liezen

Rottenmann

*Zugspitze
9,718 ft.*

Kufstein

Wörgl

Bruck an der Mur

Bavarian Alps

Kitzbühel

Bischofshofen

Knittelfeld

4

Telfs

Schwaz

Radstadt

Niedere Tauern

Judenburg

Graz

T R O L

Mittersill

Mur

Innsbruck

Hohe Tauern

St. Michael
im Langau

Köflach

Wildon

*Wildspitze
12,379 ft.*

S

△ *Grossglockner
12,454 ft.*

HUNGARY

Ötztaler
Alpen

p

Lienz

Wolfsberg

Raab

St. Veit an
der Glan

Leibnitz

Mur

Spittal-an
der Drau

Drau

Völkermarkt

5

Karnische Alpen

Villach

Klagenfurt

Murska Sobota

Maribor

Karawanken

*Triglav
9,394 ft.* △

Jesenice

Ptuj

Drava

*Julian
Alps*

Kranj

Celje

6

Tolmin

Sava

Trbovlje

46°

LJUBLJANA ■

Krško

S L O V E N I A

Nova
Gorica

Postojna

I T A L Y

Novo Mesto

Ribnica

7

Kocevje

Koper

Kozina

C R O A T I A

L Y

**BOSNIA &
HERZEGOVINA**

8

*Adriatic
Sea*

9

44°

ITALY AND MALTA

This region stretches from the Alps in the north to the Mediterranean islands of Malta in the south. Much of the Italian peninsula is mountainous, with the Apennines extending along almost the entire length of Italy, and the Dolomites are found in the northeast. In the south are volcanoes such as Etna and Vesuvius. This area also experiences earthquakes.

The northern and southern halves of the region are different from each other in several ways. The north, which has a milder climate than the south, is more developed. Big cities,

including Turin, Milan, and Genoa, are centers of industry. There manufacturing companies make cars, engines, and other products. There are also high-tech businesses and design studios specializing in everything from clothing to furniture. The north is a popular tourist destination, luring many people with its stunning scenery, fine food, and historical cities, including Venice, Florence, and Rome. Lake Garda and Lake Como also attract many visitors. In the north are two tiny countries. Vatican City, a small area in Rome, is the center of the Catholic church.

The ancient independent state of San Marino is located near the Adriatic coast.

In the south the climate is hotter, the towns are usually smaller, and industry is less well developed. The dry soils often have to be irrigated, but some crops, such as olives, citrus fruits, grapes, and tomatoes, grow well in the baking sun. Still farther south are Sicily and Malta, which have an even hotter climate. Malta is part of Italy, while the islands of Malta form a separate nation. Tourism and shipping are Malta's major sources of income.

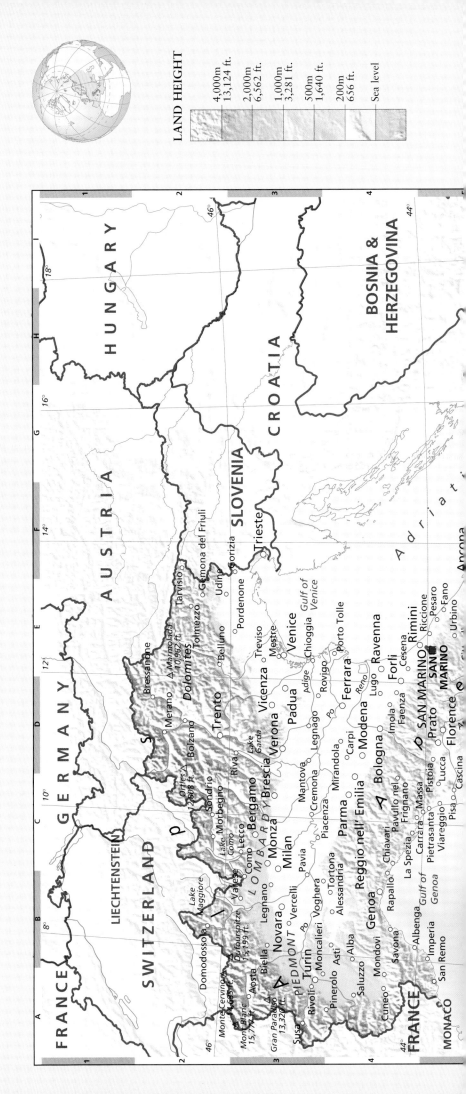

LAND HEIGHT

4,000m	13,124 ft.
2,000m	6,562 ft.
1,000m	3,281 ft.
500m	1,640 ft.
200m	656 ft.
Sea level	

Italy

San Marino

Vatican City

Malta

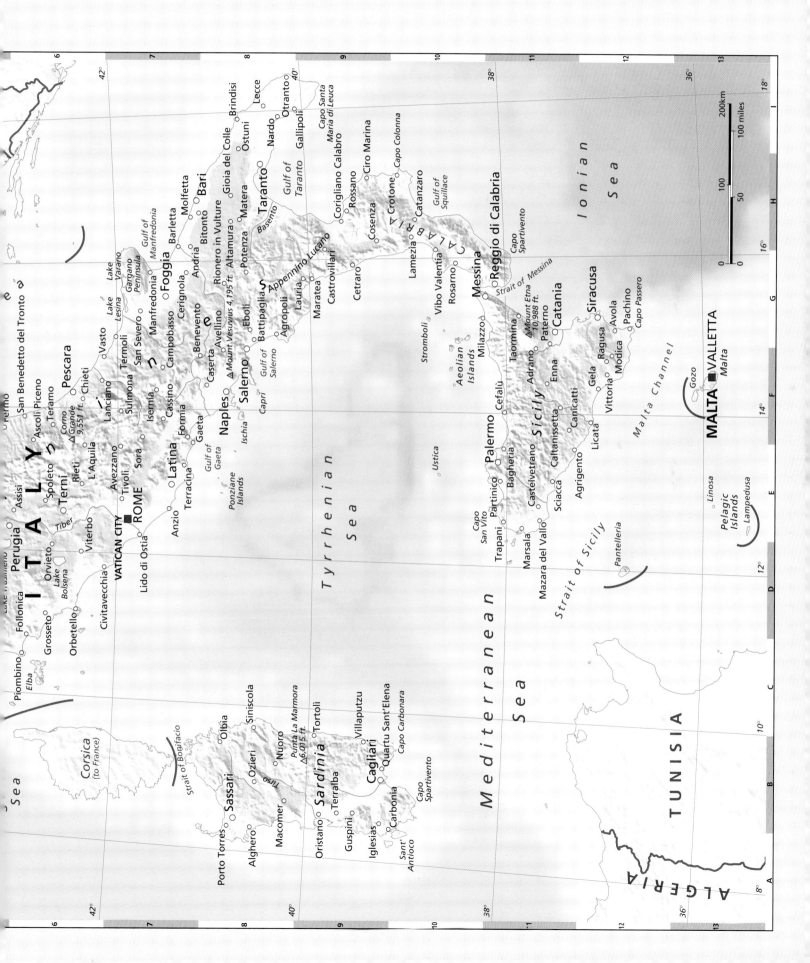

ITALY

Piombino
Elba
Follonica
Grosseto
Orbetello
Civitavecchia
Lido di Ostia
Viterbo
Orvieto
Lake Bolsena
Perugia
Assisi
Spoleto
Terni
Rieti
L'Aquila
Corno Grande △ 9,551 ft.
Teramo
Ascoli Piceno
San Benedetto del Tronto
Fermo
Pescara
Chieti
Lanciano
Vasto
Termoli
San Severo
Lake Lesina
Lake Varano
Gargano Peninsula
Manfredonia
Gulf of Manfredonia
Barletta
Molfetta
Bari
Bitonto
Andria
Foggia
Cerignola
Campobasso
Isernia
Sulmona
Avezzano
Sora
Tivoli
ROME
VATICAN CITY
Anzio
Terracina
Gulf of Gaeta
Ponziane Islands
Formia
Gaeta
Cassino
Caserta
Benevento
Avellino
Naples
Ischia
Capri
Salerno
Gulf of Salerno
Battipaglia
Eboli
△Mount Vesuvius 4,195 ft.
Agropoli
Maratea
Lauria
Rionero in Vulture
Altamura
Potenza
Matera
Castrovillari
Appennino Lucano
Basento
TARANTO
Gulf of Taranto
Gioia del Colle
Ostuni
Brindisi
Lecce
Nardo
Otranto
Gallipoli
Capo Santa Maria di Leuca
Corigliano Calabro
Rossano
Ciro Marina
Cosenza
Cetraro
Crotone
Capo Colonna
Catanzaro
Gulf of Squillace
Lamezia
Vibo Valentia
Rosarno
CALABRIA
Reggio di Calabria
Messina
Strait of Messina
Capo Spartivento
Stromboli
Aeolian Islands
Milazzo
Taormina
△Mount Etna 10,988 ft.
Catania
Siracusa
Avola
Pachino
Capo Passero
Palermo
Cefalù
Bagheria
Partinico
Capo San Vito
Castelvetrano
Trapani
Marsala
Mazara del Vallo
Sciacca
Adrano
Paterno
Enna
Caltanissetta
Canicatti
Gela
Ragusa
Modica
Vittoria
Licata
Agrigento
Sicily
Ustica
Linosa
Pelagic Islands
Lampedusa
Pantelleria
Strait of Sicily
Malta Channel
Gozo
MALTA
VALLETTA
Malta

Corsica (to France)
Strait of Bonifacio
Porto Torres
Sassari
Alghero
Macomer
Ozieri
Nuoro
Siniscola
Olbia
Tirso
Oristano
Terralba
Guspini
Iglesias
Carbonia
Sant' Antioco
Villaputzu
Tortoli
Punta La Marmora △6,015 ft.
Sardinia
Quartu Sant'Elena
Cagliari
Capo Carbonara
Capo Spartivento

Tyrrhenian Sea

Ionian Sea

Mediterranean Sea

TUNISIA

ALGERIA

Tiber

Sea

200km
100 miles
100
50
0
0

18°
16°
14°
12°
10°
8°
42°
40°
38°
36°

6 7 8 9 10 11 12 13

EASTERN EUROPE

The countries of Eastern Europe have a varied landscape that extends from the cliffs and sandy beaches of the Baltic coast through the vast Pripet Marshes in southern Belarus to the great open steppes that cover almost three fourths of the Ukraine.

Most of the countries in this region have spent long periods of their history under Russian rule. For much of the 1900s, with the exception of Moldova, they all formed part of the Soviet Union. The Soviets encouraged the growth of heavy industry and manufacturing, turning these states into industrial nations. When the Soviet Union broke up in 1991, the countries of this area became independent, and their old-fashioned factories had to compete with the modern, high-tech businesses of the rest of Europe. For a number of years there were price rises and food shortages. Recently, however, this region has developed new high-tech industries, and the countries have also formed trade links with Western Europe.

Farming is the main source of employment for much of the population. The rich black soils of the Ukraine are ideal for growing cereal crops and sugar beets. The smaller countries on the Baltic coast have many cattle and pig farms. The Baltic states have few natural resources, and they have to import goods and services from their larger, richer neighbors.

In 1986 the world's worst nuclear accident took place at the power station at Chernobyl in the Ukraine near the border with Belarus. Thirty-one people were killed immediately, and radioactive particles spread over a huge area, ruining farmland and making thousands of people sick.

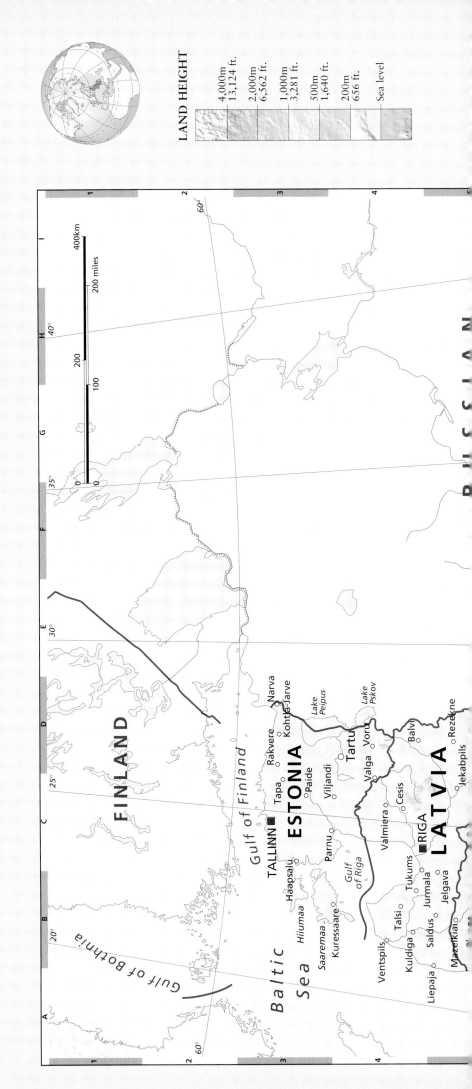

LAND HEIGHT

| 4,000m 13,124 ft. | 2,000m 6,562 ft. | 1,000m 3,281 ft. | 500m 1,640 ft. | 200m 656 ft. | Sea level |

Estonia Latvia Lithuania Belarus Ukraine Moldova

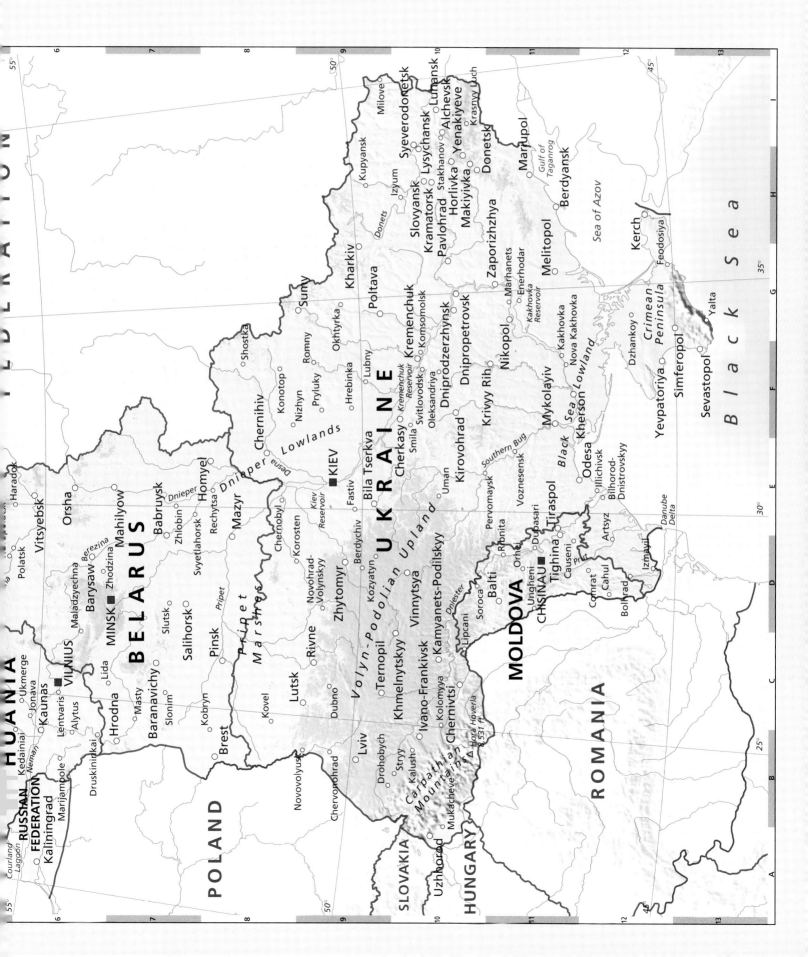

RUSSIAN FEDERATION

LITHUANIA

RUSSIAN FEDERATION
Kaliningrad

Courland
Lagoon

Polatsk
Haradok
Vitsyebsk
Orsha
Malådzyechna
Maladzyechna

BELARUS

MINSK

Barysaw
Zhodzina
Mahilyow
Babruysk
Zhlobin
Homyel
Rechytsa

Berezina

Dnieper

Svyetlahorsk

Kedainiai
Ukmerge
Jonava
VILNIUS
Lentvaris
Alytus
Druskininkai
Marijampole
Neman

Masty
Lida
Hrodna
Baranavichy
Slonim
Slutsk
Salihorsk
Pinsk
Kobryn
Brest

Pripet Marshes

Pripet

Kovel
Lutsk
Dubno

Novovolyusk
Novovolyusk

Chervonohrad

Lviv
Drohobych
Stryy
Kalusho
Mukacheve
Uzhhorod

POLAND

SLOVAKIA
HUNGARY

Carpathian Mountains
△ Hora Hoverla
8,531 ft

Rivne

Novohrad-
Volynskyy

Zhytomyr
Berdychiv
Kozyatyn

Korosten
Chernobyl

Kiev
Reservoir

Dnieper Lowlands

Desna

Chernihiv
Konotop
Nizhyn
Shostka

Romny

KIEV
Fastiv
Bila Tserkva
Kozyatyn

Uman
Pervomaysk

Ternopil
Khmelnytskyy
Ivano-Frankivsk
Kolomyya
Chernivtsi
Kamyanets-Podilskyy
Vinnytsya

Volyn-Podolian Upland

UKRAINE

Dniester

Lipcani

Soroca
Balti
Ungheni
Orhei
Rîbnita
Dubasari
CHIŞINĂU
Tighina
Causeni
Comrat
Cahul
Bolhrad

MOLDOVA

ROMANIA

Prut

Sumy
Okhtyrka
Pryluky
Lubny
Hrebinka

Kharkiv
Poltava
Kremenchuk
Kremenchuk
Reservoir
Svitlovodsk
Komsomolsk
Oleksandriya
Smila
Cherkasy
Kirovohrad
Krivyy Rih
Nikopol
Marhanets

Dnieper
Kremenchuk

Dnipropetrovsk
Dniprodzerzhynsk

Kupyansk
Izyum
Donets

Slovyansk
Kramatorsk
Pavlohrad
Horlivka
Stakhanov
Makiyivka
Zaporizhzhya

Syeverodonetsk
Lysychansk
Luhansk
Alchevsk
Yenakiyeve
Donetsk

Milove

Krasny Luch

Mariupol

Gulf of
Taganrog

Berdyansk

Sea of Azov

Kakhovka
Kakhovka
Reservoir
Nova Kakhovka
Enerhodar

Melitopol

Kherson Lowland

Mykolayiv
Kakhovka

Southern Bug

Voznesensk

Odesa
Illichivsk
Bilhorod-
Dnistrovskyy

Black Sea Lowland

Black Sea

Danube
Delta

Izmayil

Artsyz

Tiraspol

Dzhankoy
Crimean Peninsula

Yevpatoriya
Simferopol
Sevastopol
Yalta

Kerch
Feodosiya

Black Sea

55°
55°

6 7 8 9 50° 10 11 12 13

45° 45°
35°
30°
25°

I H G F E D C B A

CENTRAL EUROPE

Central Europe is made up of two plains, which are divided by a chain of mountains. To the north, in Poland, is the North European Plain. The Great Hungarian Plain, with its farmlands and grasslands, lies in the south. Much of the land area of the Czech Republic and Slovakia falls in the mountainous region in the center. For most of the 1900s these countries were united as Czechoslovakia, but in 1993 they split into two separate nations.

Central Europe's farmers grow cereal crops such as barley, oats, wheat, and rye, as well as large quantities of potatoes and sugar beets. They also raise livestock, especially pigs. In Hungary, where the climate is warmer, farmers grow grapes for wine and sweet peppers for paprika, a hot spice that is used in Hungarian cooking. Much of Slovakia is covered with forests, and the country has a large timber industry.

Poland has enormous reserves of a brown coal, called lignite, which is exported. A variety of minerals are mined in the mountains of the Czech Republic and Slovakia. Hungary has a wide range of industries, producing vehicles, metals, chemicals, textiles, and electrical goods, while the Czech Republic is famous for its breweries and fine glassware.

For much of the 1900s the countries of central Europe were ruled by communist governments, which were dominated by the powerful, Russian-led Soviet Union. The old-fashioned heavy industries that were developed under communist rule have caused terrible pollution in some places. However, the countries of central Europe are now moving toward more modern, high-tech industries.

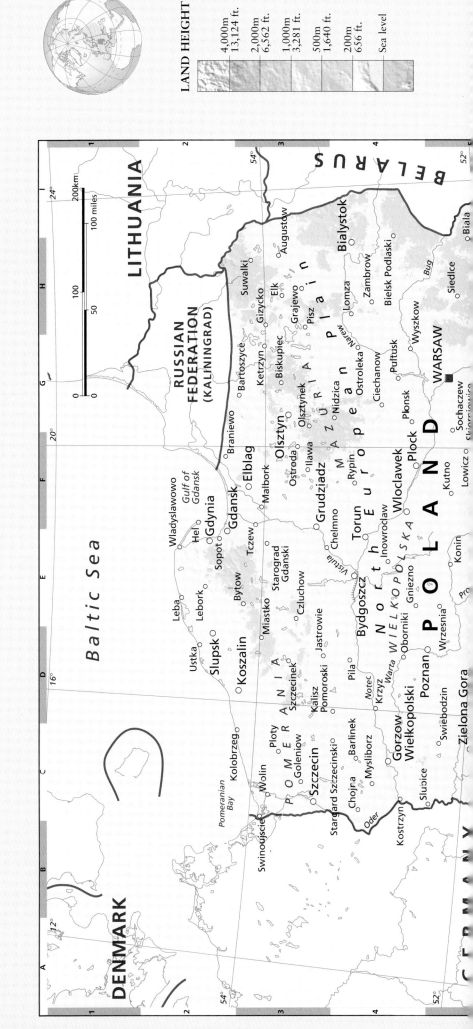

LAND HEIGHT

4,000m / 13,124 ft.	
2,000m / 6,562 ft.	
1,000m / 3,281 ft.	
500m / 1,640 ft.	
200m / 656 ft.	
Sea level	

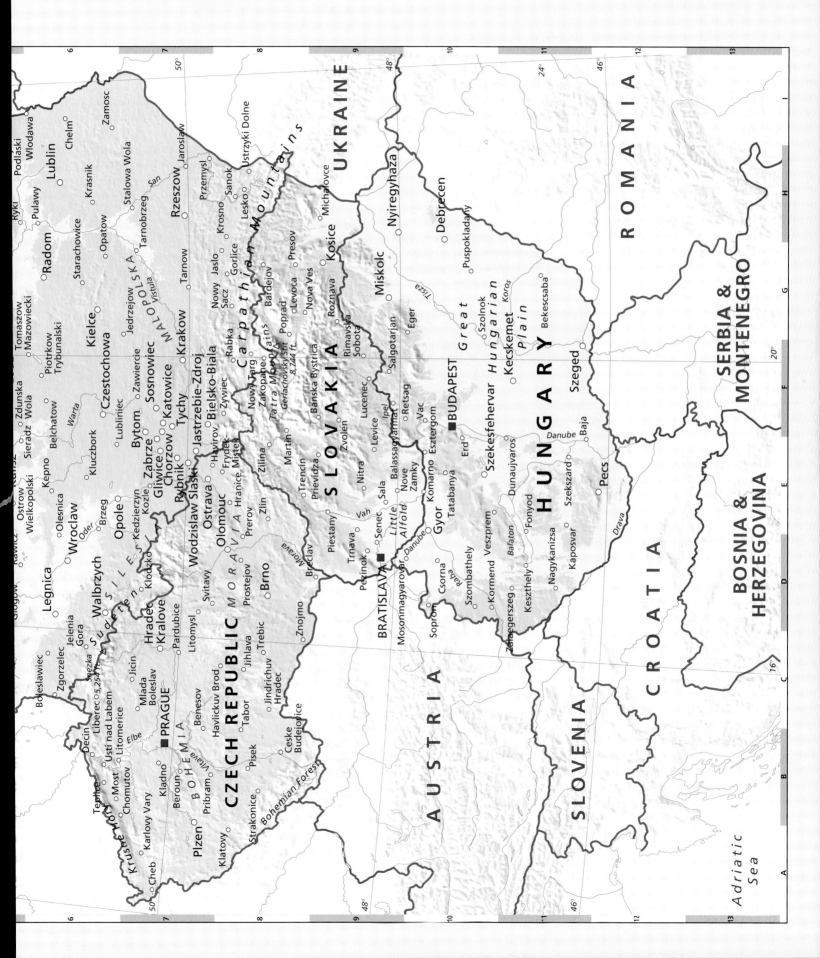

Poland

Czech Republic

Slovakia

Hungary

UKRAINE

ROMANIA

SERBIA & MONTENEGRO

SLOVAKIA

CZECH REPUBLIC

HUNGARY

AUSTRIA

CROATIA

SLOVENIA

BOSNIA & HERZEGOVINA

Ryki
Podlaski
Wlodawa
Pulawy
Lublin
Chelm
Krasnik
Opatow
Zamosc
Starachowice
Stalowa Wola
Radom
Tarnobrzeg
Tomaszow
Mazowiecki
Piotrkow
Trybunalski
Kielce
Jedrzejow
MALOPOLSKA
Rzeszow
Jaroslaw
Przemysl
San
Vistula
Tarnow
Sanok
Krosno
Lesko
Ustrzyki Dolne
Zdunska
Wola
Sieradz
Belchatow
Czestochowa
Zawiercie
Sosnowiec
Krakow
Nowy Targ
Nowy Jaslo
Sacz
Gorlice
Rabka
Presov
Michalovce
Kosice
Kepno
Kluczbork
Bytom
Katowice
Tychy
Bielsko-Biala
Zywiec
Zakopane
Tatra Mountains
Poprad
Levoca
Nova Ves
Roznava
Rimavska
Sobota
Miskolc
Nyiregyhaza
Debrecen
Puspokladany
Olesnica
Lubliniec
Zabrze
Gliwice
Chorzow
Havirov
Frydek
Mistek
Martin
Banska Bystrica
Zvolen
Lucenec
Eger
Szolnok
Kecskemet
Koros
Bekescsaba
Wroclaw
Brzeg
Opole
Kedzierzyn
Kozle
Rybnik
Jastrzebie-Zdroj
Zilina
Trencin
Prievidza
Nitra
Levice
Salgotarjan
Retsag
Vac
Szekesfehervar
Great
Hungarian
Plain
Szeged
Legnica
Wodzislaw Slaski
Ostrava
Olomouc
Hranice
Prerov
Zlin
Piestany
Vah
Sala
Balassagyarmat
Ipel
Esztergom
BUDAPEST
Erd
Dunaujvaros
Szekszard
Pecs
Walbrzych
Klodzko
Hradec
Kralove
Litomysl
Svitavy
Prostejov
Brno
Znojmo
Breclav
Trnava
Senec
Little
Alfold
Nove
Zamky
Komarno
Gyor
Tatabanya
Balaton
Fonyod
Nagykanizsa
Kaposvar
Jelenia
Gora
Zgorzelec
Jicin
Mlada
Boleslav
Pardubice
Jihlava
Trebic
Znojmo
Pezinok
Bratislava
BRATISLAVA
Mosonmagyarovar
Danube
Sopron
Csorna
Raba
Szombathely
Veszprem
Kormend
Zalaegerszeg
Keszthely
Drava
Boleslawiec
Liberec
Benesov
Havlickuv Brod
Jindrichuv
Hradec
Ceske
Budejovice
Tabor
Pisek
Teplice
Most
Chomutov
Kladno
PRAGUE
BOHEMIA
Beroun
Pribram
Strakonice
Bohemian Forest
Karlovy Vary
Plzen
Klatovy
Cheb
Decin
Usti nad Labem
Litomerice
Elbe

Carpathian Mountains

UKRAINE

Adriatic
Sea

50°
48°
46°
24°
20°
16°

SOUTHEASTERN EUROPE

Southeastern Europe extends east from the Adriatic Sea to the Black Sea, south to the Mediterranean Sea, and north to the Carpathian Mountains. The ancient country of Greece lies in the far south. It has been an independent nation since 1829. Albania, Romania, and Bulgaria were ruled by communist governments for almost 50 years until the 1990s. The rest of this region was part of a communist union of states called Yugoslavia. In 1991 a civil war led to the breakup of this union, and after the war five separate countries were created.

Southeastern Europe is mainly mountainous, but the northern part of the region has good soils where cereals, vegetables, and fruits are grown. The upland areas are used for grazing sheep and goats. Farther south and in the coastal areas grapes and olives are the main crops. Southeastern Europe has some textile, engineering, and manufacturing businesses, and these are concentrated around major cities such as Zagreb and Bucharest. Fumes from motor vehicles and factories combine to pollute the atmosphere in the urban areas. The Greek government controls the number of vehicles that come into Athens, but despite this, the air quality there is still bad. Mainland Greece and the islands in the Aegean Sea are centers of a thriving tourist trade, while tourism on the Black Sea coast is growing steadily.

LAND HEIGHT

	4,000m 13,124 ft.
	2,000m 6,562 ft.
	1,000m 3,281 ft.
	500m 1,640 ft.
	200m 656 ft.
	Sea level

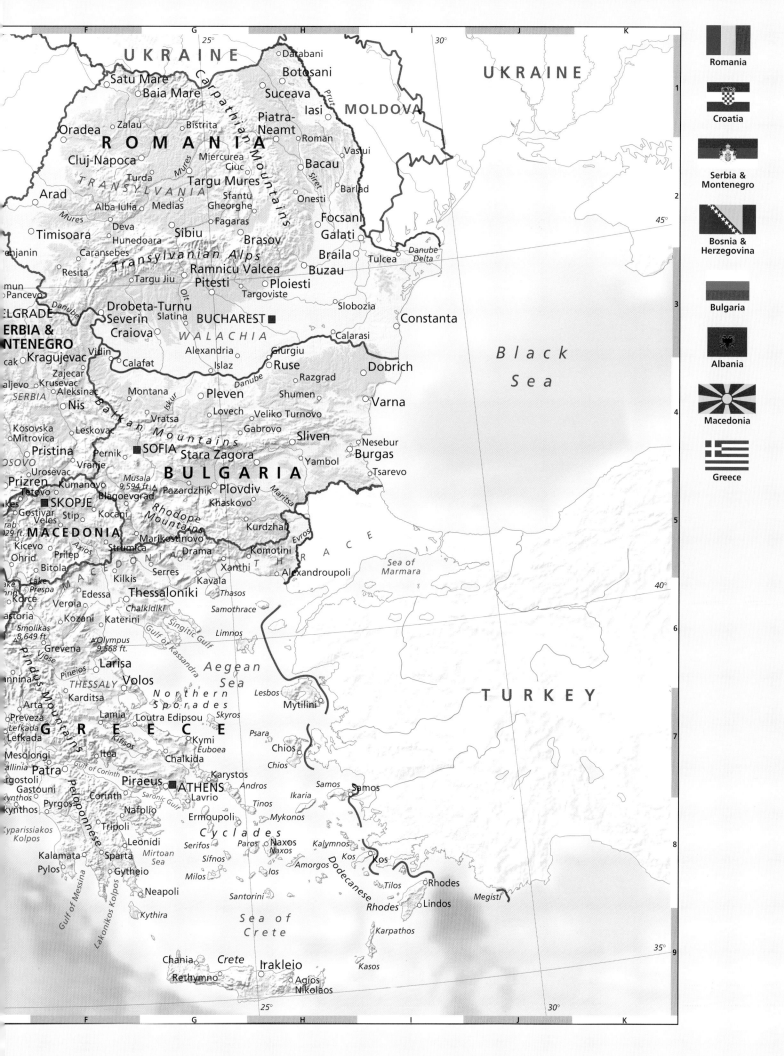

UKRAINE

Darabani
Satu Mare   Botosani
Baia Mare   Suceava   UKRAINE
Oradea   Zalau   Bistrita   Iasi   MOLDOVA
Piatra-
ROMANIA   Neamt
Cluj-Napoca   Roman
Miercurea   Vasui
Turda   Ciuc
Arad   Targu Mures   Bacau
TRANSYLVANIA   Sfantu   Barlad
Alba Iulia   Medias   Gheorghe   Onesti
Timisoara   Deva   Fagaras   Focsani
Hunedoara   Sibiu   Galati
Caransebes   Brasov
Transylvanian Alps   Braila
Resita   Targu Jiu   Ramnicu Valcea   Tulcea   Danube
Pancevo   Pitesti   Buzau   Delta
BELGRADE   Danube   Drobeta-Turnu   Targoviste   Slobozia
SERBIA &   Severin   Slatina   BUCHAREST   Constanta
MONTENEGRO   Craiova   WALACHIA   Calarasi
Cacak   Kragujevac   Vidin   Alexandria   Giurgiu   Dobrich
Zajecar   Calafat   Islaz   Ruse   Razgrad
Valjevo   Krusevac   Aleksinac   Varna
SERBIA   Montana   Pleven   Shumen
Nis   Veliko Turnovo
Kosovska   Leskovac   Vratsa   Lovech   Gabrovo   Nesebur
Mitrovica   Sliven   Burgas
Pristina   Pernik   SOFIA   Stara Zagora   Yambol
KOSOVO   Vranje   Tsarevo
Prizren   Urosevac   Musala   BULGARIA
Tetovo   Kumanovo   9,594 ft.   Pazardzhik   Plovdiv
SKOPJE   Blagoevgrad   Khaskovo   Maritsa
Gostivar   Veles   Stip   Kocani   Rhodope
Korab   MACEDONIA   Strumica   Mountains   Kurdzhali
9,029 ft.   Marikostinovo
Kicevo   Prilep   Drama   Komotini   Alexandroupoli
Ohrid   Bitola   Xanthi   THRACE
Lake   MACEDONIA   Serres   Kavala   Sea of
Prespa   Kilkis   Marmara
Lake   Edessa   Thessaloniki   Thasos
Ohrid   Korce   Veroia   Chalkidiki
Kastoria   Kozani   Katerini   Samothrace
Smolikas   Limnos
8,649 ft.   Grevena   Olympus   Aegean
Ioannina   Pindus   9,568 ft.   Gulf of Kassandra
Mountains   Vjose   Larisa   Sea   Lesbos   TURKEY
Pineios   THESSALY   Volos
Arta   Karditsa   Northern   Mytilini
Preveza   Sporades   Skyros
Lefkada   Lamia   Loutra Edipsou   Psara
Lefkada   GREECE   Kymi   Chios
Mesolongi   Euboea   Chios
Kefallinia   Itea   Chalkida
Patra   Gulf of Corinth   Karystos   Samos
Argostoli   Piraeus   Andros   Samos
Gastouni   Corinth   Saronic Gulf   ATHENS   Tinos   Ikaria
Zakynthos   Pyrgos   Nafplio   Lavrio   Mykonos
Zakynthos   Tripoli   Ermoupoli   Kalymnos
Cyparissiakos   Leonidi   Cyclades   Naxos   Kos   Kos
Kolpos   Kalamata   Sparta   Serifos   Paros   Naxos   Dodecanese
Pylos   Gytheio   Mirtoan   Sifnos   Ios   Amorgos   Rhodes
Neapoli   Sea   Milos   Tilos   Rhodes
Santorini   Rhodes   Lindos
Kythira   Megisti
Sea of   Karpathos
Crete
Chania   Crete   Irakleio   Kasos
Rethymno   Agios
Nikolaos

Black
Sea

Balkan
Mountains
Iskur
Olt

Axios

Vardar

Strymon

Evros

Gulf of Messina
Lakonikos Kolpos
Peloponnese

Kifisos

Gulf of Corinth

Romania

Croatia

Serbia &
Montenegro

Bosnia &
Herzegovina

Bulgaria

Albania

Macedonia

Greece

AFRICA

Africa, the world's second-largest continent, is separated from Asia by the Red Sea and from Europe by the Mediterranean Sea. A major feature of this huge landmass is the Sahara, Earth's biggest desert. It divides Africa's northern coast from the rest of the continent. South of the Sahara the landscape consists mainly of broad plateaus broken up by the basins of major rivers such as the Congo and the Zambezi. The Great Rift Valley cuts through the uplands of East Africa. Some of the rivers have dramatic waterfalls such as Victoria Falls, where the Zambezi plunges into

a chasm more than 390 ft. deep. Africa also has high mountains such as the Atlas range in the northwest and the Drakensberg in the south.

Most experts believe that the human race first evolved in Africa, but the continent's long history has been a troubled one. In the 1800s European powers, such as Great Britain, France, and Belgium, took over much of the continent. Most areas won independence from their foreign rulers in the 1960s, creating 53 separate African nations. These nations contain many different peoples and have a rich variety of

languages. A number of countries, however, have struggled to develop as modern states.

Some African countries rely on income from a single "cash crop" such as oranges, olives, or sugarcane. This means that their economies suffer badly if prices for the crop decrease or if the harvests fail. The continent's rapidly rising population is often hit hard by famine, and some countries have suffered from wars. Africa also has many advantages, from its plentiful natural resources to some of the planet's most spectacular scenery and fascinating wildlife.

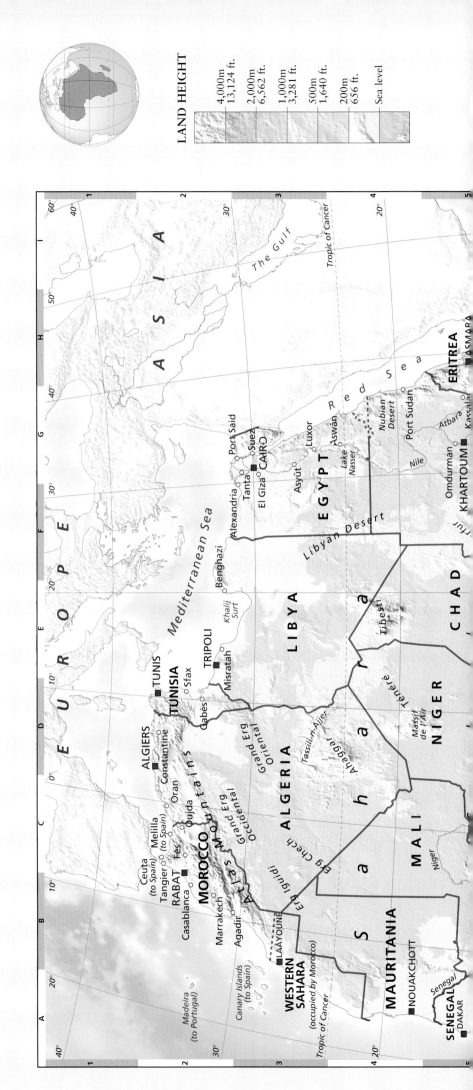

LAND HEIGHT

4,000m	13,124 ft.
2,000m	6,562 ft.
1,000m	3,281 ft.
500m	1,640 ft.
200m	656 ft.
	Sea level

ATLANTIC OCEAN

INDIAN OCEAN

MADAGASCAR

ANTANANARIVO
Toamasina
Mahajanga
Fianarantsoa
Tropic of Capricorn

Aldabra Group
(to Seychelles)

COMOROS
MORONI
Mayotte
(to France)

Mozambique Channel

SOMALIA
MOGADISHU
Kismaayo
Horn of Africa
Ogaden
Shebeli

DJIBOUTI
DJIBOUTI
Gulf of Aden
Hargeysa
Dire Dawa

ETHIOPIA
ADDIS ABABA
Ethiopian Highlands
15,154 ft.

SUDAN
Sudd
White Nile
Blue Nile
El Obeid
Juba

KENYA
NAIROBI
Lake Turkana
Kirinyaga 17,053 ft.
Kilimanjaro 19,336 ft.
Mombasa
Kisumu
Arusha

UGANDA
KAMPALA
Lake Victoria

RWANDA
KIGALI
Mwanza

BURUNDI
BUJUMBURA

TANZANIA
DODOMA
Masai Steppe
Tanga
Zanzibar
Dar es Salaam
Lake Tanganyika

Great Rift Valley

CENTRAL AFRICAN REPUBLIC
BANGUI

CHAD
NDJAMENA
Maiduguri

NIGERIA
ABUJA
Kano
Kaduna
Zaria
Ilorin
Ibadan
Lagos
PORTO-NOVO
Benue
Jos
Adamawa Highlands

CAMEROON
YAOUNDE
Douala
Aba
Port Harcourt
Benin City

EQUATORIAL GUINEA
MALABO

SÃO TOMÉ & PRÍNCIPE
SÃO TOMÉ

GABON
LIBREVILLE
Port-Gentil

CONGO
BRAZZAVILLE
Pointe-Noire

DEMOCRATIC REPUBLIC OF THE CONGO
KINSHASA
Kisangani
Mbandaka
Uele
Lualaba
Congo Basin
Kananga
Mbuji-Mayi
Kasama
Lubumbashi

ANGOLA
LUANDA
Benguela
Namibe
Huambo
Bié Plateau
Cuando
Cubango
Cuango

ANGOLA (CABINDA)

ZAMBIA
LUSAKA
Kitwe
Ndola
Kolwezi
Zambezi
Livingstone
Victoria Falls

MALAWI
LILONGWE
Blantyre
Lake Nyasa

MOZAMBIQUE
Nampula
Quelimane
Beira
Inhambane
Limpopo

ZIMBABWE
HARARE
Mutare
Gweru
Bulawayo
Francistown

BOTSWANA
GABORONE
Kalahari Desert

NAMIBIA
WINDHOEK
Namib Desert
Skeleton Coast
Walvis Bay
Okavango Delta

SOUTH AFRICA
PRETORIA
Johannesburg
BLOEMFONTEIN
Kimberley
East London
Port Elizabeth
CAPE TOWN
Cape of Good Hope
Cape Agulhas
Durban
Pietermaritzburg
Orange River
Drakensberg

SWAZILAND
MBABANE
MAPUTO

LESOTHO
MASERU

St. Helena (to U.K.)

Ascension Island (to St. Helena)

GUINEA-BISSAU
BISSAU

GUINEA
CONAKRY

SIERRA LEONE
FREETOWN

LIBERIA
MONROVIA

IVORY COAST
YAMOUSSOUKRO
Abidjan

GHANA
ACCRA

TOGO
LOMÉ

BENIN
PORTO-NOVO

BURKINA FASO
OUAGADOUGOU

MALI
BAMAKO

Lake Volta
Niger
Gulf of Guinea

Tropic of Capricorn
Equator

2000km
1000 miles
1000
500
0

NORTHWEST AFRICA

Morocco, Algeria, Tunisia, and Libya occupy the coast of northwestern Africa and part of the northern Sahara Desert. The region's uplands, including the Atlas Mountains, stretch from the north of Tunisia to the Atlantic coast of Morocco. Most of the people live in towns and villages on a fertile strip of land along the north coast, although Western Sahara and the southern parts of Algeria and Libya are thinly populated by Tuareg nomads.

On the coast farmers grow grapes and olives or raise sheep and goats. The bark of the cork tree is harvested in Morocco and Algeria, and dates are grown at oases in the desert. This region has a thriving textile industry, producing colorful rugs and fabrics, and in the past few decades oil and natural gas have brought wealth to Libya. Tourism is also a strong industry in the area, with ancient cities and hot weather attracting many overseas visitors.

The main environmental problem in northwest Africa is the northward spread of the Sahara Desert owing to droughts and the cutting down of trees and plants for fuel and animal food. As a result, farmers are losing land, and they are forced to overgraze the existing pastures. This puts more stress on the land and leads to the further expansion of the desert.

LAND HEIGHT

4,000m / 13,124 ft.
2,000m / 6,562 ft.
1,000m / 3,281 ft.
500m / 1,640 ft.
200m / 656 ft.
Sea level

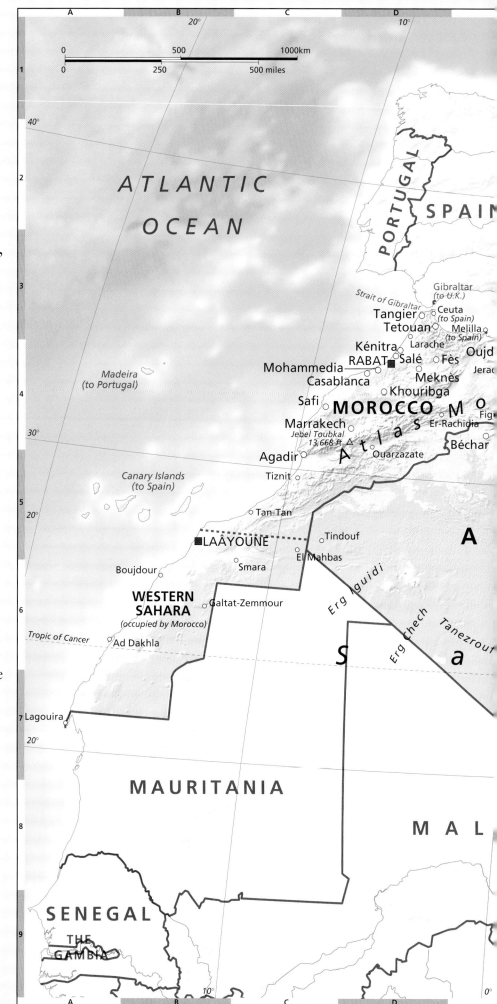

ATLANTIC OCEAN

PORTUGAL

SPAIN

Gibraltar (to U.K.)
Strait of Gibraltar
Tangier
Ceuta (to Spain)
Tetouan
Melilla (to Spain)
Kénitra   Larache   Oujd
Mohammedia   RABAT Salé Fès   Jerac
Casablanca   Meknès
Khouribga
Safi   M   O
MOROCCO
Marrakech   Er-Rachidia   Fig
Jebel Toubkal   Atlas
13,668 ft.   Ouarzazate   Béchar
Agadir
Tiznit

Madeira (to Portugal)

Canary Islands (to Spain)

Tan-Tan   A

LAÂYOUNE   Tindouf
El Mahbas
Boujdour   Smara

WESTERN   Galtat-Zemmour   Erg Iguidi
SAHARA   Erg Chech   Tanezrouf
(occupied by Morocco)

Tropic of Cancer   Ad Dakhla   S   a

Lagouira

MAURITANIA

MAL

SENEGAL
THE
GAMBIA

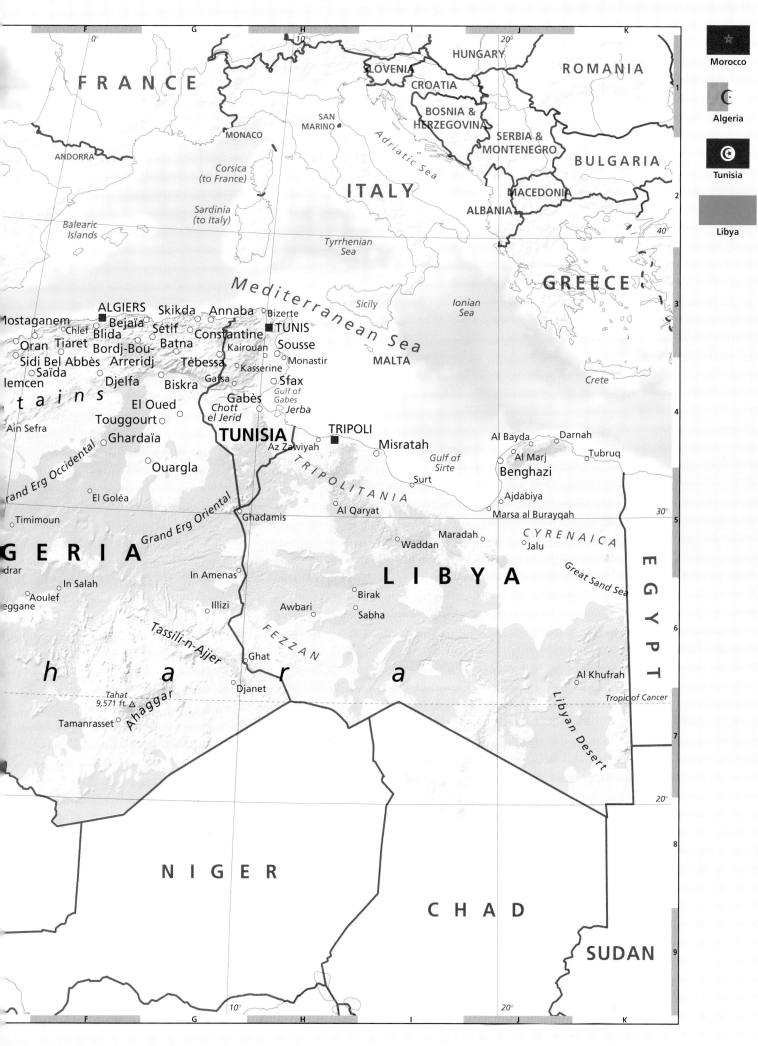

Morocco

Algeria

Tunisia

Libya

FRANCE

ANDORRA

MONACO

Corsica
(to France)

Sardinia
(to Italy)

Balearic
Islands

ITALY

SAN
MARINO

SLOVENIA

CROATIA

BOSNIA &
HERZEGOVINA

HUNGARY

SERBIA &
MONTENEGRO

ROMANIA

BULGARIA

MACEDONIA

ALBANIA

Adriatic
Sea

Tyrrhenian
Sea

Mediterranean Sea

Sicily

Ionian
Sea

GREECE

Crete

Mostaganem

ALGIERS
Bejaïa
Chlef
Blida
Oran Tiaret
Bordj-Bou-
Sidi Bel Abbès Arreridj
Saïda
lemcen
Djelfa

Skikda
Sétif
Batna

Annaba

Bizerte
TUNIS
Constantine
Kairouan Sousse
Monastir
Tébessa
Kasserine
Biskra Gafsa Sfax

MALTA

tains

El Oued
Touggourt

Ain Sefra

Ghardaïa

Grand Erg Occidental

Ouargla

El Goléa

Timimoun

GERIA

drar

In Salah

Aoulef
eggane

Gabès
Chott
el Jerid

Gulf of
Gabès

Jerba

TUNISIA

Az Zawiyah

TRIPOLI

Misratah

Gulf of
Sirte

Surt

TRIPOLITANIA

Al Qaryat

Ghadamis

Grand Erg Oriental

In Amenas

Illizi

Awbari

Birak
Sabha

FEZZAN

Tassili-n-Ajjer

Ghat

h   a   r   a

Tahat
9,571 ft. △

Ahaggar

Djanet

Tamanrasset

Al Bayda   Darnah
                         Tubruq
Al Marj
Benghazi
Ajdabiya
Marsa al Burayqah

Waddan

Maradah

CYRENAICA

Jalu

LIBYA

Great Sand Sea

Libyan Desert

Al Khufrah

EGYPT

Tropic of Cancer

NIGER

CHAD

SUDAN

NORTHEAST AFRICA

The land in the northeastern part of Africa is mainly arid. To the north Egypt and northern Sudan are desert areas. Only the Nile valley provides a narrow strip of fertile soil where people can live and farm. Smaller deserts lie in Somalia, Ethiopia, and Djibouti. There are some forests on Ethiopia's highlands, but much of the rest of this region is covered by dry scrubland and few trees.

People settled in northeast Africa more than 6,000 years ago, and by around 3000 B.C. one of the greatest early civilizations was established

in Egypt. For much of its history this region was an important international center of trade, with great cities and monuments. In 1867 the Suez Canal was opened to provide a shipping link between the Red and Mediterranean seas.

Today there are few big cities in northeast Africa, and most people live in the countryside and work the land. Farmers have to grow what crops they can in this hot, dry environment, where rainfall is rare and many rivers dry up for much of the year. Cotton and sugarcane are grown along the Nile river, dates grow well in

oases in the desert, and coffee is Ethiopia's main crop. Sheep, goats, and cattle are raised on the grasslands, while the region's factories process food. There is also a local textile industry.

In the past few decades life has been very hard for the people of this region. Rapid population growth has forced farmers to clear land in order to grow food and to cut down trees for fuel. The removal of trees and plants has allowed the wind to erode the soil, turning large areas into deserts. A series of famines and wars have brought death and suffering to millions of people in this area.

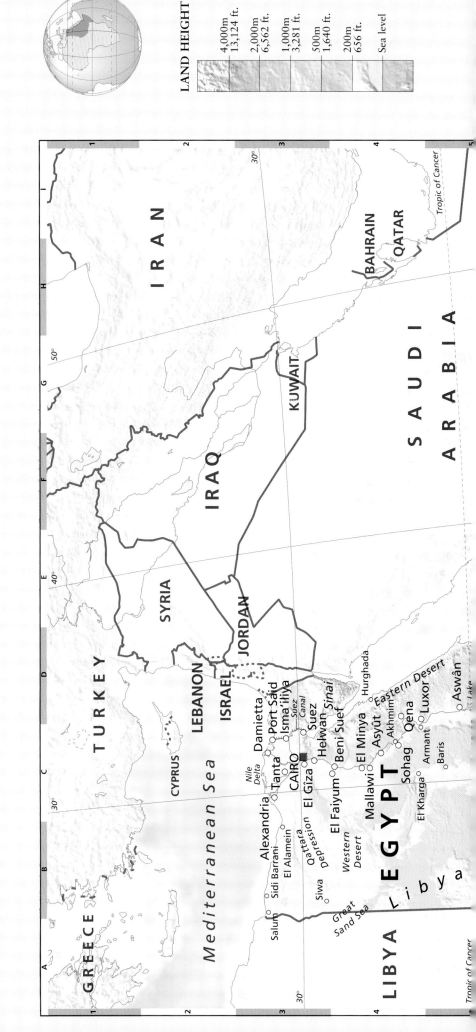

LAND HEIGHT	
4,000m	13,124 ft.
2,000m	6,562 ft.
1,000m	3,281 ft.
500m	1,640 ft.
200m	656 ft.
Sea level	

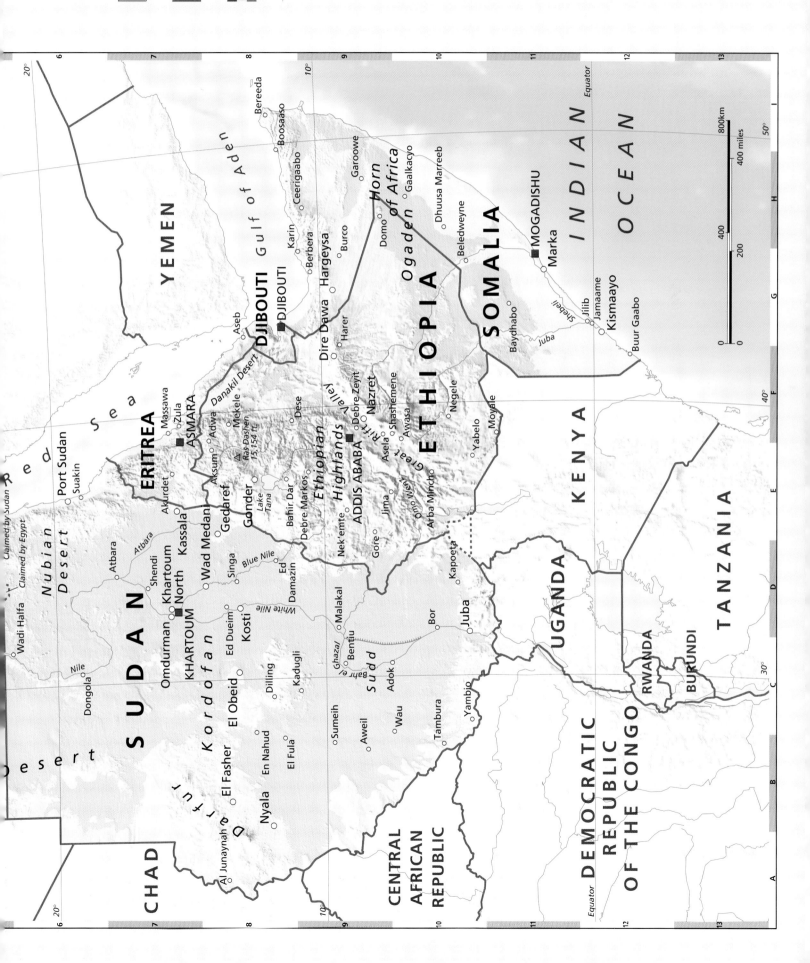

Egypt
Sudan
Eritrea
Ethiopia
Djibouti
Somalia

CHAD

SUDAN

Desert

Nubian Desert

Claimed by Sudan
Claimed by Egypt

Wadi Halfa

Dongola

Nile

Atbara

Atbara

Shendi

Omdurman
Khartoum North
KHARTOUM

Darfur

Al Junaynah
Nyala
El Fasher

En Nahud
El Fula

El Obeid

Kordofan

Dilling
Kadugli

Ed Dueim
Kosti

White Nile

Singa
Ed Damazin

Blue Nile

Wad Medani
Gedaref
Kassala

Sumeih
Aweil
Wau
Tambura

Bentiu
Ghazal
Bahr el Ghazal
Malakal
Adok

Bor
Juba

Kapoeta

Yambio

Sudd

CENTRAL AFRICAN REPUBLIC

DEMOCRATIC REPUBLIC OF THE CONGO

Equator

UGANDA

KENYA

RWANDA
BURUNDI

TANZANIA

Red Sea

Port Sudan
Suakin

ERITREA
ASMARA
Akurdet
Massawa
Zula

Danakil Desert

Aseb

Adwa
Aksum
Mekele
△ Ras Dashen
15,154 ft

Gonder
Bahir Dar
Lake Tana
Debre Markos

Dese

ETHIOPIA

Ethiopian Highlands

Nek'emte
Gore
Jima

ADDIS ABABA
Debre Zeyit
Nazret
Asela
Shashemene
Awasa

Great Rift Valley

Omo Wenz

Arba Minch
Negele
Yabelo
Moyale

DJIBOUTI
DJIBOUTI

Gulf of Aden

Dire Dawa
Harer
Hargeysa

YEMEN

Bereeda
Boosaaso

Karin
Berbera
Burco

Ceerigaabo
Garoowe

Horn of Africa

Domo

Ogaden

SOMALIA

Beledweyne
Dhuusa Marreeb
Gaalkacyo

Baydhabo

MOGADISHU
Marka

Jilib
Jamaame
Kismaayo

Shebeli
Juba

Buur Gaabo

INDIAN OCEAN

Equator

800km
400 miles

400
200

0

50°
40°
30°
20°
10°

A B C D E F G H I

6 7 8 9 10 11 12 13

WEST AFRICA

In the northern part of this region the edge of the Sahara meets a wide band of semidesert scrubland called the Sahel, which stretches from Mauritania to Niger. South of the Sahel is a strip of grassland, and farther south, along the coast, is a region of land where higher rainfall feeds areas of tropical rain forests. Many rivers cross the southern half of this area. The longest of these is the Niger, which forms a vast, swampy delta at the coast.

Cash crops, such as cotton, cocoa, and peanuts, are grown throughout the southern part of this region. Farther north farmers raise sheep and goats and grow food crops such as yams and cassava. The biggest industries are connected with food—the processing of nuts to extract oil, for example. Many people in Nigeria also work in the chemical industry or on wells that tap the region's rich supplies of gas and oil.

West Africa is an area with large deposits of minerals, ranging from iron ore to diamonds. In the past it has been home to successful civilizations such as the empires of the Mali and Asante, which benefited from these resources. In spite of new wealth from oil and tourism, most west Africans remain poor. Their lives are made difficult by frequent droughts and the growth of the desert in the north of the region.

LAND HEIGHT

4,000m
13,124 ft.

2,000m
6,562 ft.

1,000m
3,281 ft.

500m
1,640 f.t

200m
656 ft.

Sea level

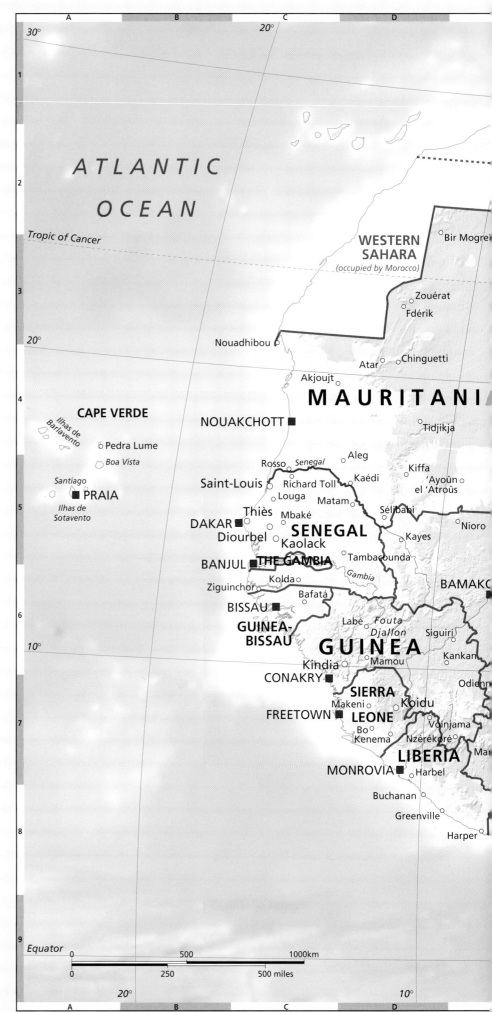

ATLANTIC

OCEAN

Tropic of Cancer

WESTERN
SAHARA
(occupied by Morocco)

Bir Mogrei

Zouérat
Fdérik

Nouadhibou

Atar Chinguetti

Akjoujt

MAURITANI

Tidjikja

CAPE VERDE

NOUAKCHOTT

Ilhas de
Barlavento

Pedra Lume

Boa Vista

Santiago

PRAIA

Ilhas de
Sotavento

Aleg

Rosso Senegal

Kiffa

Saint-Louis Richard Toll Kaédi 'Ayoûn
el 'Atroûs

Louga Matam

Thiès Mbaké Sélibabi

Nioro

DAKAR

SENEGAL

Diourbel Kayes

Kaolack

BANJUL THE GAMBIA Tambacounda

BAMAKO

Kolda Gambia

Ziguinchor Bafatá

BISSAU

GUINEA-
BISSAU

Labé Fouta
Djallon Siguiri

GUINEA Kankan

Kindia Mamou

CONAKRY

SIERRA Odienne

Makeni Koidu

FREETOWN LEONE Voinjama

Bo Nzérékoré

Kenema

LIBERIA Mar

MONROVIA Harbel

Buchanan

Greenville

Harper

MOROCCO

TUNISIA

ALGERIA

LIBYA

Erg Iguidi

Erg Chech

S a h a r a

Tessalit

Séguédine

Tropic of Cancer

Mreyyé

Araouane

Adrar des Ifôghas

Assamakka

Oualâta

Azaouâd

Kidal

Arlit

Massif de l'Aïr

Talak

Ténéré

Déma

Bassikounou

Timbuktu

M A L I

Gao

Ménaka

Agadez

N I G E R

Séfou

Niger

Mopti

Niger Delta

Tambao

Ansongo

Tahoua

e

l

Ngourti

Ségou

Bani

S a h e l

Tillabéri

Dogondoutchi

Nguigmi

CHAD

Ouahigouya

NIAMEY

Maradi

Zinder

Diffa

Koudougou

Kaya

Dosso

Sokoto

Katsina

Lake Chad

OUAGADOUGOU

B U R K I N A F A S O

Kandi

Niger

Gusau

Kano

Maiduguri

Banfora

Bolgatanga

Dapaong

Kaduna

Zaria

Bobo-Dioulasso

Natitingou

Bauchi

Kumo

Korhogo

White Volta

Tamale

Parakou

Minna

Jos

Black Volta

Sokodé

Bida

ABUJA

I V O R Y C O A S T

Ferkessédougou

GHANA

TOGO

BENIN

Ogbomosho

Ilorin

N I G E R I A

Jalingo

buaké

Oti

Atakpamé

Oyo

Oshogbo

Lokoja

Makurdi

YAMOUSSOUKRO

Lake Volta

Abeokuta

Ibadan

Akure

Benue

Abengourou

PORTO-NOVO

Enugu

Adamawa Highlands

aloa

Kumasi

Lagos

Gagnoa

Asamankese

Tema

LOMÉ

Cotonou

Benin City

Onitsha

Aba

Abidjan

ACCRA

Owerri

Calabar

CENTRAL AFRICAN REPUBLIC

n-Pédro

Sekondi-Takoradi

Cape Coast

Port Harcourt

Warri

Uyo

CAMEROON

Bight of Benin

Mouths of the Niger

Gulf of Guinea

EQUATORIAL GUINEA

CONGO

SÃO TOMÉ & PRÍNCIPE

GABON

Equator

Mauritania

Mali

Niger

Cape Verde

Senegal

The Gambia

Burkina

Nigeria

Guinea-Bissau

Guinea

Ivory Coast (Côte d'Ivoire)

Ghana

Togo

Benin

Sierra Leone

Liberia

CENTRAL AND EAST AFRICA

This region extends from Africa's Atlantic coast to the Indian Ocean. In the west is the Congo, the continent's second-longest river. Its basin is covered by Earth's largest tropical rain forest. So far this area has survived well, but some parts of it are being cut away. In the east is the Great Rift Valley, which runs from the north to the south and cuts through the uplands and grasslands of Uganda and Tanzania. The Nile river rises in the uplands and flows north on its way to the Mediterranean Sea.

To the west, among the dense forests of the Democratic Republic of the Congo, rubber and oil palm trees are grown in large plantations. The Congo river and its many tributaries provide a source of fish for the local people. Elsewhere cattle and goats are herded. In the east farmers grow crops for export such as vegetables and coffee.

The Democratic Republic of the Congo mines its rich supplies of copper, diamonds, silver, and cobalt. Other countries, such as Kenya, have developed manufacturing industries. Tourism is growing steadily in Kenya and Tanzania, where each year thousands of overseas visitors come to visit the countries' amazing wildlife. Although the tourist industry employs a large number of people there, most of the people still earn their living from the land.

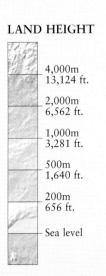

LAND HEIGHT

4,000m
13,124 ft.

2,000m
6,562 ft.

1,000m
3,281 ft.

500m
1,640 ft.

200m
656 ft.

Sea level

A

30°   40°

E G Y P T

SAUDI
ARABIA   20°

S U D A N   ERITREA   YEMEN

DJIBOUTI   10°

Birao

*Massif
es Bongo*   E T H I O P I A

Bria

Bangassou   Obo

Bondo   *Uele*   Nile   Lodwar   *Lake
Turkana*   Moyale   S O M A L I A

Bumba   Watsa   Gulu   Moroto   Marsabit

Isiro   Lira

Yangambi   Kisangani   Mungbere   Masindi   U G A N D A   Mbale   K E N Y A

Ikoli   *Lake Albert*   KAMPALA   Tororo   Eldoret   Meru   △ *Kirinyaga 17,053 ft.*   Equator

EMOCRATIC   Entebbe   Jinja   Kakamega   Nyeri   Garissa

EPUBLIC OF   *Lake Edward*   Mbarara   Kisumu   Nakuru

THE CONGO   Goma   Kabale   *Lake
Victoria*   NAIROBI   Machakos

Bukavu   KIGALI   *Lake Kivu*   Mwanza   Malindi

Kindu   RWANDA   *Serengeti
Plain*   Kilimanjaro   Mombasa

BUJUMBURA   △ *19,336 ft.*   Pemba

BURUNDI   Shinyanga   Arusha   Moshi

Kasongo   Kigoma   Singida   Tanga   I N D I A N

Kananga   Kabinda   *Lake
Tanganyika*   Tabora   *Masai
Steppe*   Zanzibar   O C E A N

Kabalo   Mpanda   DODOMA   Morogoro   Zanzibar

Mwene-Ditu   Mbuji-Mayi

Kamina   *Lake
Mweru*   Sumbawanga   Iringa   T A N Z A N I A   Dar es Salaam   Mafia

Mbeya   Rufiji   Mohoro

Dilolo   Kolwezi   Likasi   Makumbako   *Aldabra Group
(to Seychelles)*

Lubumbashi   *Lake
Nyasa*   Songea   Masasi   Lindi   10°

Z A M B I A   Mtwara

COMOROS

M A L A W I   M O Z A M B I Q U E   *Mayotte
(to France)*

30°   40°

Chad

Cameroon

Central African
Republic

Democratic
Rep. of the Congo

Kenya

Uganda

Equatorial Guinea

Congo

São Tomé &
Príncipe

Gabon

Rwanda

Tanzania

Burundi

SOUTHERN AFRICA

This region has a huge variety of scenery, from the parched Namib and Kalahari deserts of the west to the eastern grasslands and the Drakensberg mountains in the southeast. Off the eastern coast of southern Africa is Madagascar, a large island that split from the mainland around 1.3 billion years ago. Madagascar's wildlife, from lemurs to chameleons, includes many species of plants and animals that cannot be found anywhere else in the world.

Cattle are raised on the grasslands, while much of the land in the south is used for growing fruit for the export market. With rich deposits of precious minerals and metals, such as diamonds and gold, South Africa is the wealthiest part of this region. The country also has many other industries, including food canning, steel production, manufacturing, and textiles. These types of businesses are found in other countries in southern Africa but on a smaller scale.

In many areas trees have been cut down for fuel, and the soils have been blown away, leaving barren, infertile deserts. The region also has political problems. For much of the 1900s the black South Africans were denied basic human rights by the South African government. This system, known as apartheid, was abolished in 1994 when black South Africans were allowed to vote for the first time, and the country became a truly democratic state.

LAND HEIGHT

4,000m
13,124 ft.

2,000m
6,562 ft.

1,000m
3,281 ft.

500m
1,640 ft.

200m
656 ft.

Sea level

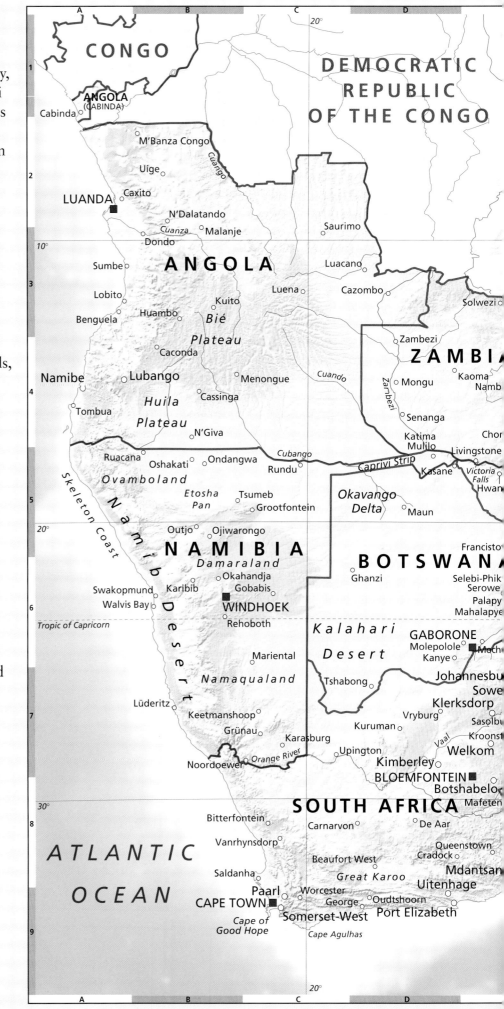

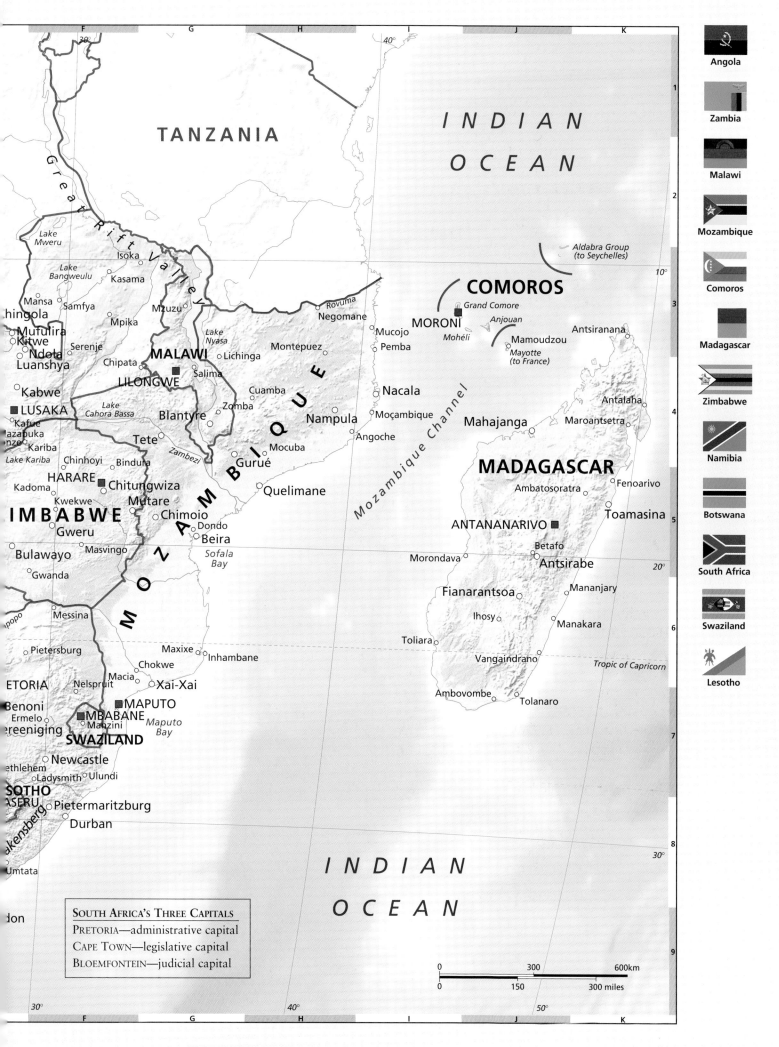

TANZANIA

INDIAN OCEAN

Great Rift Valley

Lake Mwer

Lake Bangweulu

Isoka

Kasama

Mansa

Samfya

Mpika

Mzuzu

hingola

Mutulira

Kitwe

Serenje

Ndola

Luanshya

Chipata

MALAWI

Kabwe

LILONGWE

LUSAKA

Lake Cahora Bassa

Kafue

azapuka

Blantyre

nze

Kariba

Tete

Lake Kariba

Chinhoyi

Bindura

HARARE

Kadoma

Chitungwiza

Kwekwe

Mutare

IMBABWE

Chimoio

Gweru

Dondo

Bulawayo

Masvingo

Beira

Gwanda

Sofala Bay

ipo

Messina

Pietersburg

Maxixe

Chokwe

Inhambane

ETORIA

Macia

Nelspruit

Xai-Xai

Benoni

MAPUTO

Ermelo

reeniging

MBABANE

Manzini

Maputo Bay

SWAZILAND

Newcastle

ethlehem

Ladysmith

Ulundi

SOTHO

ASERU

Pietermaritzburg

kensberg

Durban

Umtata

on

Lake Nyasa

Negomane

Rovuma

Mucojo

Montepuez

Lichinga

Pemba

Salima

Cuamba

Zomba

Nacala

Moçambique

Nampula

Mocuba

Angoche

Gurué

Quelimane

MOZAMBIQUE

Zambezi

MOZAM

Mozambique Channel

COMOROS

MORONI

Grand Comore

Anjouan

Mohéli

Mamoudzou

Mayotte (to France)

Aldabra Group (to Seychelles)

Antsiranana

Antalaha

Mahajanga

Maroantsetra

MADAGASCAR

Ambatosoratra

Fenoarivo

ANTANANARIVO

Toamasina

Betafo

Morondava

Antsirabe

Mananjary

Fianarantsoa

Ihosy

Manakara

Toliara

Vangaindrano

Tropic of Capricorn

Ambovombe

Tolanaro

INDIAN OCEAN

SOUTH AFRICA'S THREE CAPITALS

PRETORIA—administrative capital

CAPE TOWN—legislative capital

BLOEMFONTEIN—judicial capital

| 0 | 300 | 600km |
| 0 | 150 | 300 miles |

Angola

Zambia

Malawi

Mozambique

Comoros

Madagascar

Zimbabwe

Namibia

Botswana

South Africa

Swaziland

Lesotho

THE INDIAN OCEAN

From the coast of Africa in the west to Australia and the islands of Southeast Asia in the east, the Indian Ocean measures more than 6,000 mi. across at its widest point. Under the water are three ridges that form an upside-down "Y" shape. These ridges mark where three continental plates meet. Volcanic activity is common there.

The climate of the Indian Ocean varies according to latitude. The regions in the north, close to India, have a warm climate. In the south freezing temperatures have created pack ice and icebergs. Monsoon winds bring heavy rainfall to many coastal countries. They also have an effect on the ocean's currents, which reverse direction completely between March and August.

For thousands of years the Indian Ocean has provided important trade routes between the eastern and western parts of the world. Among the first traders to sail its waters were the ancient Egyptians, who traveled along the east African coast more than 4,000 years ago. In the 1400s European explorers made pioneering journeys across the Indian Ocean to Asia. They were soon followed by merchants who brought back silks, spices, and tea from India and China. Today huge tankers carry oil from the Persian Gulf to many of the ocean's international ports. A large number of these boats travel along the Red Sea and through the Suez Canal to reach Europe.

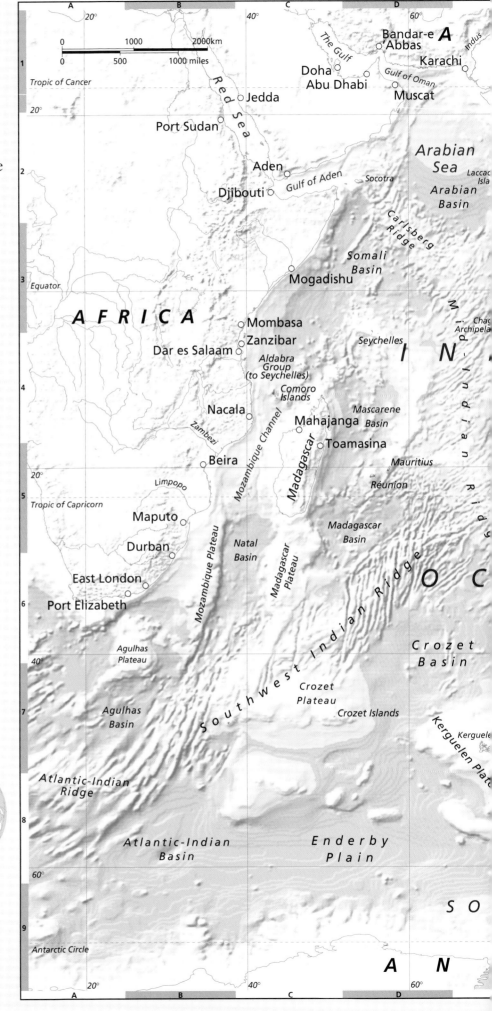

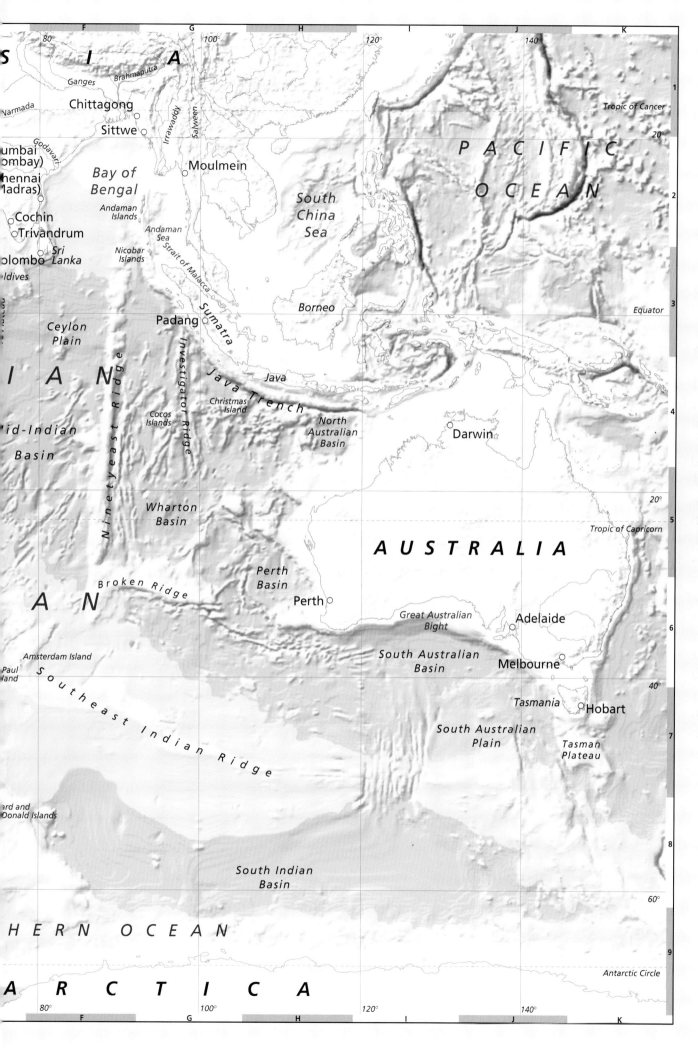

80°

S I A

Ganges
Brahmaputra

Narmada

Chittagong

Sittwe

Godavari

Irrawaddy

Salween

Moulmein

Mumbai
(Bombay)

hennai
(Madras)

Bay of
Bengal

Andaman
Islands

Cochin
Trivandrum

Sri
Lanka
olombo

Andaman
Sea

Nicobar
Islands

Strait of Malacca

ldives

100°

Tropic of Cancer

20°

P A C I F I C

O C E A N

South
China
Sea

Borneo

120°

140°

Equator

1

2

3

Ceylon
Plain

I A N

id-Indian
Basin

Ninetyeast Ridge

Investigator Ridge

Padang

Sumatra

Java Trench

Java

Christmas
Island

Cocos
Islands

North
Australian
Basin

Darwin

4

Wharton
Basin

A N

Broken Ridge

Amsterdam Island

Paul
land

Southeast Indian Ridge

rd and
Donald Islands

Perth
Basin

Perth

Great Australian
Bight

South Australian
Basin

20°

A U S T R A L I A

Tropic of Capricorn

5

Adelaide

Melbourne

6

40°

Tasmania

Hobart

South Australian
Plain

Tasman
Plateau

7

South Indian
Basin

60°

8

H E R N   O C E A N

9

Antarctic Circle

A R C T I C A

80°

100°

120°

140°

ASIA

Stretching from the Black Sea in the west to Japan in the east, Asia is the world's largest continent. There are many types of landscapes, from the snowy Mount Everest, the world's highest mountain, to the Arabian Desert. Uplands stretch across much of the middle of Asia, and there are great rivers such as China's Yangtze and India's Ganges. Earth's lowest place, the Dead Sea, is located on the border of Israel and Jordan.

Asia has a variety of people with many different beliefs, languages, and lifestyles. The huge communist state of China is the most populous country in the world. India, with more than one billion people, is the world's largest democratic nation. The breakup of the Soviet Union, which stretched from the eastern edge of the Russian Federation to Iran, created four countries in central Asia—Kazakhstan, Kyrgyzstan, Tajikistan, and Turkmenistan. These, as well as the older states to the west, are mainly Muslim nations.

Few people live in the cold and windswept areas of central and northern Asia. Those who inhabit these regions are often poor and live without many of the luxuries of modern life. Farther south are some of the world's major cities such as Mumbai (Bombay), Beijing (Peking), and Tokyo. The cities and countries in western Asia have grown rich from oil, while those on the Pacific coast have modern industries that have brought a high standard of living to many people.

LAND HEIGHT

	4,000m 13,124 ft.
	2,000m 6,562 ft.
	1,000m 3,281 ft.
	500m 1,640 ft.
	200m 656 ft.
	Sea level

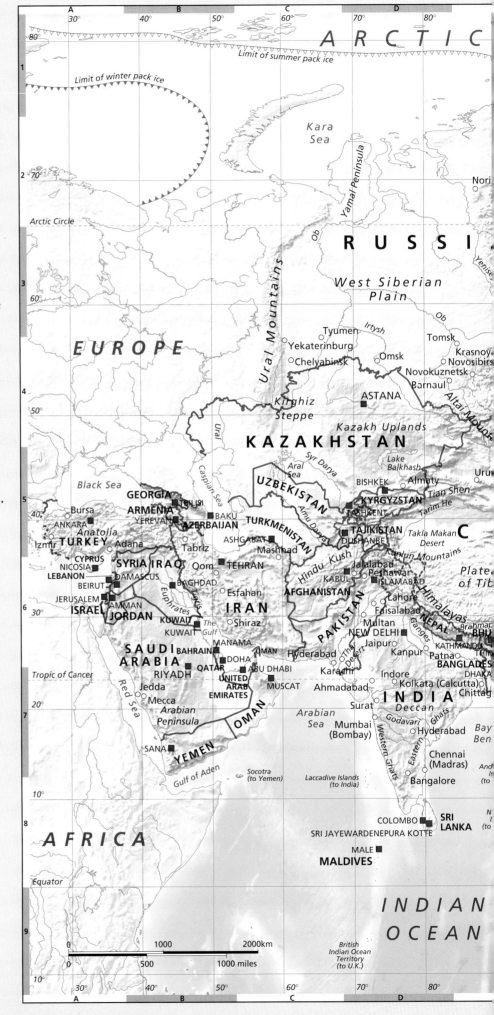

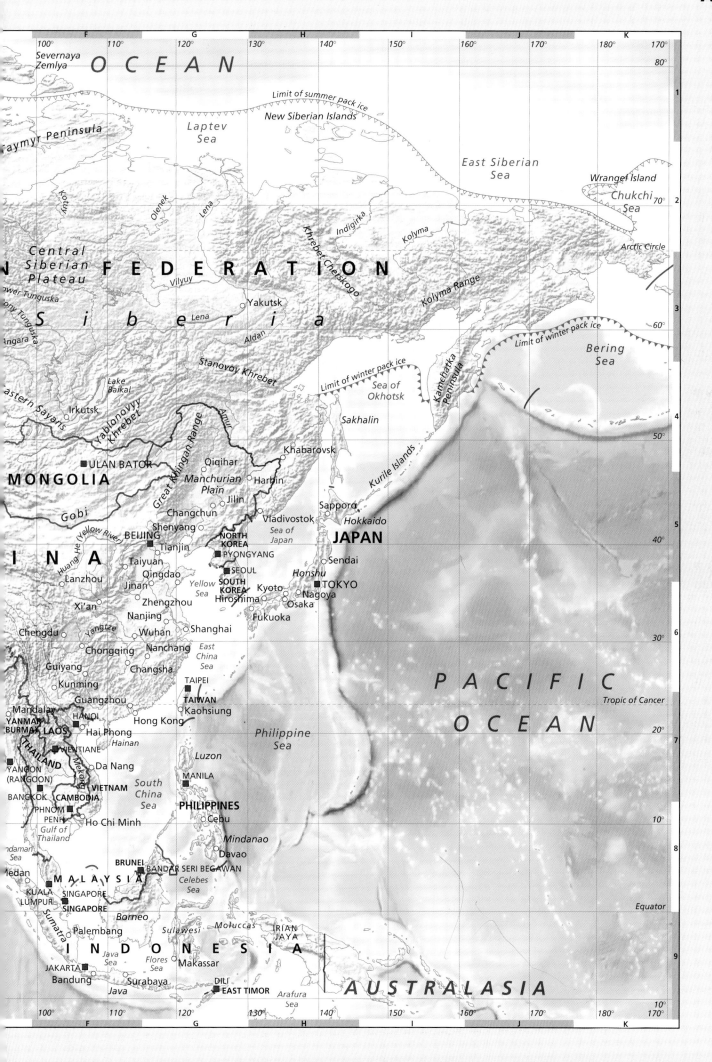

OCEAN

Severnaya Zemlya

100°   110°   120°   130°   140°   150°   160°   170°   180°   170°
80°

Limit of summer pack ice

Laptev Sea

New Siberian Islands

East Siberian Sea

Taymyr Peninsula

Kotuy

Olenek   *Lena*   *Indigirka*   *Kolyma*

Wrangel Island

Chukchi Sea

70°

2

Central Siberian Plateau

FEDERATION

Khrebet Cherskogo

Arctic Circle

Lower Tunguska

Stony Tunguska

Angara

Vilyuy

Yakutsk

Lena

Aldan

Kolyma Range

Kamchatka Peninsula

60°

3

Siberia

Stanovoy Khrebet

Limit of winter pack ice

Bering Sea

Eastern Sayans

Lake Baikal

Irkutsk

Yablonovyy Khrebet

Amur

Great Khingan Range

Limit of winter pack ice

Sea of Okhotsk

50°

4

■ ULAN BATOR

Qiqihar

Manchurian Plain

Harbin

Khabarovsk

Sakhalin

MONGOLIA

Changchun

○ Jilin

Kurile Islands

Gobi

Shenyang ○

Vladivostok

Sapporo

Hokkaido

5

Huang He (Yellow River)

BEIJING ■

○ Tianjin

NORTH KOREA

■ PYONGYANG

Sea of Japan

JAPAN

40°

INA

Taiyuan ○

SEOUL

Sendai

Lanzhou ○

Qingdao ○

SOUTH KOREA

Honshu

■ TOKYO

Jinan ○

Kyoto ○

Hiroshima

Nagoya

Xi'an ○

Zhengzhou ○

Yellow Sea

Osaka ○

30°

Nanjing ○

Fukuoka ○

Chengdu ○

Yangtze

Wuhan ○

○ Shanghai

6

Chongqing ○

Nanchang ○

East China Sea

Guiyang ○

Changsha ○

Kunming ○

TAIPEI ■

Tropic of Cancer

Guangzhou ○

TAIWAN

Mandalay ○

HANOI ■

Hong Kong ○

Kaohsiung

YANMAR

BURMA ■ LAOS

Hai Phong

Hainan

Philippine Sea

20°

7

THAILAND

■ VIENTIANE

Mekong

Da Nang ○

Luzon

YANGON (RANGOON)

VIETNAM

■ MANILA

BANGKOK ■

CAMBODIA

South China Sea

PHILIPPINES

PACIFIC

PHNOM PENH ■

Ho Chi Minh ○

Cebu ○

OCEAN

10°

Gulf of Thailand

Mindanao

8

Andaman Sea

○ Davao

Medan ○

BRUNEI ■

MALAYSIA

■ BANDAR SERI BEGAWAN

Celebes Sea

KUALA LUMPUR ○

SINGAPORE ■

Borneo

SINGAPORE

Equator

Sumatra

Palembang ○

Sulawesi

Moluccas

IRIAN JAYA

9

INDONESIA

AUSTRALASIA

JAKARTA ■

Java Sea

Flores Sea

Makassar ○

Bandung ○

Surabaya ○

Java

DILI ■

EAST TIMOR

Arafura Sea

10°

100°   110°   120°   130°   140°   150°   160°   170°   180°   170°

F   G   H   I   J   K

THE RUSSIAN FEDERATION

The western part of the Russian Federation falls in Europe, while the area east of the Ural Mountains is in Asia. Just east of the mountains is a flat region of marshes and streams called the West Siberian Plain. The plain gradually rises to the Central Siberian Plateau and then again to highlands in the south and east. Large coniferous forests cover most of this land. Much of European Russia lies on the North European Plain. This region is covered in large forests of birch and pine trees and is watered by several important rivers, including the Volga. In the far north is frozen tundra.

In the east a cold climate and harsh living conditions keep the population low. Many of those who do live there herd reindeer or work in forestry. The majority of people live in the west, where farmers grow root crops and wheat. This part of the country is highly industrialized, producing goods such as chemicals, cars, and textiles. The region is also one of Europe's main sources of oil.

The Russian Federation was created when the communist Soviet Union broke up in 1991. The communists controlled farming, and they developed heavy industries, many of which caused pollution. Today the country is modernizing its industries and tackling the environmental problems caused during the Soviet period.

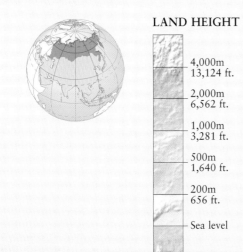

LAND HEIGHT

4,000m	13,124 ft.
2,000m	6,562 ft.
1,000m	3,281 ft.
500m	1,640 ft.
200m	656 ft.
—	Sea level

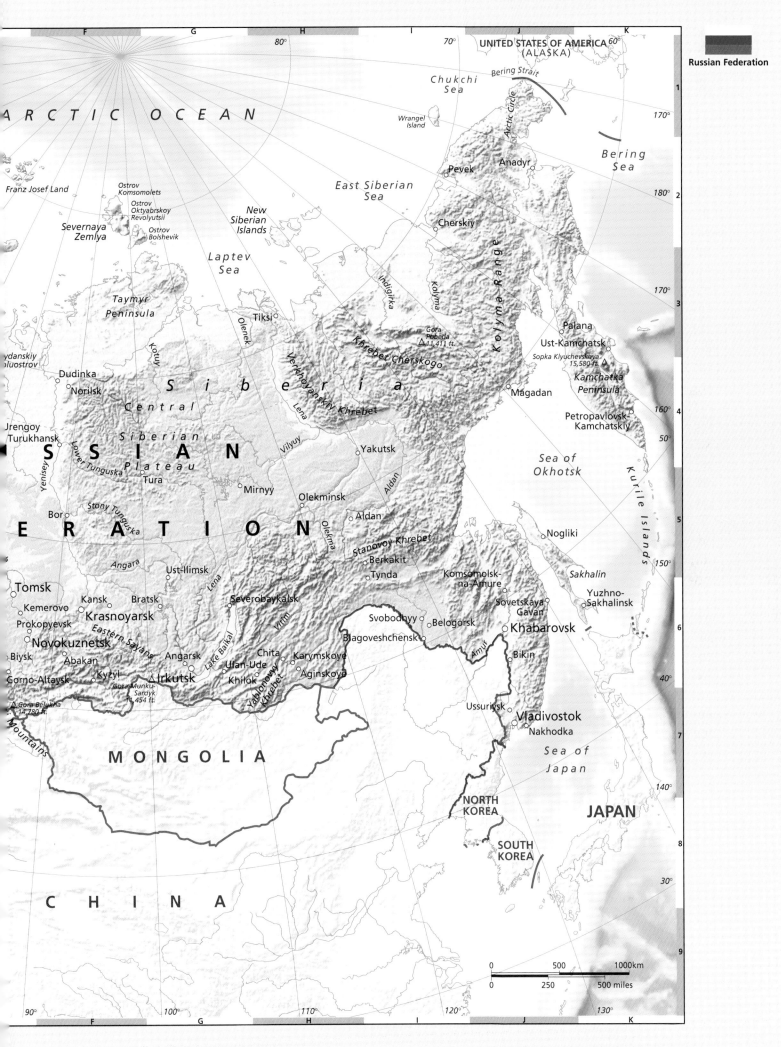

Russian Federation

UNITED STATES OF AMERICA
(ALASKA)

Chukchi
Sea

Bering Strait

Wrangel
Island

ARCTIC OCEAN

East Siberian
Sea

Pevek

Anadyr

Bering
Sea

Cherskiy

Franz Josef Land

Ostrov
Komsomolets

Ostrov
Oktyabrskoy
Revolyutsii

Severnaya
Zemlya

Ostrov
Bolshevik

New
Siberian
Islands

Laptev
Sea

Taymyr
Peninsula

Tiksi

Indigirka

Kolyma

Gora
Pobeda
11,411 ft.

Khrebet Cherskogo

Palana

Ust-Kamchatsk

Sopka Klyuchevskaya
15,580 ft.

ydanskiy
oluostrov

Olenek

Verkhoyanskiy Khrebet

Kolyma Range

Kamchatka
Peninsula

Dudinka

Kotuy

Norilsk

Siberia

Lena

Magadan

Petropavlovsk-
Kamchatskiy

Central

Yakutsk

Jrengoy
Turukhansk

Siberian
Plateau

Tura

Lower Tunguska

Vilyuy

Aldan

Sea of
Okhotsk

Kurile Islands

Mirnyy

Yenisey

Olekminsk

Bor

Stony Tunguska

Olekma

Aldan

Nogliki

Sakhalin

Angara

Ust-Ilimsk

Stanovoy Khrebet

Komsomolsk-
na-Amure

Yuzhno-
Sakhalinsk

Tomsk

Kansk

Bratsk

Severobaykalsk

Berkakit

Kemerovo

Lena

Tynda

Svobodnyy

Belogorsk

Sovetskaya
Gavan

Prokopyevsk

Krasnoyarsk

Eastern Sayans

Angarsk

Vitim

Blagoveshchensk

Khabarovsk

Novokuznetsk

Biysk

Abakan

Lake Baikal

Chita

Karymskoye

Amur

Bikin

Gorno-Altaysk

Kyzyl

Irkutsk

Ulan-Ude

Khilok

Aginskoye

Gora Munku-
Sardyk
11,454 ft.

Yablonovyy Khrebet

Ussuriysk

Vladivostok

Gora Belukha
14,780 ft.

Nakhodka

Mountains

MONGOLIA

Sea of
Japan

NORTH
KOREA

JAPAN

SOUTH
KOREA

CHINA

0		500		1000km

0	250	500 miles

WEST ASIA

In the north of west Asia lie the Taurus Mountains and the plateau of Anatolia. The eastern part of this region is also dominated by uplands, including the Elburz and Zagros mountains. In the south is the huge Arabian Peninsula, which is separated from the rest of Asia by the valleys of the Tigris and Euphrates rivers. Mountains run along the peninsula's Red Sea coast, and much of the rest of this region is covered in dry, barren deserts.

West Asia has a long history. Some of the world's first great civilizations developed in Iraq around 5,000 years ago, and the Arabian Peninsula was the home of the prophet Muhammad and the first Muslims. This region is still mainly Muslim, although it also contains the Jewish state of Israel.

Oil and natural gas are important sources of income for many of the countries in west Asia. Other industries produce a range of goods, from industrial machinery in Georgia to carpets in Iran. Cattle and sheep are raised in the north, while goats are herded on the southern tip of the Arabian Peninsula. Hazelnuts are the main crop along the Black Sea coast, root crops are produced in Anatolia, and olives, figs, grapes, and peaches are cultivated on Turkey's southern coast. Wheat is harvested in the fertile valleys of the Euphrates and Tigris rivers. Cotton, dates, and fruits for the export market are also grown there.

LAND HEIGHT

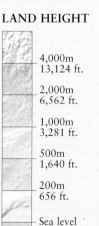

4,000m
13,124 ft.

2,000m
6,562 ft.

1,000m
3,281 ft.

500m
1,640 ft.

200m
656 ft.

Sea level

RUSSIAN FEDERATION

KAZAKHSTAN

UZBEKISTAN

Khumi *Caucasus*
GEORGIA   Kazbek
            16,554 ft.
Kutaisi   TBILISI
Batumi   Rustavi
Hopa   Vanadzor   Sumqayit
rbzon   Gyumri   Ganca   BAKU
        ARMENIA   AZERBAIJAN
urum YEREVAN
        AZERBAIJAN
Lake   Naxcivan

TURKMENISTAN

Caspian Sea

Bitlis   Van   Khvoy
Diyarbakir Lake Orumiyeh   Tabriz   Ardabil
Batman   Urmia   Maragheh   Rasht
Al Qamishli   Zanjan   Qazvin
Al Hasakah   Summel   Bukan   Qolleh ye Damavand
Mosul   Arbil   18,634 ft.
Jazirah   Kirkuk   As Sulaymaniyah   Karaj
yr az Zawr   Kamal   Tikrit   Sanandaj   TEHRAN
        Samarra'   Saray   Hamadan   Saveh
IRAQ   Ba'qubah   Ilam   Bakhtaran   Arak
        BAGHDAD   Borujerd   Khorramabad
Karbala   Al Kut   Najafabad
An Najaf   Al Hillah   Dezful   Esfahan
        Euphrates   Ar'ar   Al Amarah   Ahvaz
        Nasiriyah   Al Qurnah   Khorramshahr
        Basra   Abadan

Babol   Sari   Amol
Gonbad-e Kavus   Bojnurd
Gorgan   Neyshabur   Mashhad
Emamshahr   Sabzevar
Semnan
Garmsar   Dasht-e Kavir
Qom   Gonabad
Kashan   Tabas
IRAN
Iranian   Birjand
Qomisheh   Yazd
Plateau   Dasht-e Lut
Kerman   Zabol
Zahedan

AFGHANISTAN

Tigris
Karun
Zagros Mountains

PAKISTAN

Kazerun   Shiraz   Sirjan   Bam
Bandar-e Bushehr
Kangan   Iranshahr
Bandar-e 'Abbas

Rafhah
KUWAIT
KUWAIT   Al Ahmadi
Al Wari'ah
Hafar al Batin

Qeshm   Strait of Hormuz
Bandar-e Lengeh
Al Khasab   Jask   Chabahar
OMAN   Ajman   Sharjah   Fujairah
Ad Dammam   BAHRAIN   Dubai   Suhar
Dhahran   MANAMA
Al Majma'ah   DOHA
Al Hufuf   QATAR
        ABU DHABI   'Al Ayn   Ar Rustaq   MUSCAT
Shaqra'   RIYADH   UNITED ARAB   'Ibri   Nizwa
Al Kharj   EMIRATES   Sur
Harad

afud
Arabian
Buraydah
'Unayzah
Ad Dahna

Peninsula

SAUDI ARABIA

OMAN

Gulf of Oman
Tropic of Cancer

Zalim   Layla
Halaban   As Sulayyil
Ar Rub' al Khali   Hayma'   Gulf of Masirah
(Empty Quarter)   Mughshin

Ta'if
Al Bahah   Tathlith
fidhah
Abha   Najran
Jizan   Zufar

Masirah
Arabian Sea

Raysut   Salalah
YEMEN   Al Mahrah
SANA   Shibam   Nishtun
Hawra   Sayhut
Hodeida   Dhamar   Hadramawt
Ibb   Al Mukalla
Ta'izz   Lawdar
Mocha   Zinjibar
Bab el Mandeb   Aden
DJIBOUTI   Gulf of Aden

Socotra
(to Yemen)
'Abd Al Kuri

INDIAN OCEAN

CENTRAL ASIA

A wall of mountains cuts through central Asia in a diagonal line from the Tian Shan in the northeast through the Pamirs in the center to the Hindu Kush in the southwest. In the northwest are the sandy deserts of Uzbekistan and Turkmenistan. There are rolling grasslands in Kazakhstan in the north. Central Asia receives very little rain, and the region experiences extremes of temperature—the winters are cold, and the summers are very hot.

With very few large cities, the people of central Asia live mainly in rural areas and make their living from the land. Farming is difficult in the desert and mountain regions, so agriculture is concentrated around the river valleys in the east. A variety of cereals and fruits, including peaches, melons, and apricots, are grown there. Cotton, which is central Asia's main export, is grown on land irrigated by the Amu Darya river. Herds of cattle, sheep, and goats are raised in the south and east and on the grasslands of Kazakhstan in the north.

Fossil fuels, including oil, gas, and coal, are extracted and processed throughout the region.

There are a number of traditional industries that make products such as carpets and leather goods. The main industrial area is located in the east in the Fergana Valley, where old-fashioned factories cause air pollution.

Once the fourth-largest lake in the world, the Aral Sea has shrunk by almost half its size since 1960. This is because the rivers feeding the lake have been diverted to irrigate fields of cotton. The dry climate, combined with poor vegetation cover, means that desertification is another environmental problem in central Asia.

LAND HEIGHT

4,000m	13,124 ft.
2,000m	6,562 ft.
1,000m	3,281 ft.
500m	1,640 ft.
200m	656 ft.
Sea level	

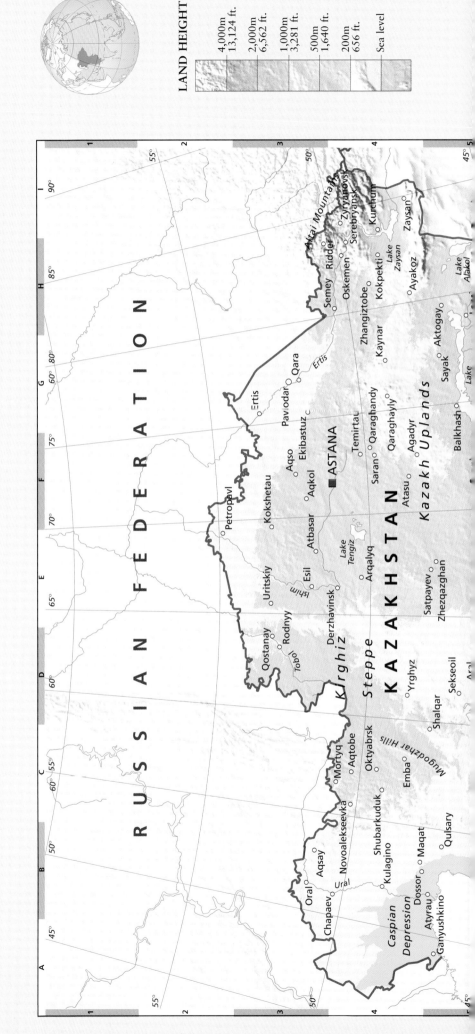

Kazakhstan | Uzbekistan | Kyrgyzstan | Turkmenistan | Tajikistan | Afghanistan | Pakistan

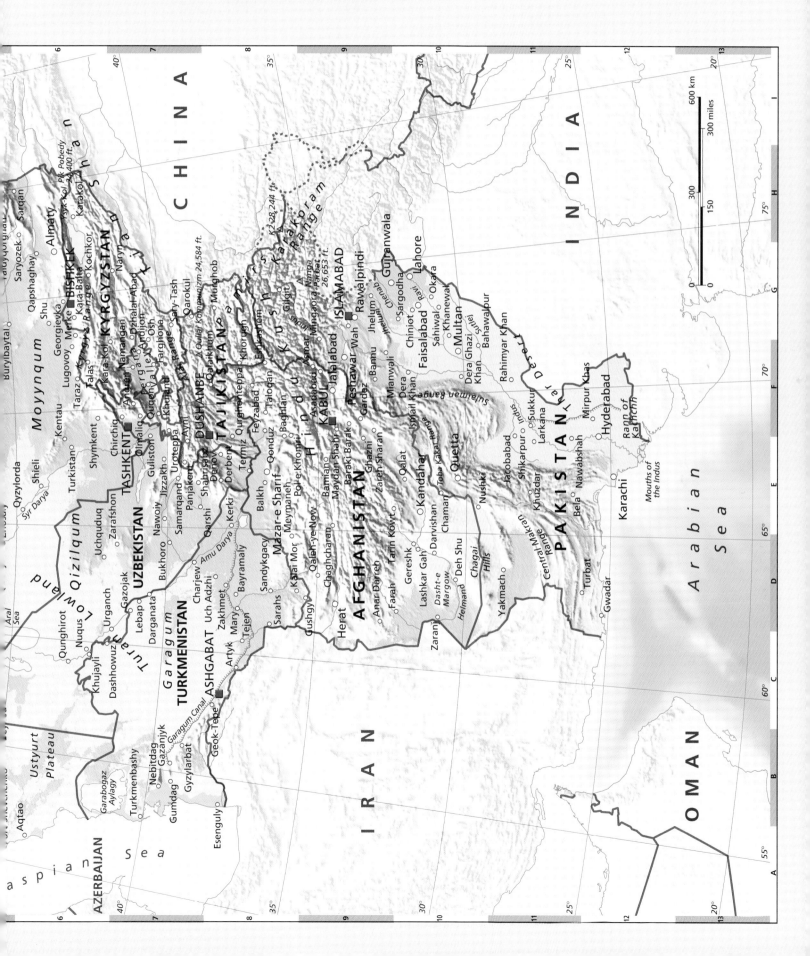

CHINA

INDIA

IRAN

OMAN

PAKISTAN

AFGHANISTAN

TAJIKISTAN

KYRGYZSTAN

UZBEKISTAN

TURKMENISTAN

AZERBAIJAN

Caspian Sea

Arabian Sea

Aral Sea

Turan Lowland

Ustyurt Plateau

Moyynqum

Qizilqum

Garagum

Thar Desert

Hindu Kush

Karakoram Range

Tian Shan

Syr Darya

Amu Darya

Indus

Garagum Canal

BISHKEK
TASHKENT
DUSHANBE
ASHGABAT
KABUL
ISLAMABAD

Almaty
Sarqan
Sarkan
Saryozek
Qapshaghay
Taldyqorghan
Sariyshaghan
Qaraghan
Burylbaytal
Shu
Georgievka
Lugovoy
Merke
Kentau
Taraz
Talas
Shymkent
Turkistan
Turkistan
Shieli
Shieli
Qyzylorda
Syr Darya
Kara-Balta
Kochkor
Navyn
Syk-Kol 3,400 ft.
Pk Pobedy 24,400 ft.
Karakol
KYRGYZSTAN
Kara-Köl
Naryn
Qarokul
Saly-Tash
Osh
Jalal-Abad
Özgön
Andijon
Namangan
Farghona
Fergana Valley
Khujand
Qurghonteppa
Panjakent
Samarqand
Jizzakh
Guliston
Chirchiq
Olmaliq
Angren
Avni
Uroteppa
Qarakhum
Khorugh
Murghob
Qazalkur
Shabrisabz
Denov
Termiz
Qonduz
Talogan
Feyzabad
Baghlan
Pol-e Khomri
Mazar-e Sharif
Balkh
Meymaneh
Kalai Mor
Qalen-ye Now
Chaghcharan
Herat
Anar Darreh
Farah
Gereshk
Lashkar Gah
Dasht-e Margow
Deh Shu
Zaranj
Nimruz
Bamian
Maydan Shahr
Ghazni
Baraki Barak
Gardez
Zareh Sharan
Qalat
Darvishan
Chaman
Kandahar
Quetta
Nushki
Chagai Hills
Yakmach
Central Makran Range
Turbat
Gwadar
Bela
Nawabshah
Karachi
Hyderabad
Mirpur Khas
Rann of Kachchh
Mouths of the Indus
Larkana
Shikarpur
Sukkur
Jacobabad
Rahimyar Khan
Bahawalpour
Bahawalnagar
Khanewal
Multan
Okara
Sahiwal
Faisalabad
Chiniot
Sargodha
Jhelum
Gujranwala
Lahore
Rawalpindi
Peshawar
Jalalabad
Asadabad
Mingora
Gilgit
Nanga Parbat 26,653 ft.
K2 28,244 ft.
Gujrat
Sialkot
Wah
Bannu
Dera Ismail Khan
Mianwali
Dera Ghazi Khan
Sulaiman Range
Khuzdar
Kalat
Zhob

Qyzylorda
Aqtao
Garabogaz Aylagy
Turkmenbashy
Nebitdag
Gyzylarbat
Gumdag
Esenguly
Geok-Tepe
Artyk
Mary
Tejen
Sarahs
Bayramaly
Uch Adzhi
Zakhmet
Kerki
Charjew
Lebap
Darganata
Gazojak
Urganch
Bukhoro
Nawoiy
Zarafshon
Uchquduq
Qarshi
Nuqus
Dashhowuz
Khujayli
Qunghirot
Gushgy

600 km
300 miles
300
150
0

SOUTH ASIA

South Asia is separated from the rest of Asia by the Thar Desert in the northwest and a wall of mountains, including the towering Himalayas, in the north and east. The great floodplains of the Ganges, Brahmaputra, and Indus rivers lie at the foothills of the mountains. Farther south are rolling plateaus, which are fringed by a line of coastal hills called the Eastern and Western Ghats. To the southeast are the mountainous islands of Sri Lanka.

More than half of south Asia's population makes its living from agriculture. Farmers grow rice in the wet areas of the east and west, while corn and millet are the main crops cn the Deccan Plateau. Elsewhere groundnuts are grown for cooking oil, and tea for the export market is harvested on huge plantations. Livestock are raised throughout the region, and fishing is common along the entire coast.

Large-scale industries, from car manufacturing to chemicals, have expanded in the region's cities in recent years. Service industries are also growing steadily. In the countryside a number of people work in traditional trades, providing goods to the local people. Products, such as clothing, leather, and jewelry, are among south Asia's leading exports.

This part of Asia's huge population is growing rapidly. The majority of the people live in rural areas, but increasing numbers are moving to the cities in search of work. There is serious overcrowding in both rural and urban regions, and slums have developed in the larger cities. Deforestation is also a major problem, with trees being cut down in the southern and Himalayan regions for fuel.

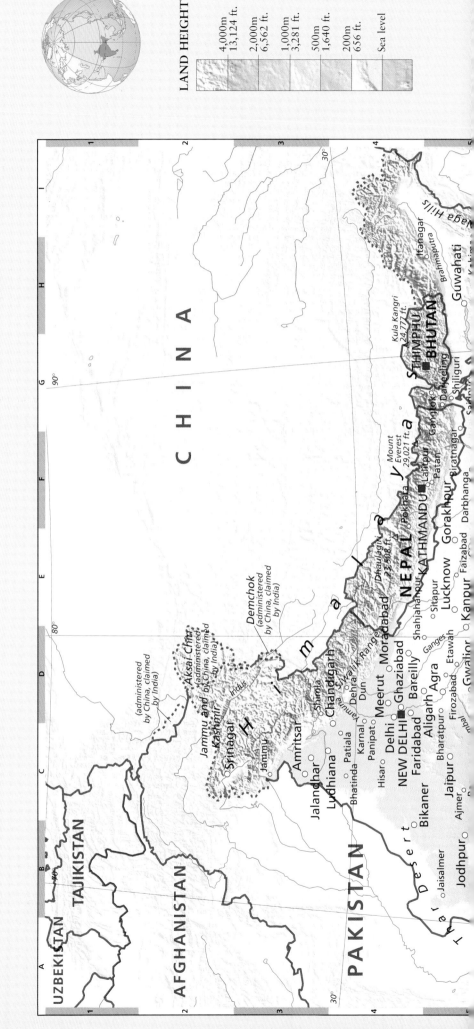

LAND HEIGHT

4,000m	13,124 ft.
2,000m	6,562 ft.
1,000m	3,281 ft.
500m	1,640 ft.
200m	656 ft.
	Sea level

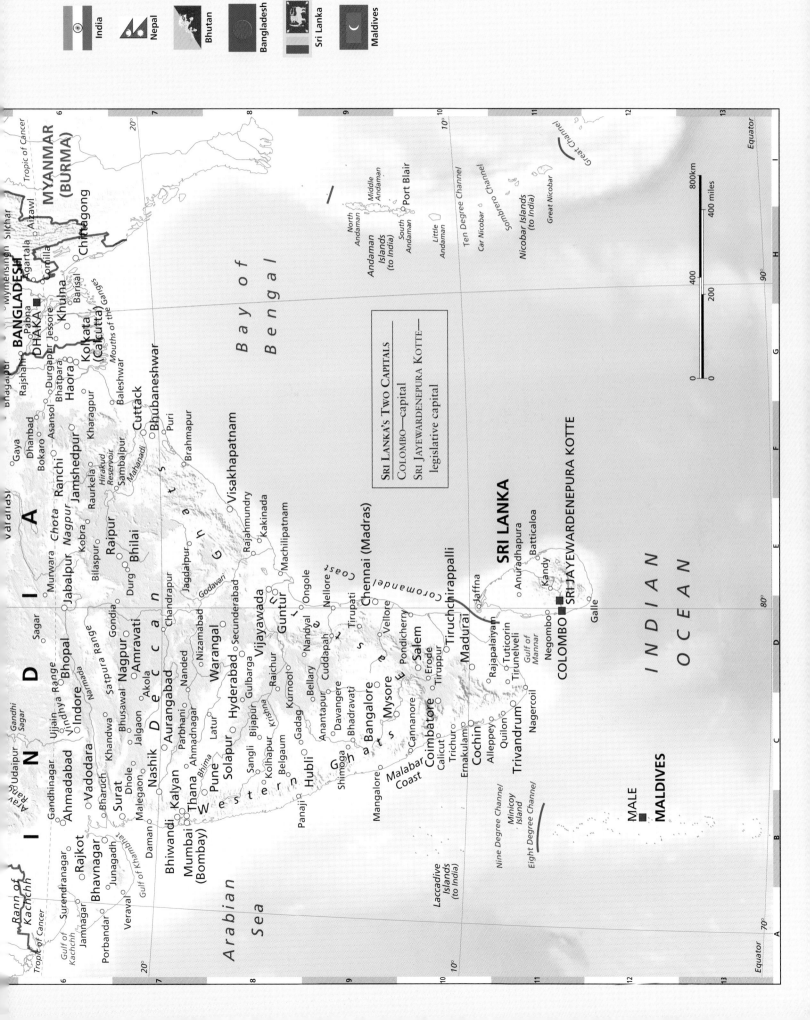

India
Nepal
Bhutan
Bangladesh
Sri Lanka
Maldives

SRI LANKA'S TWO CAPITALS
COLOMBO—capital
SRI JAYEWARDENEPURA KOTTE—
legislative capital

MYANMAR (BURMA)

Tropic of Cancer

Mymensingh Silchar
Tangail Agartala Aizawl
BANGLADESH
DHAKA Comilla
Pabna Khulna Chittagong
Rajshahi Durgapur Jessore Barisal
Bhagalpur Bhatpara Haora
Asansol Kolkata (Calcutta)
Mouths of the Ganges

Bay of Bengal

North Andaman
Middle Andaman
South Andaman
Port Blair
Little Andaman
Andaman Islands (to India)
Ten Degree Channel
Car Nicobar Channel
Sombrero Channel
Nicobar Islands (to India)
Great Nicobar
Great Channel

Equator

800km
400 miles
400
200
0
0

90°

I N D I A

Gaya
Dhanbad
Bokaro
Ranchi
Jamshedpur
Kharagpur
Baleshwar
Cuttack
Bhubaneshwar
Puri
Murwara Chota Nagpur
Jabalpur Kobra
Bilaspur Raurkela Sambalpur
Hirakud Reservoir
Mahanadi
Raipur Durg Bhilai
Brahmapur
Visakhapatnam
Rajahmundry
Kakinada
Machilipatnam

Sagar
Ujjain
Bhopal Vindhya Range
Indore Narmada Satpura Range
Chandrapur
Jagdalpur
Godavari
Ghats
Coromandel Coast

SRI LANKA
Anuradhapura
Batticaloa
Kandy
SRI JAYEWARDENEPURA KOTTE
Jaffna
Negombo
COLOMBO
Galle
Gulf of Mannar
Rajapalaiyam

INDIAN OCEAN

Udaipur Gandhi Sagar
Aravalli Range
Ratlam
Gandhinagar
Ahmadabad Vadodara
Bharuch Khandwa
Surat Dhole
Daman Malegaon Jalgaon Akola Amravati Nagpur
Deccan
Nashik Bhusawal
Bhiwandi Kalyan Thana
Mumbai (Bombay) Ahmadnagar Latur Parbhani Nanded
Western Pune Solapur
Bhima Gulbarga
Sangli Bijapur Krishna
Kolhapur Belgaum
Panaji Hubli Gadag
Goa Shimoga
Mangalore
Malabar Coast
Cannanore
Calicut
Trichur
Cochin Ernakulam
Alleppey
Quilon
Trivandrum
Nagercoil

Aurangabad
Hyderabad Secunderabad
Nizamabad
Warangal
Vijayawada
Guntur
Ongole
Nellore
Nandyal
Kurnool
Raichur
Bellary
Cuddapah
Anantapur
Tirupati
Chennai (Madras)
Vellore
Pondicherry
Salem
Erode
Tiruppur
Coimbatore
Bangalore
Mysore
Bhadravati
Davangere
Madurai
Tiruchirappalli
Tuticorin
Tirunelveli

Rann of Kachchh
Gulf of Kachchh
Jamnagar
Rajkot
Surendranagar
Bhavnagar
Junagadh
Porbandar
Veraval
Gulf of Khambhat

Arabian Sea

MALDIVES
MALE

Nine Degree Channel
Minicoy Island
Eight Degree Channel
Laccadive Islands (to India)

Tropic of Cancer
Equator

70° 80° 20° 10°

SOUTHEAST ASIA

Southeast Asia is made up of many thousands of tropical islands and a mainland area. The landscape of the mainland is dominated by a string of mountain ranges that are covered in dense forests and crossed by wide river valleys. The many islands to the southeast of the mainland are also forested. Most of these islands were formed by volcanoes, many of which are still active. In the center of the region is the island of Borneo. The third-largest island in the world, it is divided between the countries of Malaysia, Indonesia, and Brunei.

Rice is the main food crop in this region, while bananas, pineapples, and sugarcane are grown as cash crops. Large quantities of fish are caught in the surrounding waters. Over the last few decades the types of industries in Southeast Asia have changed dramatically. There are still a number of traditional companies that process the area's raw materials, including timber and metals, but many parts of the region now have large high-tech industries.

The forests of Southeast Asia are home to thousands of unique species of plants and animals. This wildlife is now under threat, however, because large numbers of trees are being cut down for use in the region's timber industry. In Indonesia trees are burned to clear land for crops. The smoke from the fires creates terrible smog.

LAND HEIGHT

4,000m
13,124 ft,

2,000m
6,562 ft.

1,000m
3,281 ft.

500m
1,640 ft.

200m
656 ft.

Sea level

Myanmar (Burma)

Laos

Vietnam

Thailand

Philippines

Cambodia

Malaysia

Brunei

Singapore

Indonesia

East Timor

TAIWAN

Tropic of Cancer

Batan Islands

Luzon Strait

Babuyan Islands

Laoag
Aparri
Luzon
Ilagan
San Fernando
Baguio
Dagupan
Cabanatuan
Angeles
San Fernando
MANILA
Catanduanes
Batangas
Naga
Mindoro
Legaspi

PACIFIC

OCEAN

South China
Sea

Calbayog
Samar
Calamian
Group
Roxas City
Masbate
PHILIPPINES
Panay
Leyte
Tacloban
Iloilo
Cadiz
Ormoc
San Carlos
Bacolod City
Cebu
Cebu
Bohol
Surigao
Spratly
Islands
Puerto
Princesa
Dumaguete
Negros
Butuan
Palawan
Sulu Sea
Cagayan de Oro
Iligan
Mindanao

MICRONESIA

Balabae Strait
Kudat
Zamboanga
Mount Apo
2,954 m
Davao
Kota Kinabalu
Gunung Kinabalu
Basilan
Jolo
△4,094 m
Sandakan
Ranau
Tawitawi
Sulu Archipelago
General Santos
SABAH
EGAWAN
PALAU

BRUNEI
Miri
Celebes
Sea
Talaud
Islands
ARAWAK
Tarakan
Sangir
Islands
Rajang
Kayan
rneo
Tanjungredeb
Morotai
Kapuas
Mountains
Manado
Equator
Samarinda
Mahakan
Gorontalo
Halmahera
Waigeo
Manokwari
ALIMANTAN
Palu
Ternate
Halmahera
Sea
Bacan
Sorong
Jazirah
Doberai
Biak
Balikpapan
Poso
Peleng
Obi
Yapen
Jayapura
Barito
Gulf of
Tomini
Molucca
Sea
Misool
Mamberamo
Banjarmasin
Sulawesi
Sula
Islands
Moluccas
Ceram Sea
Seram
IRIAN
JAYA
Puncak Jaya
5,030 m
Pegunungan
Maoke
Martapura
Malunda
Kendari
Buru
Ambon
Parepare
O   N   E   S   I   A
Muna
Kai
Islands
Aru
Islands
Makassar Strait
Makassar
Buton
Banda Sea
Selayar
PAPUA NEW GUINEA
Madura
Surabaya
Flores Sea
Wetar
Yos
Sudarso
Jember
Bali
Lombok
Sumbawa
Flores
Alor
Tanimbar
Islands
Arafura
Sea
alang
Mataram
Lomblen
DILI
Denpasar
Lesser Sunda Islands
EAST TIMOR
Sumba
Timor
ea
Kupang
Timor
Sea
AUSTRALIA

EAST ASIA

East Asia's landscape can be divided into four main areas. In the southwest is the Plateau of Tibet, where high mountain peaks surround small areas of pastureland and arid deserts. There are dry highlands in the northwest, and in the north there are cold deserts. Great plains lie to the east. These plains were formed from soils that were carried to the region by China's rivers.

Although most of China's land is either too poor or too mountainous for cultivation, almost three fourths of this country's enormous population of almost 1.3 billion people make their living from farming. The majority of the people live in the east, where the land is flatter and more fertile. Wheat, corn, soybeans, and cotton are grown on the plains, and farther south rice is the main crop. Pigs are raised there in large numbers. In Mongolia, in the north, farmers mainly herd sheep.

China became a communist country in 1949, and since then it has become a major industrial nation. The country's industries, including iron and steel production, chemicals, engineering, and textiles, are concentrated in the cities on the east coast such as Qingdao and Shanghai. Hong Kong and Beijing (Peking) are also major financial centers. Taiwan exports electronic goods, shoes, and textiles throughout the world, while Mongolia's economy is mainly based on agriculture.

LAND HEIGHT

	4,000m 13,124 ft.
	2,000m 6,562 ft.
	1,000m 3,281 ft.
	500m 1,640 ft.
	200m 656 ft.
	Sea level

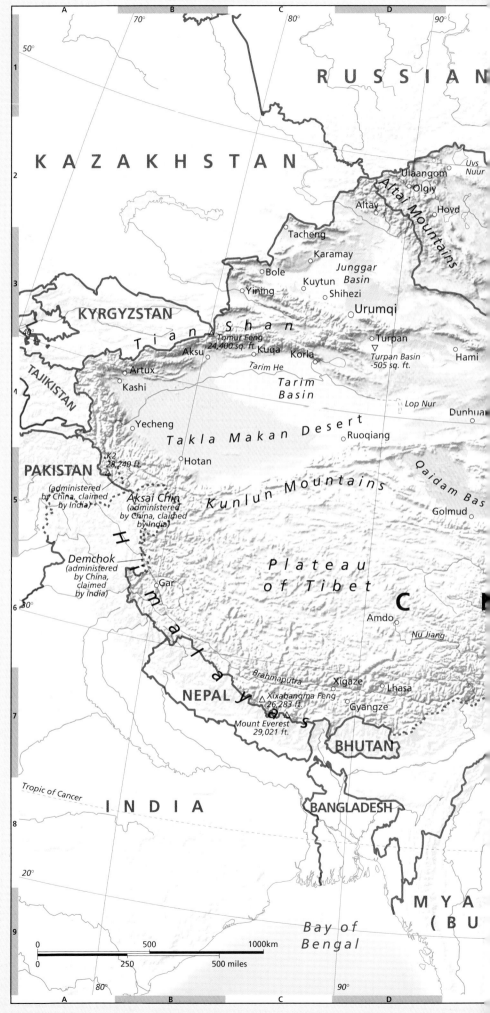

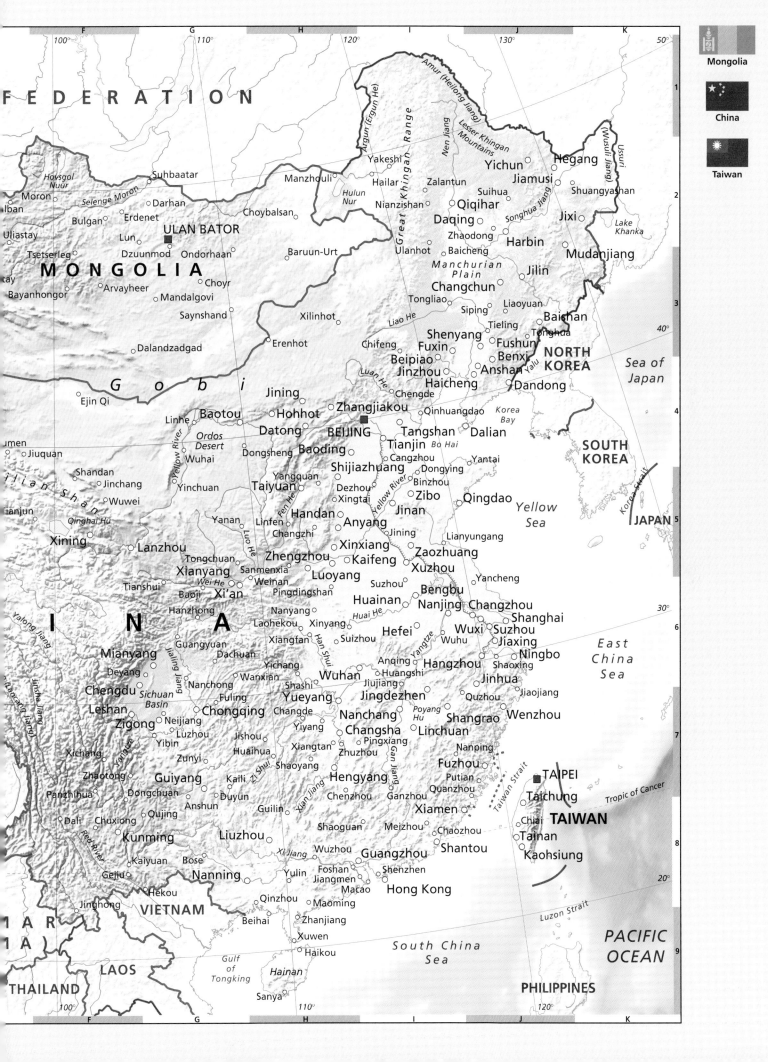

Mongolia

China

Taiwan

RUSSIAN FEDERATION

100°   110°   120°   130°   50°

Hovsgol
Nuur

Moron
Iban
Uliastay

Selenge Moron
Bulgan   Erdenet   Darhan
Lun   ULAN BATOR
Tsetserleg   Dzuunmod   Ondorhaan
Arvayheer   Choyr
Bayanhongor   Mandalgovi
Saynshand

MONGOLIA

Xilinhot

Dalandzadgad

G o b i

Ejin Qi

Linhe   **Baotou**

Suhbaatar

Choybalsan

Baruun-Urt

Erenhot

Manzhouli

Hailar
Nianzishan

Yakeshi

Zalantun

Amur (Heilong Jiang)

Nen Jiang

Great Khingan Range

Argun (Ergun He)

Lesser Khingan
Mountains

Hulun
Nur

Yichun   **Hegang**

Jiamusi

Suihua   Shuangyashan

Qiqihar

Daqing   **Jixi**

Zhaodong   Lake
Khanka

Harbin

Ulanhot   Baicheng

Mudanjiang

Manchurian
Plain

Jilin

Ussuri (Wusuli Jiang)

Songhua Jiang

Changchun

Tongliao   Siping   Liaoyuan

Tieling   Baishan

Liao He   Tonghua

Chifeng   **Shenyang**   Fushun

Fuxin   Benxi   **NORTH
KOREA**

Beipiao   Anshan

Jinzhou   Haicheng   Dandong

Sea of
Japan

Jining   Chengde

Hohhot   **Zhangjiakou**   Qinhuangdao   Korea
Bay

Datong   **BEIJING**   Tangshan   Dalian

Ordos   Baoding   Tianjin   Bo Hai

Desert   Dongsheng   **Shijiazhuang**   Cangzhou   Yantai

Wuhai   Yangquan   Dezhou   Dongying   **SOUTH
KOREA**

Yinchuan   **Taiyuan**   Xingtai   Binzhou   Zibo

Jinan   **Qingdao**   Korea Strait

Shandan   Yanan   Linfen   Handan   Anyang   **JAPAN**

Jinchang   Changzhi   Jining   Yellow
Wuwei   Zhengzhou   Sea

Qinghai Hu   Tongchuan   Xinxiang   Zaozhuang   Lianyungang

Xining   **Lanzhou**   Xianyang   Sanmenxia   Kaifeng   Xuzhou

Tianshui   Baoji   Weinan   Luoyang   Yancheng

Hanzhong   **Xi'an**   Pingdingshan   Suzhou   Bengbu

Nanyang   Huainan   Nanjing   Changzhou

Laohekou   Xinyang   Hefei   **Shanghai**

Mianyang   Guangyuan   Xiangfan   Suizhou   Wuxi   Suzhou

Deyang   Dachuan   Yichang   Anqing   Wuhu   Jiaxing

Chengdu   Nanchong   Wanxian   Huangshi   **Hangzhou**   Ningbo

Sichuan   Fuling   Shashi   **Wuhan**   Jiujiang   Jinhua   Shaoxing

Leshan   Neijiang   Changde   Yueyang   Jingdezhen   Jiaojiang

Zigong   Luzhou   Yiyang   Nanchang   Quzhou   Wenzhou

Yibin   Jishou   Xiangtan   Changsha   Shangrao

Xichang   Zunyi   Huaihua   Zhuzhou   Linchuan   Nanping

Zhaotong   Shaoyang   Hengyang   Fuzhou

Guiyang   Kaili   Pingxiang   Putian

Panzhihua   Dongchuan   Duyun   Chenzhou   Ganzhou   Quanzhou

Guilin   **Xiamen**   **TAIWAN**

Dali   Chuxiong   Qujing   Shaoguan   Meizhou   **TAIPEI**

Kunming   **Liuzhou**   Chaozhou   Taichung

Kaiyuan   Bose   Wuzhou   **Guangzhou**   Shantou   Chiai

Gejiu   **Nanning**   Yulin   Foshan   Shenzhen   **Tainan**

Jinghong   Jiangmen   Macao   **Hong Kong**   Kaohsiung

VIETNAM   Qinzhou   Maoming

Beihai   Zhanjiang

Xuwen

Haikou

East
China
Sea

Taiwan Strait

Tropic of Cancer

20°

THAILAND   **LAOS**   Gulf
of
Tongking   Hainan   South China
Sea   **PHILIPPINES**

Sanya   Luzon Strait

PACIFIC
OCEAN

C H I N A

Yellow River

Yellow River

Han Shui

Yangtze

Yangtze

Huai He

Fen He

Wei He

Luo He

Jialing Jiang

Yalong Jiang

Jinsha Jiang

Red River

Xi Jiang

Xian Jiang

Gan Jiang

Zi Shui

Poyang
Hu

Qilian Shan

100°   110°   120°

F   G   H   I   J   K

JAPAN AND THE KOREAS

South and North Korea lie on a peninsula that juts out from the southeast coast of China. To the east is Japan, a long chain of more than 4,000 islands in the Pacific Ocean. Mountains and hills dominate the landscape of these three countries, so most of this region's cities and towns are located on lower-lying land near the coasts.

Rice is grown throughout this region, and large quantities of fish are caught off the coasts. North Korea's communist government controls its industries and farms, and this country does very little trade with other nations. South Korea and Japan, however, export goods all over the globe. These two countries have few natural resources, so they have specialized in the production of high-value goods. South Korea makes cars, ships, and textiles, while Japan is a world leader in the production of high-tech goods, such as cameras, computers, and electronics, as well as cars.

Japan's environment suffers from acid rain caused by pollution from the factories of North Korea and the Russian Federation. Nuclear waste is dumped in the Sea of Japan. This country is also located in a major earthquake zone. Although buildings are constructed to withstand tremors, major quakes, such as the one that destroyed Kobe in 1995, are still a big threat in Japan.

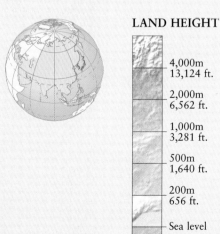

LAND HEIGHT

	4,000m 13,124 ft.
	2,000m 6,562 ft.
	1,000m 3,281 ft.
	500m 1,640 ft.
	200m 656 ft.
	Sea level

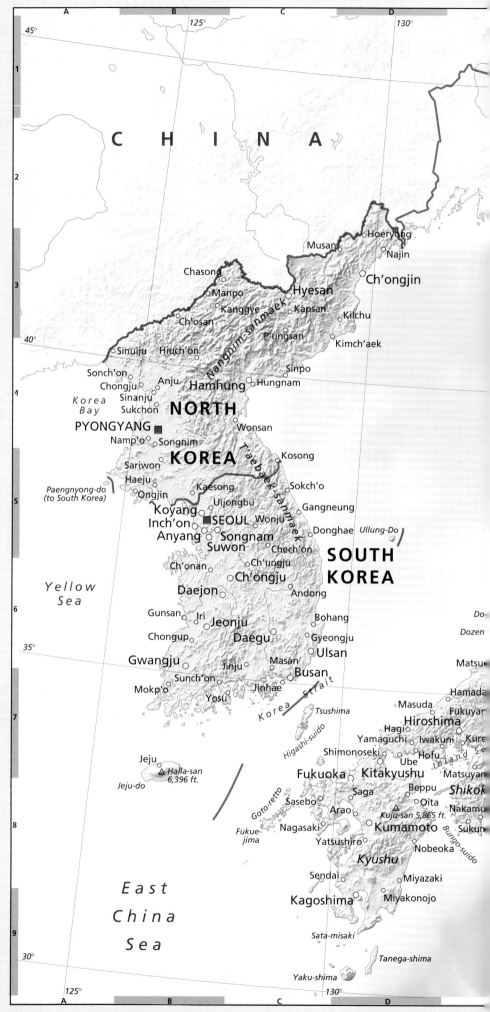

CHINA

Hoeryong
Musan
Najin
Chasong
Ch'ongjin
Manpo
Hyesan
Kanggye
Kapsan
Kilchu
Ch'osan
P'ungsan
Sinuiju
Hiuch'on
Kimch'aek
Sonch'on
Sinpo
Chongju
Anju
Hamhung
Hungnam
Korea Bay
Sinanju
Sukchon
NORTH
Wonsan
PYONGYANG
Namp'o
Songnim
KOREA
Kosong
Sariwon
Haeju
Kaesong
Sokch'o
Paengnyong-do (to South Korea)
Ongjin
Uijongbu
Gangneung
Koyang
Wonju
Ullung-Do
Inch'on
SEOUL
Donghae
Anyang
Songnam
Suwon
Chech'on
SOUTH
Ch'ungju
KOREA
Ch'onan
Ch'ongju
Daejon
Andong
Gunsan
Iri
Bohang
Do
Jeonju
Dozen
Chongup
Daegu
Gyeongju
Gwangju
Jinju
Masan
Ulsan
Matsu
Mokp'o
Sunch'on
Jinhae
Busan
Korea Strait
Yosu
Tsushima
Hamada
Jeju
Masuda
Fukuyar
Higashi-suido
Hiroshima
Hagi
Halla-san 6,396 ft.
Yamaguchi
Iwakuni
Kure
Jeju-do
Shimonoseki
Hofu
Inland Se
Ube
Matsuyan
Fukuoka
Kitakyushu
Beppu
Shikok
Goto-retto
Saga
Oita
Nakamu
Sasebo
Kuju-san 5,865 ft.
Arao
Kumamoto
Sukun
Fukue-jima
Nagasaki
Yatsushiro
Bungo-suido
Nobeoka
Kyushu
Sendai
Miyazaki
Kagoshima
Miyakonojo

Yellow Sea

East China Sea

Sata-misaki

Tanega-shima

Yaku-shima

Nangnim-sanmaek
Taebaek-sanmaek

F
G
H
I
J
K
1
2
3
4
5
6
7
8
9
135°
140°
145°
45°
40°
35°
30°
RUSSIAN
FEDERATION
La Perouse Strait
Soya-misaki
Sea of
Okhotsk
Kurile Islands
(administered by Russian Federation)
Rebun-to
Rishiri-to
Wakkanai
Shiretoko-misaki
Nayoro
Monbetsu
Abashiri
Kitami
Rumoi
Asahikawa
Asahi-dake
7,511 ft.
Shibetsu
Kussharo-ko
Nemuro
Takikawa
Otaru
Ebetsu
Hokkaido
Sapporo
Iwanai
Chitose
Obihiro
Kushiro
Tomakomai
Muroran
Uchiura-wan
Okushiri-to
Hakodate
Erimo-misaki
Tsugaru-kaikyo
Shimokita-hanto
Mutsu-
wan
Aomori
Hirosaki
Hachinohe
Sea of
Japan
Noshiro
Oga
Akita
Morioka
Miyako
Yokote
PACIFIC
OCEAN
Kesennuma
Sakata
Furukawa
Ishinomaki
Sado-shima
Yamagata
Sendai
Ryotsu
Sendai-
wan
Niigata
Fukushima
Nagaoka
Koriyama
Noto-hanto
Joetsu
Honshu
JAPAN
Toyama-
wan
Iwaki
Nikko
Kuroiso
Takaoka
Toyama
Kanazawa
Nagano
Utsunomiya
Hitachi
Matto
Ueda
Maebashi
Mito
Komatsu
Matsumoto
Takasaki
Oyama
Tsuchiura
ki-shoto
Fukui
Wakasa-
wan
Takayama
Chino
Urawa
Funabashi
Tsuruga
Kofu
TOKYO
Choshi
Tottori
Kawasaki
Chiba
Maizuru
Gifu
Ichihara
onago
Ogaki
Fujinomiya
Mount
Fuji
12,385 ft.
Yokohama
Biwa-ko
Nagoya
Otsu
Yokkaichi
Toyota
Fuji
kayama
Himeji
Kyoto
Okazaki
Fujieda
Shizuoka
Nojima-zaki
Kobe
Nara
Yaizu
Sagami-nada
Kurashiki
Toyohashi
Sakai
Osaka
Tsu
Hamamatsu
Ise-wan
Ise
Takamatsu
Wakayama
ihama
Tokushima
Izu-shoto
ochi
Kii-suido
Tanabe
osa-
wan
Muroto-zaki
Shiono-misaki
PACIFIC
OCEAN
0
200
400km
0
100
200 miles
Amami-o-
shima
Naze
Tokuno-
shima
East China
Sea
Ryukyu Islands
Okinawa
Okinawa
Kume-
jima
Naha
Miyako-
jima
Philippine
Sea
Iriomote-
jima
Ishigaki-
jima

Japan

North Korea

South Korea

AUSTRALASIA AND OCEANIA

Australasia and Oceania is made up of 14 countries. They include the enormous landmass of Australia, the islands of New Zealand and Papua New Guinea, and the many thousands of coral atolls and islands that extend into the Pacific Ocean.

Before European explorers started to visit this part of the globe during the 1500s the region was occupied by native people who lived by traditional means such as hunting and gathering. Eventually the Europeans began to settle and take over these lands. Some of the islands became overseas territories of the United Kingdom, France, and the U.S. In the past 20 years a number of these dependencies, such as Palau, have become independent nations.

Natural resources are of major economic importance throughout Australasia and Oceania. Australia exports raw materials such as coal, iron ore, and bauxite. Sheep are raised for their wool and meat in New Zealand and Australia, and fishing is important throughout the Pacific islands. Manufacturing companies are found only in the large coastal cities of Australia and New Zealand. Until recently both of these countries relied on Europe for trade. However, they have now begun to form trade links with the neighboring countries of east and Southeast Asia.

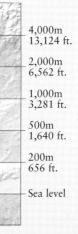

LAND HEIGHT

4,000m
13,124 ft.

2,000m
6,562 ft.

1,000m
3,281 ft.

500m
1,640 ft.

200m
656 ft.

Sea level

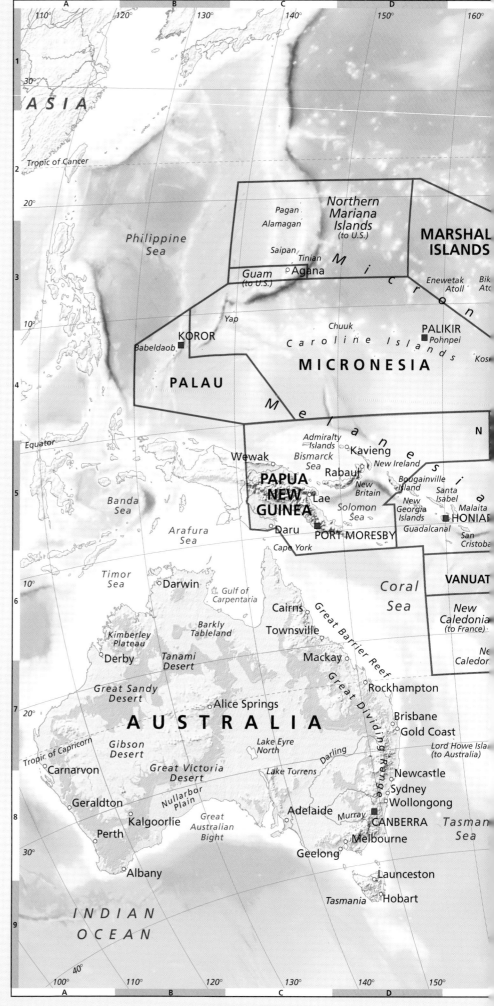

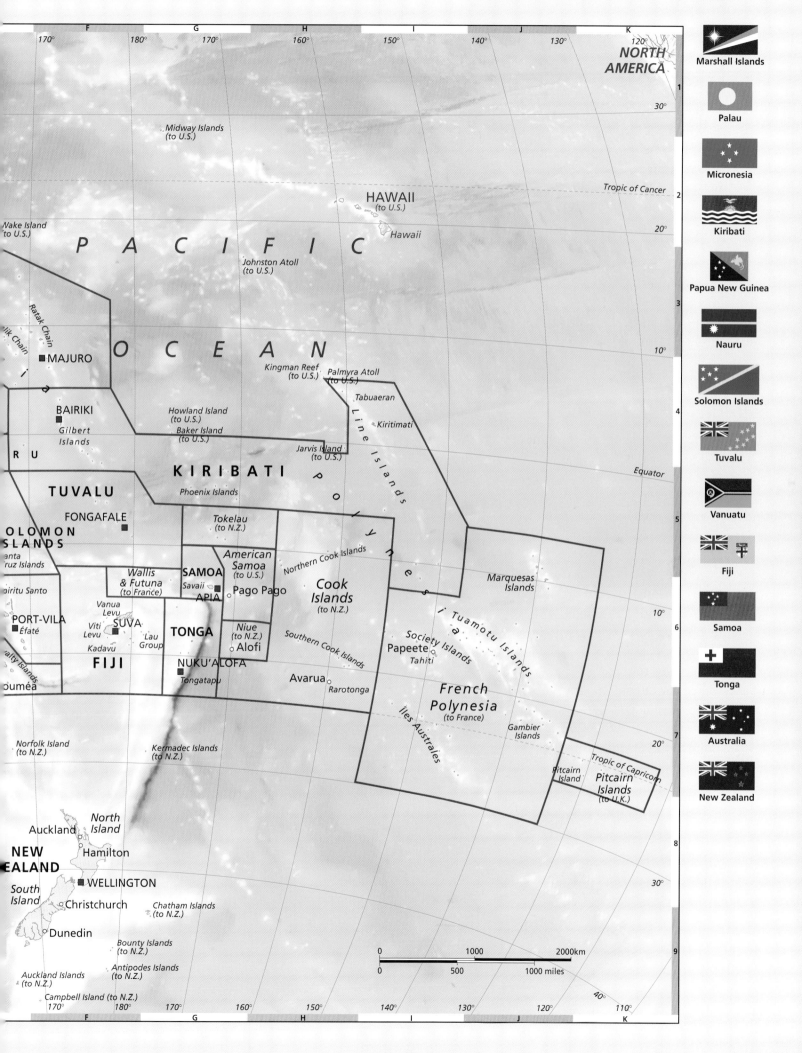

NORTH
AMERICA

170° F   180° G   170°   160° H   150° I   140° J   130°   120° K

30°

Midway Islands
(to U.S.)

Tropic of Cancer

HAWAII
(to U.S.)

20°

Wake Island
(to U.S.)

Hawaii

P   A   C   I   F   I   C

Johnston Atoll
(to U.S.)

Ratak Chain

O   C   E   A   N

10°

MAJURO

Kingman Reef
(to U.S.)

Palmyra Atoll
(to U.S.)

ilik Chain

Tabuaeran

BAIRIKI

Howland Island
(to U.S.)

Kiritimati

Gilbert
Islands

Baker Island
(to U.S.)

Equator

R U

Jarvis Island
(to U.S.)

Line Islands

KIRIBATI

Po

TUVALU

Phoenix Islands

ly

FONGAFALE

Tokelau
(to N.Z.)

ne

Marquesas
Islands

SOLOMON
ISLANDS

American
Samoa
(to U.S.)

Northern Cook Islands

s

10°

anta
ruz Islands

Wallis
& Futuna
(to France)

SAMOA

Savaii

Cook
Islands
(to N.Z.)

i

Tuamotu Islands

piritu Santo

APIA

Pago Pago

a

Vanua
Levu

PORT-VILA

Niue
(to N.Z.)

Society Islands

Éfaté

Viti
Levu

SUVA

TONGA

Alofi

Southern Cook Islands

Papeete

Tahiti

Lau
Group

Kadavu

FIJI

NUKU'ALOFA

Avarua

French
Polynesia
(to France)

Gambier
Islands

alty Islands

Tongatapu

Rarotonga

oumêa

Îles Australes

20°

Norfolk Island
(to N.Z.)

Kermadec Islands
(to N.Z.)

Tropic of Capricorn

Pitcairn
Island

Pitcairn
Islands
(to U.K.)

Auckland

North
Island

NEW
EALAND

Hamilton

South
Island

WELLINGTON

30°

Christchurch

Chatham Islands
(to N.Z.)

Dunedin

Bounty Islands
(to N.Z.)

0   1000   2000km

Antipodes Islands
(to N.Z.)

0   500   1000 miles

Auckland Islands
(to N.Z.)

40°

Campbell Island (to N.Z.)

170° F   180° G   170°   160° H   150° I   140° J   130°   120°   110° K

Marshall Islands

Palau

Micronesia

Kiribati

Papua New Guinea

Nauru

Solomon Islands

Tuvalu

Vanuatu

Fiji

Samoa

Tonga

Australia

New Zealand

AUSTRALIA

One of the world's largest countries, Australia is located in the southern Pacific Ocean. Despite its huge size, this nation has a relatively small population of more than 19.5 million people because much of the land is dry. In the west are semiarid plains of scrubs and grassland, while in the east the land rises to the peaks of the Great Dividing Range. In the north there are tropical rain forests and mangrove swamps.

Sugarcane is harvested near the east coast. In the south and west grapes for Australia's successful wine industry are produced, along with wheat. Large numbers of sheep and cattle are raised in the southwest and on the Great Artesian Basin in the east. These provide meat and wool for export.

The first inhabitants of Australia were the aborigines. Today they are a tiny minority, and the majority of Australians are of European origin. Most people work and live in cities in the south and east, as well as around Perth in the west. In these urban areas are engineering and manufacturing businesses and thriving service industries.

Australia has one of the world's biggest mining industries, which exploits the rich resources of gold, copper, coal, and iron ore. Tourism is another important source of income, especially along the northeast coast, where people come to visit the sunny beaches and the Great Barrier Reef.

LAND HEIGHT

4,000m
13,124 ft.

2,000m
6,562 ft.

1,000m
3,281 ft.

500m
1,640 ft.

200m
656 ft.

Sea level

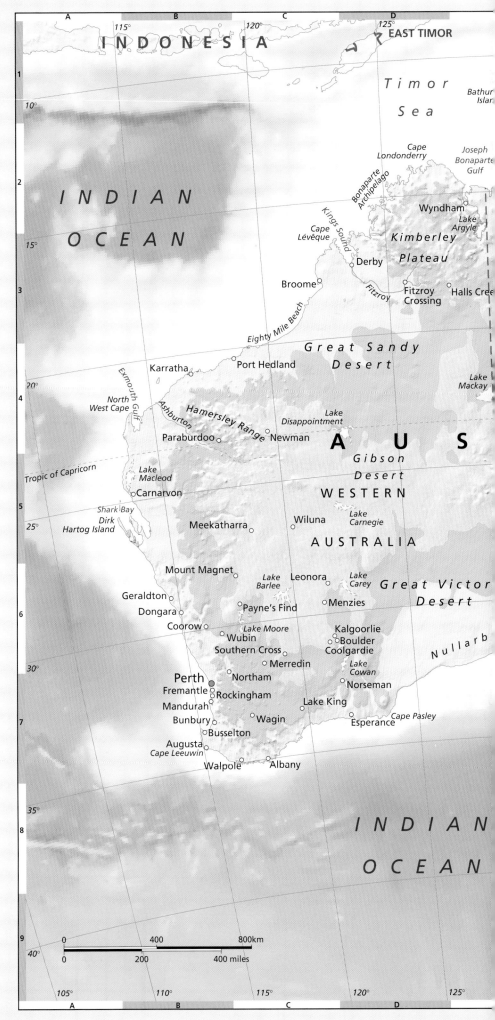

Australia

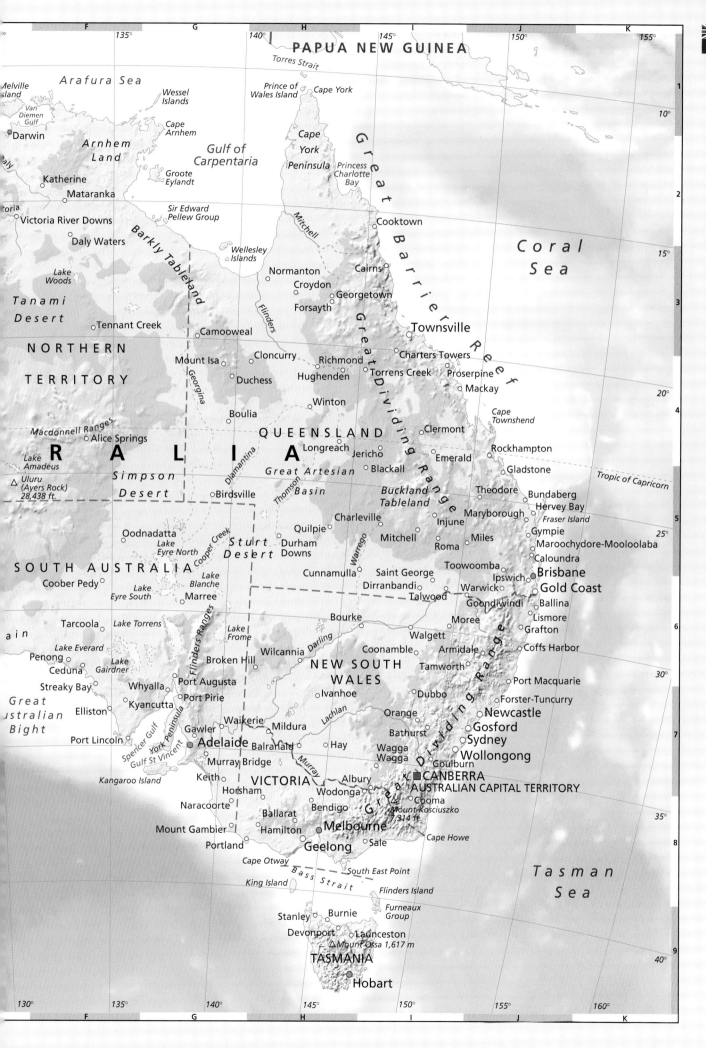

PAPUA NEW GUINEA

Torres Strait

Prince of
Wales Island
Cape York

Arafura Sea

Melville
Island

*Van
Diemen
Gulf*
Darwin

*Wessel
Islands*

Cape
Arnhem

*Arnhem
Land*

Groote
Eylandt

Katherine
Mataranka

*Gulf of
Carpentaria*

*Sir Edward
Pellew Group*

*Wellesley
Islands*

*Coral
Sea*

Cape
York

Princess
Charlotte
Bay

Cooktown

Cairns

Great Barrier Reef

Victoria River Downs

Daly Waters

*Lake
Woods*

*Tanami
Desert*

Tennant Creek

Barkly Tableland

Normanton

Croydon

Mitchell

Georgetown
Forsayth

Flinders

Townsville

Great Dividing Range

NORTHERN

TERRITORY

Camooweal

Mount Isa

Cloncurry

Duchess

Georgina

Richmond
Hughenden

Charters Towers

Torrens Creek
Proserpine
Mackay

Winton

Boulia

QUEENSLAND

Macdonnell Ranges
Alice Springs

*Lake
Amadeus*
△ Uluru
(Ayers Rock)
28,438 ft.

R A L I A

*Simpson
Desert*

Diamantina

Longreach
Jericho

Great Artesian

Blackall

Clermont

*Cape
Townshend*

Emerald

Rockhampton

Gladstone

Tropic of Capricorn

Birdsville

Thomson

Basin

Buckland
Tableland

Theodore
Bundaberg
Hervey Bay
Fraser Island

Oodnadatta

*Lake
Eyre North*

Cooper Creek

*Sturt
Desert*

Quilpie
Durham
Downs

Charleville

Mitchell

Injune

Maryborough

Gympie

Maroochydore-Mooloolaba
Caloundra

Roma
Miles

SOUTH AUSTRALIA

Coober Pedy

*Lake
Eyre South*

*Lake
Blanche*
Marree

Cunnamulla

Saint George

Dirranbandi
Talwood

Toowoomba

Warwick

Ipswich

Brisbane

Gold Coast

Ballina

Goondiwindi

Lismore

Tarcoola

Lake Torrens

Flinders Ranges

Bourke

Moree

Grafton

Walgett

Coffs Harbor

ain

Penong

Lake Everard

*Lake
Gairdner*

*Lake
Frome*

Wilcannia

Darling

Coonamble

Armidale

Ceduna
Streaky Bay

Whyalla

Broken Hill

NEW SOUTH

Tamworth

Port Macquarie

Kyancutta

Port Augusta
Port Pirie

WALES

Dubbo

Forster-Tuncurry

Elliston

*Great
Australian
Bight*

Port Lincoln

Waikerie

Gawler

Spencer Gulf

York Peninsula

Ivanhoe

Orange

Bathurst

Newcastle

Gosford

Sydney

Adelaide

Balranald

Hay

Wagga
Wagga

Wollongong

Goulburn

Gulf St Vincent

Murray Bridge

Murray

Mildura

Lachlan

Albury

× CANBERRA

AUSTRALIAN CAPITAL TERRITORY

Keith

Kangaroo Island

VICTORIA

Horsham

Wodonga

Cooma

× Mount Kosciuszko
7,314 ft.

Naracoorte

Ballarat

Bendigo

Mount Gambier

Hamilton

Melbourne

Sale

Cape Howe

Portland

Geelong

Cape Otway

Bass Strait

South East Point

King Island

Flinders Island

*Furneaux
Group*

*Tasman
Sea*

Stanley

Burnie

Devonport

Launceston

△ Mount Ossa 1,617 m

TASMANIA

Hobart

NEW ZEALAND

New Zealand lies in the southern Pacific Ocean 992 mi. southeast of Australia. This country consists of two large islands—North Island and South Island—and many smaller ones. In the far north of North Island are coastal inlets fringed by mangrove swamps. Farther south are geysers, boiling mud pools, and fertile plains that rise to volcanic peaks such as Mount Egmont and Mount Ruapehu. There are also volcanoes in South Island, where the landscape is dominated by the Southern Alps. This towering mountain range stretches more than 298 mi. along the western

side of the island. Many rivers flow down from these uplands to the east coast.

The first inhabitants of New Zealand were the Maori, a Polynesian people. In the 1800s Europeans began to settle there, and they now make up more than 90 percent of the entire population. The people are mainly concentrated in the country's coastal towns and cities, especially in Auckland on North Island.

New Zealand has rich and fertile land that provides good pastures for millions of sheep

and cattle. Fruits, such as apples, peaches, oranges, and kiwifruit, are grown and exported to many countries throughout the world.

New Zealand has a strong timber industry, and in the cities high-tech businesses that produce electronic goods and computers are expanding. Agricultural products, however, such as lamb, wool, and milk, remain the country's major exports. Tourism is also an important source of income. New Zealand's environment is generally unpolluted owing to its low population and lack of heavy industries.

LAND HEIGHT

4,000m	13,124 ft.
2,000m	6,562 ft.
1,000m	3,281 ft.
500m	1,640 ft.
200m	656 ft.
	Sea level

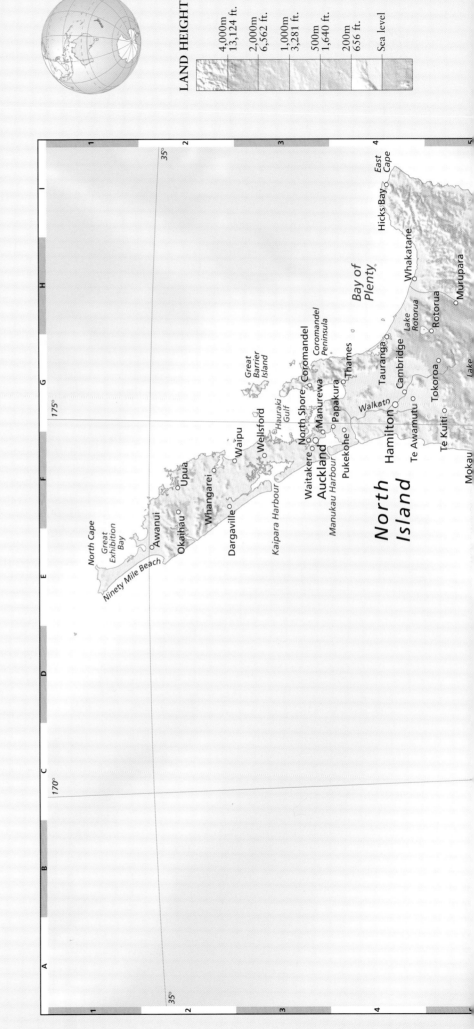

New Zealand

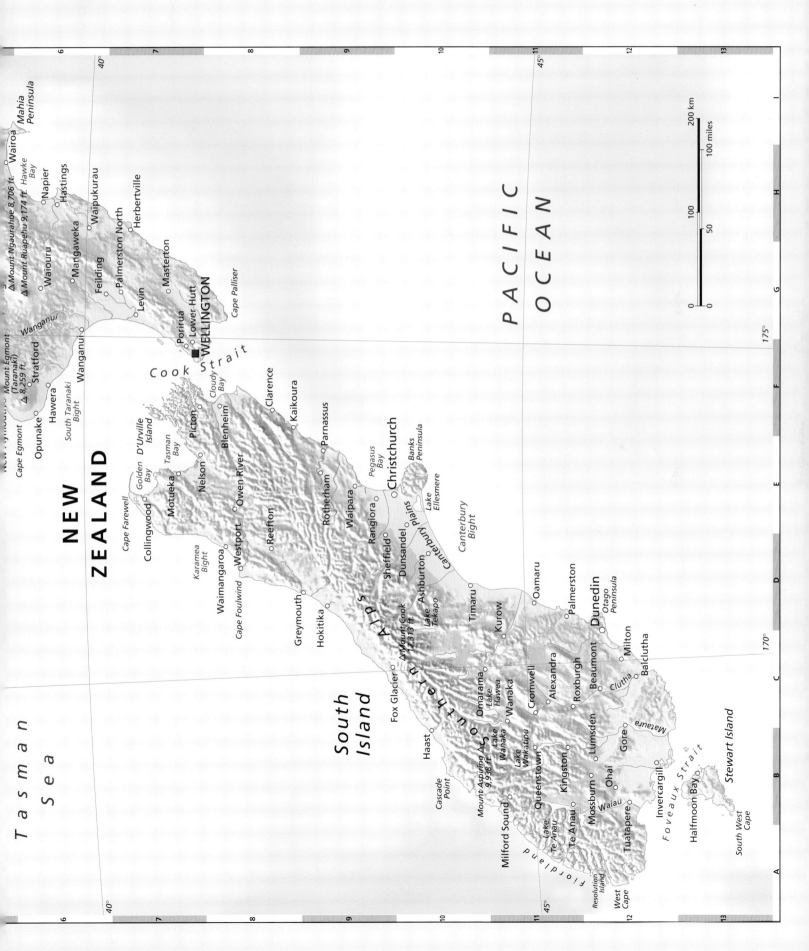

NEW ZEALAND .105

NEW
ZEALAND

NEW
ZEALAND

Tasman Sea

PACIFIC OCEAN

South
Island

Southern Alps

Fiordland

Stewart Island

Cook Strait

200 km
100 miles
100
50
0

Mahia Peninsula
Wairoa
Hawke Bay
Napier
Hastings
Waipukurau
Herbertville
△Mount Ngauruhoe 8,706 ft.
△Mount Ruapehu 9,174 ft.
Waiouru
Mangaweka
Palmerston North
Feilding
Masterton
Levin
Cape Palliser
Lower Hutt
Porirua
WELLINGTON
Wanganui
Stratford
Hawera
Opunake
Cape Egmont
Mount Egmont (Taranaki) △8,259 ft.
New Plymouth
South Taranaki Bight

Cloudy Bay
Clarence
Kaikoura
Parnassus
Picton
Blenheim
D'Urville Island
Tasman Bay
Golden Bay
Nelson
Motueka
Owen River
Cape Farewell
Collingwood
Karamea Bight
Westport
Reefton
Waimangaroa
Cape Foulwind
Greymouth
Hokitika
Fox Glacier
Haast
Cascade Point
Mount Aspiring 9,938 ft. △
Milford Sound
Lake Te Anau
Te Anau
Resolution Island
West Cape
Tuatapere
Waiau
Ohai
Mossburn
Lake Wakatipu
Kingston
Queenstown
Lake Wanaka
Lake Hawea
Wanaka
Omarama
△Mount Cook 12,313 ft.
Lake Tekapo
Ashburton
Sheffield
Dunsandel
Rangiora
Waipara
Rotherham
Pegasus Bay
Christchurch
Banks Peninsula
Lake Ellesmere
Canterbury Plains
Canterbury Bight
Timaru
Kurow
Oamaru
Palmerston
Dunedin
Otago Peninsula
Milton
Balclutha
Clutha
Beaumont
Roxburgh
Alexandra
Cromwell
Lumsden
Gore
Mataura
Invercargill
Foveaux Strait
Halfmoon Bay
South West Cape

THE PACIFIC OCEAN

Stretching over around one third of Earth's surface, the Pacific is the planet's largest ocean. It extends east from Japan to the Americas and south from the Arctic Ocean to Antarctica. The ocean's floor is generally deeper in the west than in the east, and at its deepest point, the Mariana Trench, the Pacific plunges to –36,191 ft.

The many thousands of islands scattered across the Pacific Ocean were created by volcanic eruptions. Some of these islands became fringed with coral, and the islands eventually dropped back into the sea, leaving circles of coral, or atolls. A string of active volcanoes, known as the "Ring of Fire," surrounds the ocean. The Pacific region is plagued by tropical storms, called typhoons. The area is also prone to tidal waves, which are caused by volcanic eruptions or underwater earthquakes.

The people of the Pacific mainly grow food for their own consumption, although a few islands grow crops, such as coconuts and oil palms, for export. Many of the small islands rely heavily on fishing for much-needed foreign income. These fish industries tend to be small and are forced to compete with the large fishing fleets of Japan and the Russian Federation. With palm-fringed beaches, spectacular coral reefs, and a warm, sunny climate, the islands of the Pacific Ocean have become popular tourist destinations.

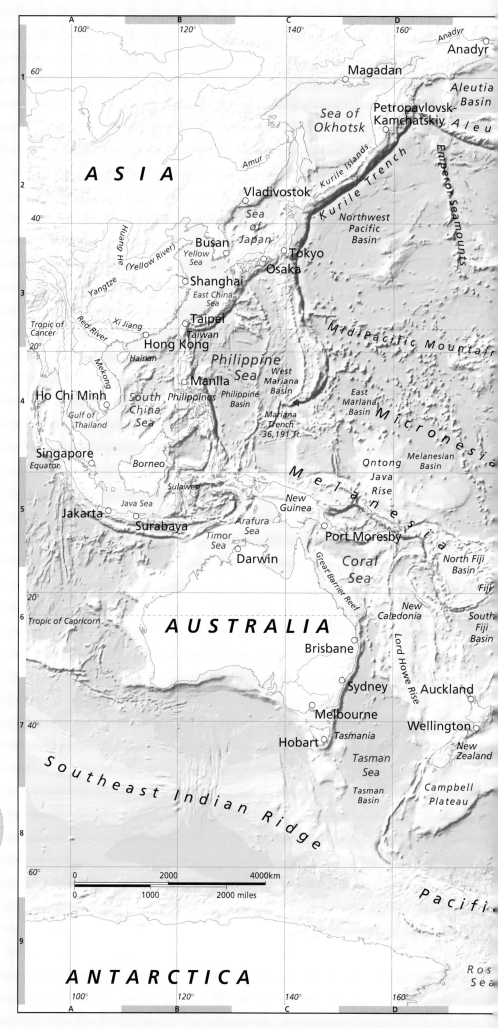

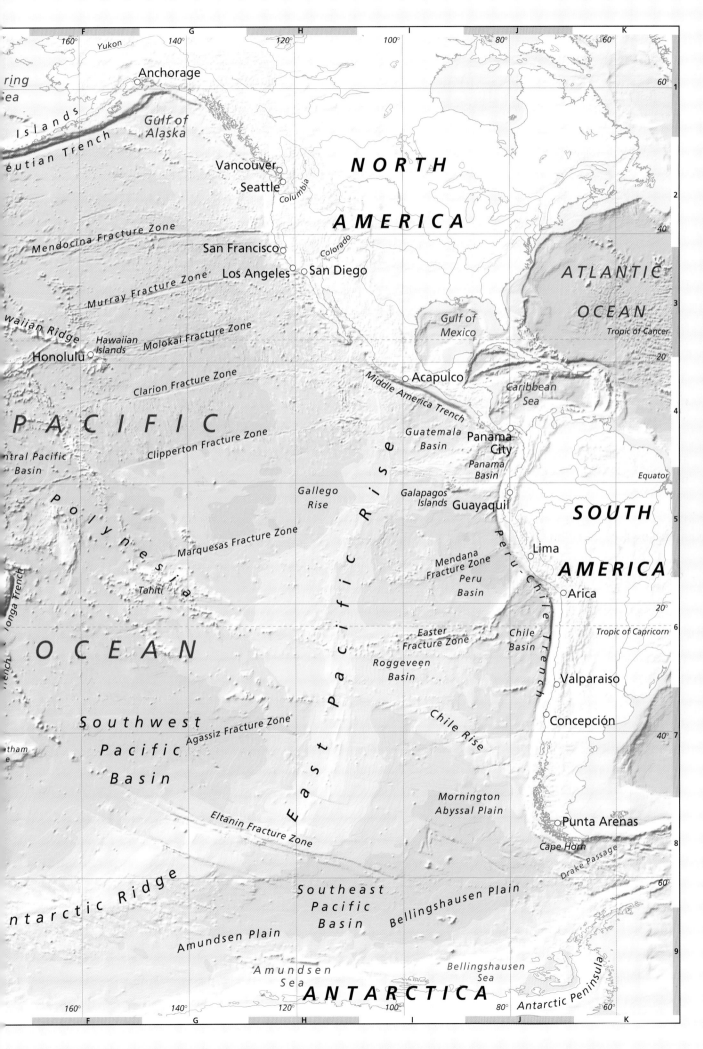

F   160°   Yukon   140°   G   120°   H   100°   I   80°   J   60°   K

Anchorage   60°   1

ring
ea

Islands   Gulf of
eutian Trench   Alaska   NORTH

Vancouver
Seattle   Columbia   AMERICA   40°   2
Mendocina Fracture Zone   ATLANTIC

San Francisco   Colorado   OCEAN

Murray Fracture Zone   Los Angeles San Diego   3
waiian Ridge   Gulf of   Tropic of Cancer
Hawaiian   Molokai Fracture Zone   Mexico
Honolulu   Islands   20°

Acapulco   Caribbean
Clarion Fracture Zone   Middle America Trench   Sea

PACIFIC   4
Clipperton Fracture Zone   Guatemala   Panama
ntral Pacific   Basin   City
Basin   Panama
P   Basin   Equator
o   Gallego   Galapagos
l   Rise   Islands Guayaquil   SOUTH
y   5
n   Marquesas Fracture Zone   AMERICA
e
s   Mendana
i   Tahiti   Fracture Zone   Lima
a   Peru   20°
onga Trench   Basin   Arica

OCEAN   Easter   Tropic of Capricorn   6
                                                    Fracture Zone   Chile
                                                                     Basin
                                                    Roggeveen
                                                    Basin   Valparaiso

Southwest   Concepción
Pacific   Agassiz Fracture Zone   Chile Rise   40°   7
tham
e   Basin
                                                                        Mornington
                 Eltanin Fracture Zone   Abyssal Plain
                                                                                        Punta Arenas   8
                                                                        Cape Horn   Drake Passage

ntarctic Ridge   Southeast   60°
                                          Pacific   Bellingshausen Plain
                Amundsen Plain   Basin   9

                        Amundsen   Bellingshausen
                        Sea   ANTARCTICA   Sea   Antarctic Peninsula

F   160°   140°   G   120°   H   100°   I   80°   J   60°   K

GLOSSARY

The following glossary explains certain geographical and technical terms used in this atlas.

Acid rain
Rain and snow that have absorbed gases released by power plants and vehicle exhausts. Acid rain can cause severe environmental damage.

Arctic Circle
An imaginary line (latitude) that runs from east to west around Earth. The Arctic Circle lies at a latitude of 66° 32'N.

Biodiversity
The quantity of different plant or animal species in a given area.

Cash crops
Crops grown for sale, often for the export market rather than for consumption in the area in which they are grown.

Climate
The average weather conditions in a given region.

Deforestation
The cutting down of large areas of forests for timber, farmland, or urban development. It can lead to soil erosion, flooding, and landslides.

Delta
A low-lying, fan-shaped area at a river mouth. It is formed when the river drops layers of sediment as it slows down when entering the sea.

Desertification
The gradual spread of desert conditions in arid or semiarid regions. Desertification may be caused by changes in the climate or by human activities such as overgrazing and deforestation.

Equator
The imaginary line (latitude) that circles the center of Earth. Lying at 0°, it is equidistant from the North and South poles.

European Union (EU)
A group of European countries that have joined together to promote trade, industry, and agriculture. The EU was formed in 1965 and was formerly known as the European Economic Community (EEC) and then the European Community (EC).

Floodplain
The broad, flat part of a river valley bordering the river. Floodplains are formed by sediment deposited during flooding.

Heavy industry
A type of industry that uses large amounts of energy and raw materials to make heavy goods such as machinery and ships.

High-tech industry
A type of industry that produces high-value, technologically advanced goods such as computers and other electronic equipment.

Ice shelf
Floating ice attached to the edge of a coast. The edge facing the sea is usually a steep cliff up to 100 ft. high.

Irrigation
The artificial supply of water to land. It usually involves the construction of canals and the diversion of natural watercourses.

Manufacturing
A type of industry that makes large quantities of finished goods, from clothing to cars, that are sold to large numbers of people.

Natural resources
Fuel and raw materials, such as oil, ores, and timber, that occur naturally and are found in large quantities in a given area.

Peninsula
A thin strip of land that juts out into the sea and is surrounded by water on three of its sides. Large examples include Florida and the Koreas.

Plain
A flat, level region of land. It is often fairly low-lying.

Service industry
A type of industry that does not produce goods but provides services such as banking and tourism.

Shantytown
An area in or around a city where people live in makeshift shacks, usually without basic facilities such as running water.

Tropics
The area between the **Tropic of Cancer** and the **Tropic of Capricorn** where the **climate** is hot.

Tropic of Cancer
An imaginary circle around Earth north of the equator. It lies at a latitude of 23° 28'N.

Tropic of Capricorn
An imaginary circle around Earth south of the equator. It lies at a latitude of 23° 28'S.

United Nations (UN)
An association of countries that was established in 1945. It seeks to maintain international peace and security and to promote cooperation over economic, social, cultural, and humanitarian problems.

INDEX

The following index lists all of the place names and features on the regional and continental maps in this atlas. The entry names are settlements unless otherwise indicated by the use of italicized definitions. Each name is located within a region, country, sea, or ocean. Physical feature names that are made up of a proper name and a description, such as Mount Etna, are positioned alphabetically by the proper name. The description appears after the proper name. For example, Mount Etna appears as "Etna, Mount" in the index.

The first number at the end of each entry is the page number of the map on which the feature or place may be found. The letter and figure after the page number give the grid square in which the name is located.

COLORADO–DUNGUN .113

Colorado *river* Mexico/U.S. 23 C9, 27 G9, 28 C7, 30 D5
Colorado *state* U.S. 28 D7
Colorado Plateau *plateau* W. U.S. 23 C8, 27 G8
Colorado Springs Colorado, U.S. 28 E7
Columbia *river* Canada/U.S. 23 C7, 26 D1
Columbia Missouri, U.S. 29 J7
Columbia *state capital* South Carolina, U.S. 23 G9, 31 J4
Columbia Basin *physical region* Washington, U.S. 26 D2
Columbia Plateau *plateau* Idaho/Oregon, U.S. 26 E5
Columbus Georgia, U.S. 31 H5
Columbus Mississippi, U.S. 31 G4
Columbus Nebraska, U.S. 29 H6
Columbus *state capital* Ohio, U.S. 23 F9, 32 E7
Comilla Bangladesh 93 H6
Como Italy 62 B3
Comodoro Rivadavia Argentina 43 D10
Como, Lake *lake* Italy 62 C2
Comoro Islands *island group* Comoros 82 C4
Comoros *country* W. Indian Ocean 71 H9, 81 J3
Compiègne France 55 F2
Comrat Moldova 65 D11
Conakry *country capital* Guinea 71 A6, 76 C7
Concepción Chile 43 B7
Concepción Paraguay 42 G2
Conception, Point *headland* California, U.S. 27 B10
Conchos *river* Mexico 34 C3
Concord California, U.S. 27 B8
Concord *state capital* New Hampshire, U.S. 33 I5
Concordia Argentina 43 G5
Congo *country* C. Africa 71 E8, 78 D6
Congo *river* Congo/Democratic Republic of the Congo 71 E8, 78 D7
Congo Basin *physical region* C Africa 71 E7, 78 E6
Congo, Democratic Republic of the *country* C. Africa 71 F8, 79 F6
Connaught *cultural region* Republic of Ireland 51 B8
Connecticut *state* U.S. 33 I5
Constance Germany 59 D12
Constance, Lake *lake* Germany/Switzerland 59 D12, 60 D4
Constanta Romania 47 G7, 69 I3
Constantine Algeria 70 D2, 73 G3
Constitución Chile 43 B7
Coober Pedy South Australia, Australia 103 F6
Cook Islands *N.Z. dependent territory* C. Pacific Ocean 101 H6
Cook, Mount *mountain* New Zealand 105 C10
Cook Strait *strait* New Zealand 105 F7
Cooktown Queensland, Australia 103 I2
Coolgardie Western Australia, Australia 102 C6
Cooma New South Wales, Australia 103 I8
Coonamble New South Wales, Australia 103 I6
Cooper Creek *seasonal river* Queensland/South Australia, 103 G5
Coorow Western Australia, Australia 102 B6
Coos Bay Oregon, U.S. 26 A4
Copenhagen *country capital* Denmark 46 E4, 49 C12
Copiapó Chile 42 C4
Coquimbo Chile 42 C5
Coral Sea *sea* S.W. Pacific Ocean 100 D6, 103 J2, 106 D5
Corcovado, Golfo de *gulf* Chile 43 C9
Córdoba Argentina 39 D9, 43 E5
Córdoba Spain 46 A7, 56 D7
Corfu *island* Greece 68 E6
Corigliano Calabro Italy 63 H9
Corinth Greece 69 F7
Corinth, Gulf of *gulf* Aegean Sea/Ionian Sea 69 F7
Cork Republic of Ireland 51 B10
Corner Brook Newfoundland & Labrador, Canada 25 J7
Corno Grande *mountain* Italy 63 F6
Coro Venezuela 40 D1
Coromandel New Zealand 104 G3
Coromandel Coast *coastal region* India 93 D10
Coromandel Peninsula *peninsula* New Zealand 104 G3
Coronel Oviedo Paraguay 42 G3
Coronel Pringles Argentina 43 F7
Coropuna, Nevado *mountain* Peru 40 D6
Corpus Christi Texas, U.S. 30 D7
Corrib, Lough *lake* Republic of Ireland 51 B9
Corrientes Argentina 42 F4
Corrientes, Cabo *headland* Mexico 34 C5
Corse, Cap *headland* Corsica, France 55 K8
Corsica *island* France 46 D7, 55 K9
Cortona Italy 63 D5
Coruche Portugal 56 B6
Corum Turkey 88 D1
Corumba Brazil 41 F7
Corvallis Oregon, U.S. 26 B4
Cosenza Italy 63 H9
Costa Rica *country* Central America 23 F13, 35 I8
Cotonou Benin 77 H7
Cotopaxi *volcano* Ecuador 40 B3
Cotswold Hills *hill range* England, United Kingdom 51 G11
Cottbus Germany 59 I6
Council Bluffs Iowa, U.S. 29 H6
Courland Lagoon *lagoon* Lithuania/Russian Federation 65 A6
Coventry England, United Kingdom 51 G10
Covilha Portugal 56 B5
Cowan, Lake *seasonal lake* Western Australia, Australia 102 D6
Cozumel, Isla *island* Mexico 35 H5
Cradock South Africa 80 D8
Craiova Romania 69 G3
Crawley England, United Kingdom 51 H11
Creil France 55 F2
Cremona Italy 62 C3
Cres *island* Croatia 68 B3
Crescent City California, U.S. 27 A5
Crete *island* Greece 47 F9, 69 G9
Créteil France 55 F3
Crete, Sea of *sea* N.E. Mediterranean Sea 69 H9
Creuse *river* France 55 E5
Crimean Peninsula *peninsula* Ukraine 47 H6, 65 G12
Croatia *country* S.E. Europe 47 E7, 68 C2
Cromwell New Zealand 105 C11
Crotone Italy 63 H10
Croydon Queensland, Australia 103 H3
Crozet Basin *undersea feature* S. Indian Ocean 82 D6
Crozet Islands *island group* S.W. Indian Ocean 82 C7
Crozet Plateau *undersea feature* S.W. Indian Ocean 82 C7
Csorna Hungary 67 D10
Cuamba Mozambique 81 H4
Cuando *river* S. Africa 71 E10, 80 C4
Cuango *river* Angola/Democratic Republic of the Congo 71 E9, 80 B2
Cuanza *river* Angola 80 B3
Cuautla Mexico 34 E6
Cuba *country* W. West Indies 23 F11, 36 C3
Cubango *river* S. Africa 71 E10, 80 C5
Cúcuta Colombia 38 B2, 40 C2
Cuddapah India 93 D9
Cuenca Ecuador 40 B4
Cuenca Spain 57 F5
Cuernavaca Mexico 34 E6
Cuiabá Brazil 41 G6
Culiacán Mexico 34 C4
Cumaná Venezuela 40 E1
Cuneo Italy 62 A4
Cunnamulla Queensland, Australia 103 H5
Curaçao *island* Netherlands Antilles 37 G8
Curitiba Brazil 39 G8, 41 H8
Cusco Peru 40 D6
Cuttack India 93 F7
Cuxhaven Germany 58 D3
Cyclades *island group* Greece 69 G8
Cyprus *country* W. Asia 84 A6, 88 C3
Cyrenaica *cultural region* Libya 73 I5
Czech Republic *country* C. Europe 46 E6, 67 B8
Czestochowa Poland 67 F6
Czluchow Poland 66 E3

D

Dachau Germany 59 D11
Dachuan China 97 G6
Daegu South Korea 98 C6
Daejon South Korea 98 B6
Dagupan Philippines 95 G3
Dakar *country capital* Senegal 70 A5, 76 C5
Dalälven *river* Norway/Sweden 49 D9
Dalandzadgad Mongolia 97 F3
Da Lat Vietnam 94 D4
Dali China 97 F8
Dalian China 97 J4
Dallas Texas, U.S. 23 E9, 30 E5
Dalmatia *cultural region* Croatia 68 D4
Daloa Ivory Coast 77 E7
Daly *river* Northern Territory, Australia 103 E2
Daly Waters Northern Territory, Australia 103 F2
Daman India 93 B7
Damaraland *physical region* Namibia 80 B6
Damascus *country capital* Syria 84 A6, 88 D3
Damavand, Qolleh ye *mountain* Iran 89 H3
Damietta Egypt 74 C3
Danakil desert *desert* Ethiopia 75 F8
Da Nang Vietnam 85 F7, 94 D4
Dandong China 97 J4
Dannenberg Germany 59 G11
Danube *river* C. Europe 47 F7, 59 C9, 61 J3, 67 E11, 69 F3
Danube Delta *delta* Romania/Ukraine 65 E12, 69 I3
Danville Virginia, U.S. 33 F9
Dapaong Togo 77 G6
Daqing China 97 J2
Darabani Romania 69 H1
Darbhanga India 92 F5
Dar es Salaam Tanzania 71 H8, 79 J8
Darfur *cultural region* Ethiopia/Sudan 70 F5, 75 C8
Darganata Turkmenistan 91 D7
Dargaville New Zealand 104 F2
Darhan China 97 G2
Darien, Golfo de *gulf* S. Caribbean Sea 35 K8, 40 C2
Darjeeling Bhutan 92 G5
Darling *river* S.W. Australia 100 C7, 103 H6
Darmstadt Germany 59 C9
Darnah Libya 73 J4
Darnley, Cape *headland* Antarctica 21 E2
Daroca Spain 57 G4
Dart *river* England, United Kingdom 51 E12
Dartmoor *moorland* England, United Kingdom 51 E12
Daru Papua New Guinea 100 C5
Darvishan Afghanistan 91 D10
Darwin *state capital* Northern Territory, Australia 100 B6, 103 E1
Dashhowuz Turkmenistan 91 C6
Datong Mongolia 97 H4
Daugavpils Latvia 64 D5
Davangere India 93 C9
Davao Philippines 85 G8, 95 H5
Davenport Iowa, U.S. 29 J6
David Panama 35 J9
Davis Strait *strait* Baffin Bay/Labrador Sea 22 H4, 25 H3, 44 C2
Davos Switzerland 60 D5
Dawson Yukon Territory, Canada 24 B3
Dax France 54 D7
Dayr az Zawr Syria 89 E3
Dayton Ohio, U.S. 32 D7
Daytona Beach Florida, U.S. 31 J6
De Aar South Africa 80 D8
Deán Funes Argentina 42 E5
Death Valley *valley* California, U.S. 23 C8, 27 D9
Debrecen Hungary 67 H10
Debre Markos Ethiopia 75 E9
Debre Zeyit Ethiopia 75 F9
Decatur Alabama, U.S. 31 H4
Decatur Illinois, U.S. 32 B7
Deccan *plateau* India 84 D7, 93 C7
Decin Czech Republic 67 B6
Dee *river* Scotland, United Kingdom 50 F5
Deggendorf Germany 59 G10
Dehra Dun India 92 D4
Deh Shu Afghanistan 91 D10
Delano California, U.S. 27 C9
Delaware *state* U.S. 33 H7
Delaware Bay *inlet* N.E. U.S. 33 H7
Delémont Switzerland 60 B4
Delft Netherlands 53 D6
Delfzijl Netherlands 52 I2
Delhi India 92 D4
Delicias Mexico 34 C3
Delmenhorst Germany 58 D4
Del Rio Texas, U.S. 30 C6
Deltona Florida, U.S. 31 J6
Demchok *disputed region* China/India 92 D3, 97 B6
Demerara Plain *undersea feature* W. Atlantic Ocean 45 D7
Den Helder Netherlands 52 E3
Denia Spain 57 H6
Denizli Turkey 88 C2
Denmark *country* N. Europe 46 D4, 49 B12
Denmark Strait *strait* Greenland/Iceland 20 B5, 25 J1, 44 E2
Denov Uzbekistan 91 E8
Denpasar Indonesia 95 F9
Denver *state capital* Colorado, U.S. 23 D8, 28 E7
Dera Ghazi Khan Pakistan 91 F10
Dera Ismail Khan Pakistan 91 F10
Derbent Uzbekistan 91 E8
Derby England, United Kingdom 51 G9
Derby Western Australia, Australia 100 A6, 102 D3
Derry *see* Londonderry
Derzhavinsk Kazakhstan 90 E4
Dese Somalia 75 F8
Deseado *river* Argentina 43 D10
Des Moines *river* C. U.S. 29 I5
Des Moines *state capital* Iowa, U.S. 29 I6
Desna *river* Russian Federation/Ukraine 65 E8
Dessau Germany 59 G6
Desventurados, Islas de los *island group* Chile 39 A8
Detmold Germany 59 D6
Detroit Michigan, U.S. 23 F8, 32 F5
Deva Romania 69 F2
Deventer Netherlands 52 G5
Devon Island *island* Nunavut, Canada 25 F2
Devonport Tasmania, Australia 103 H9
Deyang China 97 G6
Dezful Iran 89 G4
Dezhou China 97 I5
Dhahran Saudi Arabia 89 G6
Dhaka *country capital* Bangladesh 84 E7, 93 H6
Dhamar Yemen 89 F9
Dhanbad India 93 F6
Dhaulagiri *mountain* Nepal 92 E4
Dhole India 93 C7
Dhuusa Marreeb Somalia 75 H10
Diamantina *seasonal river* Queensland/South Australia, Australia 103 G5
Dickinson North Dakota, U.S. 29 F3
Diekirch Luxembourg 53 G12
Diepholz Germany 58 C5
Dieppe France 55 E2
Diest Belgium 53 E9
Diffa Niger 77 J6
Digne France 55 I7
Dijon France 55 H4
Dili *country capital* East Timor 85 G9, 95 H9
Dilling Sudan 75 C8
Dillon Montana, U.S. 29 B3
Dilolo Democratic Republic of the Congo 79 E9
Dinajpur Bangladesh 92 G5
Dinant Belgium 53 E11
Dinaric Alps *mountain range* Bosnia & Herzegovina 68 D4
Dingle Bay *bay* Republic of Ireland 51 A10
Diourbel Senegal 76 C5
Dire Dawa Ethiopia 71 H6, 75 F9
Dirk Hartog Island *island* Western Australia, Australia 102 A5
Dirranbandi Queensland, Australia 103 I6
Disappointment, Lake *seasonal lake* Western Australia, Australia 102 C4
Divinópolis Brazil 41 H7
Diyarbakir Turkey 89 E2
Djambala Congo 78 C7
Djanet Algeria 73 G6
Djelfa Algeria 73 F4
Djibouti *country* E. Africa 71 H5, 75 G8
Djibouti *country capital* Djibouti 71 H6, 75 G8
Dnieper *river* E. Europe 47 G6, 65 E7
Dnieper Lowlands *physical region* Ukraine Belarus 65 E8
Dniester *river* Moldova/Ukraine 47 F6, 65 D10
Dniprodzerzhynsk Ukraine 65 G10
Dnipropetrovsk Ukraine 47 H6, 65 G10
Doberai, Jazirah *peninsula* Indonesia 95 I7
Doboj Bosnia & Herzegovina 68 D3
Dobrich Bulgaria 69 I4
Dodecanese *island group* Greece 69 H8
Dodge City Kansas, U.S. 29 G8
Dodoma *country capital* Tanzania 71 G8, 79 I8
Dogo *island* Japan 98 E6
Dogondoutchi Niger 77 H6
Doha *country capital* Qatar 84 B6, 89 H6
Dolisie Congo 78 C7
Dolomites *mountain range* Italy 62 D2
Dombås Norway 49 B7
Dominica *country* E. West Indies 23 I12, 37 J6
Dominican Republic *country* C. West Indies 23 H11, 37 G4
Domo Ethiopia 75 H9
Domodossola Italy 62 B2
Don *river* Russian Federation 47 H5, 86 A5
Don *river* Scotland, United Kingdom 50 F5
Donaueschingen Germany 59 C12
Donauwörth Germany 59 D10
Don Benito Spain 56 D6
Doncaster England, United Kingdom 51 G9
Dondo Angola 80 B3
Dondo Mozambique 81 G5
Donegal Republic of Ireland 51 C7
Donegal Bay *bay* N.E. Atlantic Ocean 51 B8
Donets *river* Russian Federation/Ukraine 65 H9
Donetsk Ukraine 47 H6, 65 H10
Dongara Western Australia, Australia 102 B6
Dongchuan China 97 F8
Donghae South Korea 98 C5
Dong Hoi Vietnam 94 D3
Dongola Sudan 75 C6
Dongsheng China 97 G4
Dongying China 97 I5
Donostia-San Sebastián Spain 57 F2
Dordogne *river* France 55 F6
Dordrecht Netherlands 53 E6
Dorfen Germany 59 G11
Dornbirn Switzerland 60 D4
Dorotea Sweden 49 E6
Dortmund Germany 59 B6
Dortmund-Ems-Canal *canal* Germany 59 B6
Dos Hermanas Spain 56 D8
Dosso Niger 77 H6
Dossor Kazakhstan 90 B4
Dostyk Kazakhstan 90 I5
Dothan Alabama, U.S. 31 H5
Douala Cameroon 71 D7, 78 B5
Douglas Isle of Man 51 E8
Dourados Brazil 41 G7
Douro *river* Portugal/Spain 46 A7, 56 B4 *see also* Duero
Dover England, United Kingdom 51 I11
Dover *state capital* Delaware, U.S. 33 H7
Dover, Strait of *strait* France/United Kingdom 51 I11, 55 E1
Dovrefjell *plateau* Norway 49 B7
Dozen *island* Japan 98 E6
Drachten Netherlands 52 G2
Drakensberg *mountain range* Lesotho/South Africa 71 F12, 81 E8
Drake Passage *strait* E. Atlantic Ocean 45 C12
Drama Greece 69 G5
Drammen Norway 49 C9
Drau *river* Austria 61 H5
Drava *river* C. Europe 61 J6, 67 E12, 68 D2
Dresden Germany 59 H7
Drina *river* Bosnia & Herzegovina/Serbia & Montenegro 68 E3
Drobeta-Turnu Severin Romania 69 F3
Drogheda Republic of Ireland 51 D8
Drohobych Ukraine 65 B9
Dronning Maud Land *physical region* Antarctica 21 C1
Drummond Montana, U.S. 28 B3
Drummondville Québec, Canada 25 I8
Druskininkai Lithuania 65 B6
Duba Saudi Arabia 88 D5
Dubai United Arab Emirates 89 I6
Dubasari Moldova 65 D11
Dubawnt Lake *lake* Nunavut, Canada 24 E5
Dubbo New South Wales, Australia 103 I7
Dublin *country capital* Republic of Ireland 46 B4, 51 D9
Dubno Ukraine 65 C9
Dubrovnik Croatia 68 D4
Dubuque Iowa, U.S. 29 J5
Duchess Queensland, Australia 103 G4
Dudinka Russian Federation 87 F4
Duero *river* Portugal/Spain 57 F3 *see also* Douro
Dufourspitze *mountain* Italy/Switzerland 60 C6, 62 B3
Duisburg Germany 59 B6
Duluth Minnesota, U.S. 29 I3
Dumaguete Philippines 95 G5
Dumfries Scotland, United Kingdom 51 E7
Dumont d'Urville Sea *sea* S. Pacific Ocean 21 D5
Dunaujvaros Hungary 67 E11
Dundalk Republic of Ireland 51 D8
Dundee Scotland, United Kingdom 51 F5
Dunedin New Zealand 101 F9, 105 D12
Dunfermline Scotland, United Kingdom 51 F6
Dungeness *headland* England, United Kingdom 51 I12
Dungun Malaysia 94 C6

N'DALATANDO–ORKNEY ISLANDS .121

N'dalatando Angola 80 B2
Ndjamena *country capital* Chad 71 E5, 78 D3
Ndjolé Gabon 78 B6
Ndola Zambia 71 F9, 81 E3
Neagh, Lough *lake* Northern Ireland, United Kingdom 51 C7
Neapoli Greece 69 G8
Nebitdag Turkmenistan 91 B7
Nebraska *state* U.S. 29 F6
Neckar *river* Germany 59 D10
Necochea Argentina 43 F8
Negele Ethiopia 75 F10
Negomane Mozambique 81 H3
Negombo Sri Lanka 93 D11
Negro *river* N. South America 38 D3, 41 E3
Negro, Río *river* Argentina 39 D10, 43 E8
Negros *island* Philippines 95 G5
Neijiang China 97 G7
Neisse *river* Germany 59 I7
Neiva Colombia 40 C3
Nek'emte Ethiopia 75 E9
Nellore India 93 D9
Nelson *river* Manitoba, Canada 25 F6
Nelson New Zealand 105 E7
Nelspruit South Africa 81 F7
Néma Mauritania 76 E5
Neman *river* N. Europe 65 B6
Nemuro Japan 99 J2
Nen Jiang *river* China 97 I2
Nepal *country* S. Asia 84 D6, 92 E4
Nesebur Bulgaria 69 I4
Neskaupstadhur Iceland 48 D2
Ness, Loch *lake* Scotland, United Kingdom 50 E5
Netherlands *country* N.W. Europe 46 C5, 52 E5
Netherlands Antilles *Dutch dependent territory* E. West Indies 37 I5
Netherlands Antilles *Dutch dependent territory* S. West Indies 23 H12, 37 G7
Nettilling Lake *lake* Nunavut, Canada 25 G4
Neubrandenburg Germany 58 H4
Neuchâtel Switzerland 60 B5
Neuchâtel, Lake *lake* Switzerland 60 B5
Neufchâteau Belgium 53 F12
Neumünster Germany 58 E3
Neunkirchen Austria 61 J4
Neuquén Argentina 43 D8
Neuruppin Germany 58 G4
Neusiedler See *lake* Austria/Hungary 61 K3
Neuss Germany 59 B7
Neustrelitz Germany 58 G4
Neu-Ulm Germany 59 E11
Neuwied Germany 59 B8
Nevada *state* U.S. 27 D8
Nevada, Sierra *mountain range* Spain 57 E8
Nevers France 55 G4
Nevis *island* St. Kitts & Nevis 37 J5
Newark New Jersey, U.S. 33 H6
New Britain *island* Papua New Guinea 100 D5
New Brunswick *province* Canada 25 I7
Newbury England, United Kingdom 51 G11
New Caledonia *French dependent territory* S.W. Pacific Ocean 100 E6
Newcastle New South Wales, Australia 100 D8, 103 J7
Newcastle South Africa 81 F7
Newcastle-upon-Tyne England, United Kingdom 51 G7
New Delhi *country capital* India 84 D6, 92 D4
New England *cultural region* N.E. U.S. 33 I5
New Forest *physical region* England, United Kingdom 51 G12
Newfoundland *island* Newfoundland & Labrador, Canada 23 I7, 25 J6, 44 D4
Newfoundland & Labrador *province* Canada 25 I6
Newfoundland Basin *undersea feature* N.W. Atlantic Ocean 44 D4
New Georgia Islands *island group* Solomon Islands 100 D5
New Guinea *island* W. Pacific Ocean 106 C5
New Hampshire *state* U.S. 33 I4
New Ireland *island* Papua New Guinea 100 D5
New Jersey *state* U.S. 33 H7
Newman Western Australia, Australia 102 C4
New Mexico *state* U.S. 30 B4
New Orleans Louisiana, U.S. 23 E10, 31 G6
New Plymouth New Zealand 105 F5
Newport Wales, United Kingdom 51 F11
Newport News Virginia, U.S. 33 H8
New Providence *island* Bahamas 36 D2
Newquay England, United Kingdom 51 D12
Newry Northern Ireland, United Kingdom 51 D8
New Siberian Islands *island group* Russian Federation 87 H2
New South Wales *state* Australia 103 H6
Newtownabbey Northern Ireland, United Kingdom 51 D7
New Ulm Minnesota, U.S. 29 I4
New York *state* U.S. 33 G5
New York City New York, U.S. 23 G9, 33 I6
New Zealand *country* S.W. Pacific Ocean 101 E8, 104–105
Neyshabur Iran 89 I2
Ngaoundéré Cameroon 78 C4
Ngauruhoe, Mount *mountain* New Zealand 105 G5
N'giva Angola 80 B4
Ngourti Niger 77 J5
Nguigmi Niger 77 J5
Nha Trang Vietnam 94 D4
Niagara Falls *waterfall* Canada/U.S. 33 F5
Niagara Falls New York, U.S. 33 F5
Niamey *country capital* Niger 71 C5, 77 H6
Nianzishan China 97 I2
Nias *island* Indonesia 94 B7
Nicaragua *country* Central America 23 F12, 35 I8
Nicaragua, Lake *lake* Nicaragua 23 F12, 35 I8
Nice France 46 D7, 55 I7
Nicobar Islands *island group* India 83 G3, 84 E8, 93 I11
Nicosia *country capital* Cyprus 84 A6, 88 D3
Nidzica Poland 66 G4
Niedere Tauern *mountain range* Austria 61 H4
Nienburg Germany 58 D5
Nieuwegein Netherlands 53 E6
Niger *country* W. Africa 70 D5, 77 I5
Niger *river* W. Africa 70 C5, 77 I7
Niger Delta *delta* Mali 45 G7, 77 F5
Nigeria *country* W. Africa 71 D6, 77 I7
Niger, Mouths of the *wetland* Nigeria 77 I8
Niigata Japan 99 H5
Niihama Japan 98 E7
Nijmegen Netherlands 53 G6
Nikko Japan 99 H6
Nikopol Ukraine 65 G11
Niksic Serbia & Montenegro 68 D4
Nile *river* N.E. Africa 70 G4, 75 E9
Nile Delta *delta* Egypt 75 C6
Nîmes France 55 G7
Nine Degree Channel *channel* India/Maldives 93 B11
Ninetyeast Ridge *undersea feature* E. Indian Ocean 83 F4
Ninety Mile Beach *coastal region* New Zealand 104 E1
Ningbo China 97 J6
Niobrara *river* Nebraska/Wyoming, U.S. 29 F5
Nioro Mali 76 E5
Niort France 54 D5
Nipigon, Lake *lake* Ontario, Canada 25 F8, 23 F7
Nis Serbia & Montenegro 69 F4
Nishtun Yemen 89 H8
Nitra Slovakia 67 E9
Niue *N.Z. dependent territory* C. Pacific Ocean 101 G6
Nivelles Belgium 53 D10
Nizamabad India 93 D7
Nizhnevartovsk Russian Federation 86 E5
Nizhniy Novgorod Russian Federation 47 H4, 86 B4
Nizhniy Tagil Russian Federation 86 D5
Nizhyn Ukraine 65 F8
Nizwa Oman 89 I6
Nkongsamba Cameroon 78 B5
Nobeoka Japan 98 D8
Nogales Arizona, U.S. 27 H12
Nogliki Russian Federation 87 J5
Noirmoutier, Île de *island* France 54 C4
Nojima-zaki *headland* Japan 99 H7
Nokia Finland 49 G8
Nome Alaska, U.S. 26 G1
Nonthaburi Thailand 94 C4
Noordoewer Namibia 80 C7
Noormarkku Finland 49 F8
Nora Sweden 49 D9
Norden Germany 58 B3
Norderstedt Germany 58 E3
Nordhausen Germany 59 E6
Nordhorn Germany 58 B5
Norfolk Nebraska, U.S. 29 H5
Norfolk Virginia, U.S. 33 H8
Norfolk Island *N.Z. dependent territory* S.W. Pacific Ocean 101 E7
Norilsk Russian Federation 84 E2, 87 F4
Norman Oklahoma, U.S. 30 E4
Normandy *cultural region* France 54 D3
Normanton Queensland, Australia 103 H3
Norrköping Sweden 49 E10
Norrtälje Sweden 49 E9
Norseman Western Australia, Australia 102 D7
Norte, Punta *headland* Argentina 43 G7
Northam Western Australia, Australia 102 B6
North America *continent* 22–37
Northampton England, United Kingdom 51 G10
North Andaman *island* Andaman Islands, India 93 H9
North Australian Basin *undersea feature* E. Indian Ocean 83 H4
North Bay Ontario, Canada 25 H8
North Cape *headland* New Zealand 104 E1
North Cape *headland* Norway 47 F1, 48 G1
North Carolina *state* U.S. 31 K3
North Charleston South Carolina, U.S. 31 J4
North Dakota *state* U.S. 29 F2
North Downs *hill range* England, United Kingdom 51 H11
North-East Canal *canal* Germany 58 D3
Northern Cook Islands *island group* Cook Islands 101 H5
Northern Dvina *river* Russian Federation 47 H2, 86 C3
Northern Ireland *national region* United Kingdom 51 C7
Northern Mariana Islands *U.S. dependent territory* W. Pacific Ocean 100 C2
Northern Sporades *island group* Greece 69 G7
Northern Territory *state* Australia 103 F3
North European Plain *physical region* N. Europe 47 E5, 66 E4, 86 B4
North Fiji Basin *undersea feature* S.W. Pacific Ocean 106 D5
North Frisian Islands *island group* N. Europe 58 C1
North Island *island* New Zealand 101 F8, 104 E4
North Korea *country* E. Asia 85 G5, 98 B4
North Las Vegas Nevada, U.S. 27 E9
North Little Rock Arkansas, U.S. 31 F4
North Platte Nebraska, U.S. 29 F6
North Platte *river* C. U.S. 29 E6
North Pole *pole* Arctic Ocean 20 C3
North Saskatchewan *river* Alberta/Saskatchewan, Canada 24 C7
North Sea *sea* N.E. Atlantic Ocean 44 G3, 46 D4, 50 H5, 58 B2
North Shore New Zealand 104 F3
North Taranaki Bight *bay* New Zealand 104 E5
North Uist *island* Scotland, United Kingdom 50 C4
Northwest Atlantic Mid-Ocean Canyon *undersea feature* N.W. Atlantic Ocean 44 D4
North West Cape *headland* Western Australia, Australia 102 A4
Northwest Highlands *mountain range* Scotland, United Kingdom 50 E4
Northwest Pacific Basin *undersea feature* N. Pacific Ocean 106 D2
Northwest Territories *province* Canada 24 C4
North York Moors *moorland* England, United Kingdom 51 G8
Norway *country* N.W. Europe 46 D4, 49 B8
Norwegian Sea *sea* N.E. Atlantic Ocean 44 G2, 46 D2
Norwich England, United Kingdom 51 I10
Noshiro Japan 99 H4
Notec *river* Poland 66 D4
Noto-hanto *peninsula* Japan 99 F5
Nottingham England, United Kingdom 51 G9
Nouadhibou Mauritania 76 C3
Nouakchott *country capital* Mauritania 70 A4, 76 C4
Nouméa New Caledonia 101 E6
Nova Gorica Slovenia 61 H6
Nova Iguaçu Brazil 39 G7
Nova Kakhovka Ukraine 65 F11
Novara Italy 62 B3
Nova Scotia *province* Canada 25 J8
Nova Ves Slovakia 67 G8
Novaya Zemlya *island group* Russian Federation 47 H1, 86 D3
Nove Zamky Slovakia 67 E9
Novgorod Russian Federation 86 B3
Novi Serbia & Montenegro 68 E3
Novoalekseevka Kazakhstan 90 C4
Novohrad-Volynskyy Ukraine 65 D9
Novokuznetsk Russian Federation 84 E4, 87 E6
Novo Mesto Slovenia 61 I7
Novosibirsk Russian Federation 84 D4, 87 E6
Novovolyusk Ukraine 65 B9
Novyy Urengoy Russian Federation 86 E4
Nowy Sacz Poland 67 G8
Nowy Targ Poland 67 F8
Nubian Desert *desert* Sudan 70 G4, 74 C3
Nueva Lubecka Argentina 43 C10
Nuevo Laredo Mexico 34 E3
Nu Jiang *river* S.E. Asia 96 D6 *see also* Salween
Nuku'alofa *country capital* Tonga 101 G6
Nullarbor *physical region* Australia 100 B8
Nullarbor Plain *plateau* South Australia/Western Australia, Australia 102 D6
Nunavut *province* Canada 24 E4
Nunivak Island *island* Alaska, U.S. 26 G2
Nuoro Italy 63 B8
Nuqus Uzbekistan 91 C6
Nuremberg Germany 59 F9
Nurmes Finland 49 I6
Nushki Pakistan 91 E10
Nuuk Greenland 20 A5, 22 H5
Nyala Sudan 75 B8
Nyasa, Lake *lake* E. Africa 71 G9, 79 H9, 81 G3
Nyborg Denmark 49 B12
Nyeri Kenya 79 I6
Nyiregyhaza Hungary 67 H9
Nykøbing Denmark 49 C13
Nyköping Sweden 49 E10
Nzérékoré Guinea 76 E7

O

Oahe, Lake *lake* North Dakota/South Dakota, U.S. 29 F3
Oahu *island* Hawaii, U.S. 27 B12
Oakland California, U.S. 27 B8
Oak Ridge Tennessee, U.S. 31 H3
Oamaru New Zealand 105 D11
Oates Land *physical region* Antarctica 21 C5
Oaxaca Mexico 35 F6
Ob *river* Russian Federation 84 D3, 86 D4
Oban Scotland, United Kingdom 51 D6
Oberhausen Germany 59 B6
Oberwald Switzerland 60 C5
Obi *island* Indonesia 95 I7
Obihiro Japan 99 I2
Obo Central African Republic 79 F5
Oborniki Poland 66 D4
Oceanside California, U.S. 27 D11
Odemira Portugal 56 A7
Odense Denmark 49 B12
Oder *river* C. Europe 47 E5, 58 I5, 67 D6
Oderhaff *bay* S. Baltic Sea 58 H3
Odesa Ukraine 47 G6, 65 E12
Odessa Texas, U.S. 30 C5
Odienné Ivory Coast 76 E7
Oeiras Portugal 56 A6
Offenbach am Main Germany 59 C8
Offenburg Germany 59 C11
Oga Japan 99 H4
Ogaden *plateau* Ethiopia/Somalia 71 H6, 75 G10
Ogaki Japan 99 G7
Ogbomosho Nigeria 77 H7
Ogden Utah, U.S. 27 G6
Ogdensburg New York, U.S. 33 H4
Ogulin Croatia 68 C3
Ohai New Zealand 105 B12
Ohio *river* N. U.S. 32 C8
Ohrid Macedonia 69 E5
Ohrid, Lake *lake* Albania/Macedonia 69 E5
Ohura New Zealand 104 G5
Oise *river* France 55 G2
Oita Japan 98 D8
Ojiwarongo Namibia 80 B5
Ojos del Salado *mountain* Argentina 39 C8, 42 C4
Oka *river* Russian Federation 47 H4
Okahandja Namibia 80 B6
Okaihau New Zealand 104 F2
Okara Pakistan 91 G10
Okavango Delta *delta* Botswana 71 F10, 80 D5
Okayama Japan 99 E7
Okazaki Japan 99 G7
Okeechobee, Lake *Lake* Florida, U.S. 31 J7
Okhotsk, Sea of *sea* N.W. Pacific Ocean 85 I4, 87 J4, 99 J1
Okhtyrka Ukraine 65 G9
Okinawa Japan 99 J8
Okinawa *island* Japan 99 J8
Oki-shoto *island group* Japan 99 E6
Oklahoma *state* U.S. 30 D4
Oklahoma City *state capital* Oklahoma, U.S. 23 E9, 30 D4
Oktyabrsk Kazakhstan 90 C4
Oktyabrskoy Revolyutsii, Ostrov *island* Russian Federation 87 F2
Okucani Croatia 68 D3
Okushiri-to *island* Japan 99 H3
Öland *island* Sweden 47 E4, 49 E12
Olavarría Argentina 43 F7
Olbia Italy 63 B8
Oldenburg Germany 58 C4
Olekma *river* Russian Federation 87 H5
Olekminsk Russian Federation 87 H5
Oleksandriya Ukraine 65 F10
Olenek *river* Russian Federation 85 G2, 87 G3
Oléron, Île d' *island* France 54 D5
Olesnica Poland 67 D6
Olgiy Mongolia 96 D2
Olhão Portugal 56 B8
Olinda Brazil 41 J5
Olivet France 55 F4
Ollagüe Chile 42 C2
Olmaliq Uzbekistan 91 F7
Olomouc Czech Republic 67 D8
Olsztyn Poland 66 G3
Olsztynek Poland 66 G3
Olt *river* Romania 69 F6
Olten Switzerland 60 C4
Olympia *state capital* Washington, U.S. 26 B2
Olympic Mountains *mountain range* Washington, U.S. 26 B1
Olympus *mountain* Greece 69 F6
Olympus, Mount *mountain* Washington, U.S. 26 B1
Omagh Northern Ireland, United Kingdom 51 C7
Omaha Nebraska, U.S. 29 H6
Oman *country* S.W. Asia 84 C7, 89 I7
Oman, Gulf of *gulf* N. Arabian Sea 82 D1, 89 J6
Omarama New Zealand 105 C10
Omdurman Sudan 70 G5, 75 D7
Omo Wenz *river* Ethiopia 75 E10
Omsk Russian Federation 84 D4, 86 D6
Ondangwa Namibia 80 B5
Ondorhaan Mongolia 97 G3
Onega, Lake *lake* Russian Federation 47 G3, 86 C3
Onesti Romania 69 H2
Ongjin North Korea 98 B5
Ongole India 93 D9
Onitsha Nigeria 77 J8
Ontario *province* Canada 25 F7
Ontario, Lake *lake* Canada/U.S. 23 G8, 25 H9, 33 G4
Ontong Java Rise *undersea feature* W. Pacific Ocean 106 D5
Oodnadatta South Australia, Australia 103 F5
Oosterhout Netherlands 53 E7
Oosterschelde *inlet* Netherlands 53 C7
Opatow Poland 67 G6
Opole Poland 67 E6
Opunake New Zealand 105 F6
Oradea Romania 69 F2
Oral Kazakhstan 90 B3
Oran Algeria 70 C2, 73 E3
Orán Argentina 42 E2
Orange New South Wales, Australia 103 I7
Orange France 55 H7
Orangeburg South Carolina, U.S. 31 J4
Orange River *river* Namibia/South Africa 71 E12, 80 C7
Oranienburg Germany 58 H5
Oranjestad Aruba 37 G8
Orbetello Italy 63 D6
Ordos Desert *desert* China 97 G4
Ordu Turkey 88 E1
Örebro Sweden 49 D10
Oregon *state* U.S. 26 C4
Orel Russian Federation 86 B4
Orem Utah, U.S. 27 G7
Orenburg Russian Federation 47 J4, 86 C5
Orhei Moldova 65 D11
Orihuela Spain 57 G7
Orinoco *river* Colombia/Venezuela 38 D2, 40 E2
Oristano Italy 63 B9
Orivesi *lake* Finland 49 I7
Orizaba Mexico 35 F6
Orizaba, Pico de *volcano* Mexico 23 D11, 35 E6
Orkney Islands *island group* Scotland, United Kingdom 46 C3, 50 E2

PRESQUE ISLE–ST. KITTS & NEVIS .123

69 E6
Presque Isle Maine, U.S. 33 K2
Preston England, United Kingdom 51 F8
Pretoria *administrative capital* South Africa 71 F11, 81 E7
Preveza Greece 69 E7
Priboj Serbia & Montenegro 68 E4
Pribram Czech Republic 67 B7
Prievidza Slovakia 67 E9
Prijedor Bosnia & Herzegovina 68 C3
Prilep Macedonia 69 F5
Prince Albert Saskatchewan, Canada 24 D7
Prince Charles Island *island* Nunavut, Canada 25 G4
Prince Edward Island *province* Canada 25 J7
Prince George British Columbia, Canada 24 B6
Prince Of Wales Island *island* Queensland, Australia 103 H1
Prince of Wales Island *island* Nunavut, Canada 22 F4, 25 E3
Prince Rupert British Columbia, Canada 24 A6
Princess Charlotte Bay *bay* Queensland, Australia 103 H2
Princess Elizabeth Land *physical region* Antarctica 21 E3
Príncipe *island* São Tomé & Príncipe 78 B6
Prinses Margriet Canal *canal* Netherlands 52 F3
Pripet *river* Belarus/Ukraine 65 D8
Pripet Marshes *marsh* Belarus/Ukraine 65 C8
Pristina Serbia & Montenegro 47 F7, 69 E4
Prizren Serbia & Montenegro 69 E5
Prokopyevsk Russian Federation 87 E6
Prome Myanmar 94 B3
Proserpine Queensland, Australia 103 I4
Prosna *river* Poland 66 E5
Prostejov Czech Republic 67 D8
Provence *cultural region* France 55 H8
Providence *state capital* Rhode Island, U.S. 33 J5
Provo Utah, U.S. 27 G7
Prudhoe Bay Alaska, U.S. 26 H1
Prut *river* E. Europe 65 D12, 69 H1
Pryluky Ukraine 65 F9
Przemysl Poland 67 H7
Psara *island* Greece 69 H7
Pskov Russian Federation 86 B3
Pskov, Lake *lake* Estonia/Russian Federation 64 D4
Ptuj Slovenia 61 J6
Pucallpa Peru 40 C5
Pudasjärvi Finland 49 H5
Puebla Mexico 35 E6
Pueblo Colorado, U.S. 28 E7
Puerto Aisén Chile 43 C10
Puerto Baquizero Moreno Galapagos Islands 40 B9
Puerto Barrios Guatemala 35 H7
Puerto Deseado Argentina 43 E11
Puertollano Spain 56 E6
Puerto Montt Chile 43 C9
Puerto Natales Chile 43 C12
Puerto Princesa Philippines 95 F5
Puerto Rico *U.S. dependent territory* C. West Indies 23 H12, 37 H5
Puerto Rico Trench Plain *undersea feature* W. Atlantic Ocean 45 C6
Puerto San Julián Argentina 43 D11
Puerto Santa Cruz Argentina 43 D11
Puerto Vallarta Mexico 34 C5
Pukekohe New Zealand 104 G4
Pula Croatia 68 B3
Pulawy Poland 67 H6
Pultusk Poland 66 G4
Pune India 93 B7
P'ungsan North Korea 98 C3
Puno Peru 40 D6
Punta Alta Argentina 43 F6
Punta Arenas Chile 43 D12
Puntarenas Costa Rica 35 I8
Puri India 93 F7
Purmerend Netherlands 52 E4
Purus *river* Brazil/Peru 38 D5, 40 E4
Puspokladany Hungary 67 G10
Putian *lake* China 97 J7
Puttgarden Germany 58 F2
Putumayo *river* N.W. South America 38 B4, 40 C4
Pyhäjoki Finland 49 G6
Pylos Greece 69 F8
Pyongyang *country capital* North Korea 85 G5, 98 B4
Pyramid Lake *lake* Nevada, U.S. 27 C7
Pyrenees *mountain range* France/Spain 46 B7, 54 D8, 57 G2
Pyrgos Greece 69 F8

Q

Qaanaaq Greenland 20 B3
Qaidam Basin *physical region* China 96 D5
Qalaikhum Tajikistan 91 F8
Qalat Afghanistan 91 E10
Qaleh-ye Now Afghanistan 91 D9
Qapshaghay Kazakhstan 91 G6
Qaqortoq Greenland 20 A5
Qara Kazakhstan 90 G3
Qaraghandy Kazakhstan 90 F4
Qaraghayly Kazakhstan 90 G4
Qarokul Tajikistan 91 G7
Qarshi Uzbekistan 91 E7
Qatar *country* S.W. Asia 84 B6, 89 H6
Qattara Depression *physical region* Egypt 74 B3
Qazaly Kazakhstan 91 D5
Qazvin Iran 89 G3
Qena Egypt 74 D4
Qeshm *island* Iran 89 I5
Qilian Shan *mountain range* China 97 E5
Qingdao China 85 G5, 97 I5
Qinghai Hu *lake* China 97 F5
Qinhuangdao China 97 I4
Qinzhou China 97 H8
Qiqihar China 85 G4, 97 I2
Qizilqum *desert* Kazakhstan/Uzbekistan 91 D6
Qom Iran 84 B6, 89 H3
Qomisheh Iran 89 H4
Qonduz Afghanistan 91 F8
Qostanay Kazakhstan 90 D3
Quanzhou China 97 J7
Quartu Sant'Elena Italy 63 B9
Québec Québec, Canada 25 I8
Québec *province* Canada 23 H8
Queen Charlotte Islands *island group* British Columbia, Canada 23 B2, 24 A6
Queen Elizabeth Islands *island group* Nunavut, Canada 22 F3, 25 E2
Queensland *state* Australia 103 H4
Queenstown New Zealand 105 B11
Queenstown South Africa 80 E8
Quelimane Mozambique 71 G10, 81 H5
Querétaro Mexico 34 E5
Quetta Pakistan 91 E10
Quibdó Colombia 40 C2
Quilon India 93 C11
Quilpie Queensland, Australia 103 H5
Quimper France 54 B3
Quito *country capital* Ecuador 38 A3, 40 B3
Qujing China 97 G8
Qulsary Kazakhstan 90 B5
Qunghirot Uzbekistan 91 C6
Quqon Uzbekistan 91 F7
Qurghonteppa Tajikistan 91 F8
Quy Nhon Vietnam 94 D4
Quzhou China 97 I7
Qyzylorda Kazakhstan 91 E6

R

Raab *river* Austria/Hungary 61 J5
Raahe Finland 49 G6
Raba *river* Austria/Hungary 67 D10
Rabat *country capital* Morocco 70 C2, 72 D4
Rabaul Papua New Guinea 100 D5
Rabigh Saudi Arabia 88 E6
Rabka Poland 67 F8
Race, Cape *headland* Newfoundland & Labrador, Canada 25 K7
Radom Poland 67 G6
Radstadt Austria 61 H4
Radzyn Podlaski Poland 67 H5
Rafaela Argentina 42 F5
Rafhah Saudi Arabia 89 F5
Ragusa Italy 63 F12
Rahimyar Khan Pakistan 91 F11
Raichur India 93 D8
Rainier, Mount *mountain* Washington, U.S. 23 C7, 26 C2
Raipur India 93 E7
Rajahmundry India 93 E8
Rajang *river* Malaysia 95 E7
Rajapalaiyam India 93 D10
Rajkot India 93 B6
Rajshahi Bangladesh 93 G6
Rakvere Estonia 64 D3
Raleigh *state capital* North Carolina, U.S. 31 J3
Ralik Chain *island group* Marshall Islands 101 E3
Ramnicu Valcea Romania 69 G3
Ranau Malaysia 95 F6
Rancagua Chile 43 C6
Ranchi India 93 F6
Randers Denmark 49 B11
Rangiora New Zealand 105 E9
Rangoon *see* Yangon
Rangpur Bangladesh 92 G5
Rapallo Italy 62 B4
Rapid City South Dakota, U.S. 29 E4
Rarotonga *island* Cook Islands 101 H6
Rasa, Punta *headland* Argentina 39 E11, 43 F8
Ras Dashen *mountain* Ethiopia 71 H5, 75 E8
Rasht Iran 89 G2
Ratak Chain *island group* Marshall Islands 101 E3
Ratan Sweden 49 D7
Rättvik Sweden 49 D8
Rauma Finland 49 F8
Raurkela India 93 F6
Ravenna Italy 62 E4
Ravi *river* India/Pakistan 91 G10
Rawalpindi Pakistan 91 G9
Rawicz Poland 67 D5
Rawlins Wyoming, U.S. 28 D5
Rawson Argentina 43 E9
Rayong Thailand 94 C4
Raysut Oman 89 I8
Razgrad Bulgaria 69 H4
Raz, Pointe du *headland* France 54 B3
Reading England, United Kingdom 51 G11
Rebun-to *island* Japan 99 H1
Rechytsa Belarus 65 E8
Recife Brazil 38 I5, 41 J5
Recklinghausen Germany 59 B6
Reconquista Argentina 42 F4
Red Bluff California, U.S. 27 B7
Red Deer Alberta, Canada 24 C7
Redding California, U.S. 27 B6
Red Hill *mountain* Hawaii, U.S. 27 B12
Red River *river* Canada/U.S. 29 H2
Red River *river* China/Vietnam 94 C2, 97 F8
Red River *river* S. U.S. 30 D4
Red Sea *sea* N.W. Indian Ocean 70 G4, 75 E6, 82 C2, 84 B7, 89 D6
Reefton New Zealand 105 D8
Ree, Lough *lake* Republic of Ireland 51 C9
Regensburg Germany 59 G10
Reggane Algeria 73 E6
Reggio di Calabria Italy 63 G11
Reggio nell' Emilia Italy 62 C4
Regina Saskatchewan, Canada 24 D8
Rehoboth Namibia 80 B6
Ré, Île de *island* France 54 D5
Reims France 55 G2
Reina Adelaida, Archipiélago *island group* Chile 39 C13, 43 C12
Reindeer Lake *lake* Manitoba/Saskatchewan, Canada 23 E6, 24 E6
Remscheid Germany 59 B7
Rendsburg Germany 58 E2
Rennes France 46 C6, 54 D3
Reno *river* Italy 62 D4
Reno Nevada, U.S. 27 C7
Republican *river* Kansas/Nebraska, U.S. 29 G6
Resistencia Argentina 42 F4
Resita Romania 69 F3
Resolution Island *island* New Zealand 105 A12
Rethymno Greece 69 G9
Retsag Hungary 67 F10
Réunion *island* W. Indian Ocean 82 D5
Reus Spain 57 I4
Reutlingen Germany 59 D11
Revillagigedo, Islas *island group* Mexico 34 A5
Reykjanes Ridge *undersea feature* N. Atlantic Ocean 44 E3
Reykjavik *country capital* Iceland 46 B1, 48 B3
Reynosa Mexico 35 E4
Rezekne Latvia 64 D5
Rhaetian Alps *mountain range* Italy/Switzerland 60 E6
Rheine Germany 58 B5
Rhine *river* W. Europe 46 D6, 53 F6, 55 I3, 59 C10, 60 C4
Rhode Island *state* U.S. 33 J6
Rhodes Greece 69 I8
Rhodes *island* Greece 47 G9, 69 I8
Rhodope Mountains *mountain range* Bulgaria/Greece 69 G5
Rhön *mountain range* Germany 59 E8
Rhône *river* France/Switzerland 46 C7, 55 H7, 60 B6
Rhum *island* Scotland, United Kingdom 50 D5
Riau Islands *island group* Indonesia 94 C7
Ribeirão Prêto Brazil 39 G7, 41 H7
Ribnica Slovenia 61 I7
Ribnita Moldova 65 D11
Riccione Italy 62 E5
Richard Toll Senegal 76 C5
Richmond Queensland, Australia 103 H4
Richmond *state capital* Virginia, U.S. 33 G8
Ricobayo, Embalse de *reservoir* Spain 56 C3
Ridder Kazakhstan 90 H3
Rieti Italy 63 E6
Riga *country capital* Latvia 47 F4, 64 C4
Riga, Gulf of *gulf* E. Baltic Sea 64 B4
Riihimäki Finland 49 G8
Riiser-Larsen Ice Shelf *ice shelf* Antarctica 21 B1
Riiser-Larsen Peninsula *peninsula* Antarctica 21 D1
Rijeka Croatia 46 E7, 68 B3
Rimavska Sobota Slovakia 67 F9
Rimini Italy 62 E5
Ringebu Norway 49 C8
Ringsted Denmark 49 C12
Ringvassoy *island* Norway 48 E2
Rinteln Germany 59 D5
Rio Branco Brazil 40 D5
Río Colorado Argentina 43 E8
Río Cuarto Argentina 43 E6
Rio de Janeiro Brazil 39 H8, 41 I7
Río Gallegos Argentina 43 D12
Río Grande Argentina 43 D13
Rio Grande Brazil 41 G9
Rio Grande Rise *undersea feature* S.W. Atlantic Ocean 45 E10
Ríohacha Colombia 40 C1
Rionero in Vulture Italy 63 G8
Ripoll Spain 57 I3
Rishiri-to *island* Japan 99 H1
Riva Italy 62 D3
Rivera Uruguay 42 G5
Riverside California, U.S. 27 D11
Rivne Ukraine 47 F6, 65 C9
Rivoli Italy 62 A3
Riyadh *country capital* Saudi Arabia 84 B6, 89 G6
Roanne France 55 G5
Roanoke Virginia, U.S. 33 F8
Roan Plateau *plateau* Utah, U.S. 27 H7
Rochefort France 54 D5
Rochester Minnesota, U.S. 29 I4
Rochester New York, U.S. 33 G5
Rockford Illinois, U.S. 32 B5
Rockhampton Queensland, Australia 100 D7, 103 J4
Rockingham Western Australia, Australia 102 B7
Rock Springs Wyoming, U.S. 28 C6
Rocky Mountains *mountain range* Canada/U.S. 22 D5, 24 B5, 26 F2, 28 B2, 30 A1
Rødbyhavn Denmark 49 C13
Rodez France 55 F7
Rodnyy Kazakhstan 90 D3
Roermond Netherlands 53 G8
Roeselare Belgium 53 B9
Rogers, Mount *mountain* Virginia, U.S. 33 E9
Roggeveen Basin *undersea feature* E. Pacific Ocean 107 I6
Rolvsøya *island* Norway 48 G1
Roma Queensland, Australia 103 I5
Roman Romania 69 H2
Romania *country* S.E. Europe 47 F7, 69 G2
Rome *country capital* Italy 46 D7, 63 E7
Romny Ukraine 65 F9
Ronda Spain 56 D8
Rønne Denmark 49 D13
Ronne Ice Shelf *ice shelf* Antarctica 21 B2
Ronse Belgium 53 C9
Roosendaal Netherlands 53 D7
Roosevelt Island *island* Antarctica 21 C4
Røros Norway 49 C7
Rosario Argentina 39 E9, 43 F6
Rosarno Italy 63 G10
Roscoff France 54 B3
Roseau *country capital* Dominica 37 J6
Roseburg Oregon, U.S. 26 B4
Rosenheim Germany 59 G12
Roses Spain 57 J2
Rossano Italy 63 H9
Ross Ice Shelf *ice shelf* Antarctica 21 C4
Ross Island *island* Antarctica 21 C4
Rosso Mauritania 76 C5
Ross Sea *sea* Antarctica 21 C4
Rostock Germany 58 G3
Rostov-na-Donu Russian Federation 47 H6, 86 A5
Røsvatnet *lake* Norway 49 D5
Roswell New Mexico, U.S. 30 B4
Rotenburg Germany 58 D4
Rotherham New Zealand 105 E9
Rotorua New Zealand 104 H5
Rotorua, Lake *lake* New Zealand 104 H4
Rottenmann Austria 61 I4
Rotterdam Netherlands 53 D6
Roubaix France 55 G1
Rouen France 55 E2
Rovaniemi Finland 48 G4
Rovigo Italy 62 D3
Rovuma *river* Mozambique/Tanzania 81 H3
Roxas City Philippines 95 G4
Roxburgh New Zealand 105 C11
Royan France 54 D6
Roznava Slovakia 67 G9
Ruacana Namibia 80 B5
Ruapehu, Mount *mountain* New Zealand 105 G6
Rubtsovsk Russian Federation 86 E6
Rudolstadt Germany 59 F8
Rufiji *river* Kenya 79 I9
Rufino Argentina 43 E6
Rügen *island* Germany 58 H2
Rumford Maine, U.S. 33 J4
Rumoi Japan 99 I2
Rundu Namibia 80 C5
Ruoqiang China 96 D4
Rupel *river* Belgium 53 D8
Ruse Bulgaria 69 H4
Russian Federation *country* Asia/Europe 47 H3, 84 D3, 86 E4
Rustavi Georgia 89 F1
Rutland Vermont, U.S. 33 I4
Ruvuma *river* Mozambique/Tanzania 79 I9
Rwanda *country* C. Africa 71 G7, 79 G7
Ryazan Russian Federation 47 H4, 86 B4
Rybinsk Russian Federation 86 B4
Rybnik Poland 67 E7
Ryki Poland 67 H5
Ryotsu Japan 99 G5
Rypin Poland 66 F4
Ryukyu Islands *island group* Japan 99 I9
Rzeszow Poland 67 H7

S

Saale *river* Germany 59 F6
Saalfeld Germany 59 F8
Saarbrücken Germany 59 B10
Saaremaa *island* Estonia 64 B3
Sabac Serbia & Montenegro 68 E3
Sabadell Spain 57 I3
Sabah *political region* Malaysia 95 F6
Sabha Libya 73 I6
Sabine *river* Louisiana/Texas, U.S. 31 E5
Sable, Cape *headland* Nova Scotia, Canada 25 J8
Sable, Cape *headland* Florida, U.S. 31 J7
Sabzevar Iran 89 I3
Saco Montana, U.S. 28 D2
Sacramento *river* California, U.S. 27 B7
Sacramento *state capital* California, U.S. 27 B8
Sacramento Mountains *mountain range* New Mexico, U.S. 30 B4
Sado-shima *island* Japan 99 G5
Säffle Sweden 49 C10
Safi Morocco 72 C4
Saga Japan 98 D8
Sagami-nada *inlet* Japan 99 H7
Sagar India 93 D6
Saginaw Michigan, U.S. 32 D5
Sagres Portugal 56 A8
Sagunto Spain 57 H5
Sahara *desert* N. Africa 70 C4, 72 C6, 77 G4, 78 D2
Sahel *physical region* W. Africa 70 D5, 77 G5, 78 D3
Sahiwal Pakistan 91 G10
Saïda Algeria 73 F4
Saidpur India 92 G5
Saimaa *lake* Finland 49 H8
St. Anton Switzerland 60 E5
St. Barthélémy *French dependent territory* E. West Indies 37 J5
St.-Brieuc France 54 C3
St. Catharines Ontario, Canada 25 H9
St.-Chamond France 55 H6
St. Charles Missouri, U.S. 29 K7
St. Cloud Minnesota, U.S. 29 I3
St.-Dié France 55 I3
Saintes France 54 D5
St.-Étienne France 55 G6
St. Gallen Switzerland 60 D4
Saint George Queensland, Australia 103 I6
St. George's *country capital* Grenada 37 J8
St. George's Channel *channel* Celtic Sea/Irish Sea 51 D10
St. Helena *island* S.W. Africa 45 F8
Saint Helens, Mount *mountain* Washington, U.S. 26 B3
St. Helier Jersey, Channel Islands 51 G13
Saint John New Brunswick, Canada 25 J8
St. John's *country capital* Antigua & Barbuda 37 J5
St. John's Newfoundland & Labrador, Canada 25 K6
Saint Joseph Missouri, U.S. 29 I7
Saint Kilda *island* Scotland, United Kingdom 50 B4
St. Kitts *island* St. Kitts & Nevis 37 J5
St. Kitts & Nevis *country* E. West Indies 23 I12, 37 J6

SIERRA MADRE DEL SUR–TALWOOD .125

35 F7
Sierra Madre del Sur *mountain range* Mexico 23 D11, 34 E6
Sierra Madre Occidental *mountain range* Mexico 23 C10, 34 C3
Sierra Madre Oriental *mountain range* Mexico 34 D3
Sierra Nevada *mountain range* W. U.S. 27 B6
Sierre Switzerland 60 B6
Sifnos *island* Greece 69 G8
Siglufjördhur Iceland 48 B2
Sigmaringen Germany 59 D11
Siguiri Guinea 76 E6
Siilinjärvi Finland 49 H7
Sikasso Mali 77 E6
Silchar India 93 H5
Silesia *cultural region* Poland 67 D6
Simbirsk Russian Federation 47 I4, 86 B5
Simeulue *island* Indonesia 94 A6
Simferopol Ukraine 65 G13
Simpson Desert *desert* Northern Territory/South Australia, Australia 103 F5
Sinai *peninsula* Egypt 74 D3
Sinanju North Korea 98 B4
Sincelejo Colombia 40 C1
Sines Portugal 56 A7
Singa Sudan 75 D8
Singapore *country* S.E. Asia 85 F8, 94 C7
Singapore *country capital* Singapore 85 F8, 94 C7
Singen Germany 59 C12
Singida Tanzania 79 H7
Singitic Gulf *gulf* N. Adriatic Sea 69 G6
Singkawang Indonesia 94 D7
Siniscola Italy 63 C8
Sinop Turkey 88 D1
Sinpo North Korea 98 C4
Sintra Portugal 56 A6
Sinuiju North Korea 98 A4
Sion Switzerland 60 B6
Sioux City Iowa, U.S. 29 H5
Sioux Falls South Dakota, U.S. 29 H5
Siping China 97 J3
Siple Island *island* Antarctica 21 A4
Siracusa Italy 63 G12
Sir Edward Pellew Group *island group* Northern Territory, Australia 103 G2
Siret *river* Romania 69 H2
Sirjan Iran 89 I4
Sirte, Gulf of *gulf* S. Mediterranean Sea 70 E2, 73 I4
Sisak Croatia 68 C3
Sisimiut Greenland 20 A4
Sitapur India 92 E5
Sittwe Myanmar 94 A2
Sivas Turkey 88 D2
Siwa Egypt 74 B3
Siwalik Range *mountain range* India/Nepal 92 D4
Skagerrak *channel* N.W. Europe 49 B10
Skeleton Coast *coastal region* Namibia 71 D10, 80 A5
Skellefteå Sweden 49 F6
Skellefteälven *river* Sweden 49 F5
Skibotn Norway 48 F3
Skien Norway 49 B9
Skierniewice Poland 66 F5
Skiftet Kihti *strait* Baltic Sea/Gulf of Bothnia 49 F9
Skikda Algeria 73 G3
Skopje *country capital* Macedonia 47 F7, 69 F5
Skye *island* Scotland, United Kingdom 50 D4
Skyros *island* Greece 69 G7
Slatina Romania 69 G3
Slave *river* Alberta/Northwest Territories, Canada 24 D6
Slavonia *cultural region* Croatia 68 D3
Slavonski Brod Croatia 68 D3
Sligo Republic of Ireland 51 B8
Sliven Bulgaria 69 H4
Slobozia Romania 69 H3
Slonim Belarus 65 DC7
Slough England, United Kingdom 51 H11
Slovakia *country* C. Europe 47 E6, 67 E9
Slovenia *country* S.E. Europe 46 E6, 61 I6
Slovyansk Ukraine 65 H10
Slubice Poland 66 C5
Slupsk Poland 66 D2
Slutsk Belarus 65 D7
Smallwood Reservoir *reservoir* Newfoundland & Labrador, Canada 23 H7, 25 I6
Smara Western Sahara 72 C5
Smila Ukraine 65 F10
Smoky Hill *river* Kansas, U.S. 29 F7
Smøla *island* Norway 49 B6
Smolensk Russian Federation 47 G5, 86 B3
Smolikas *mountain* Greece 69 E6
Snake *river* N.W. U.S. 26 D3
Snake River Plain *physical region* Idaho, U.S. 26 F5
Snezka *mountain* Czech Republic 67 C6
Snowdon *mountain* Wales, United Kingdom 51 E9
Snyder Texas, U.S. 30 C5
Sobradinho, Represa de *reservoir* Brazil 39 G5, 41 H5
Sobral Brazil 41 I4
Sochaczew Poland 67 C6
Society Islands *island group* French Polynesia 101 I6
Socompa Chile 42 C3
Socorro, Isla *island* Mexico 34 B6
Socotra *island* Yemen 82 D2, 84 C7, 89 I9
Sodankylä Finland 48 G4
Söderhamn Sweden 49 E8
Södertälje Sweden 49 E10
Sofala Bay *bay* W. Indian Ocean 81 G5
Sofia *country capital* Bulgaria 47 F7, 69 F4
Sognefjorden *fjord* Norway 49 A8
Sohag Egypt 74 C4
Soignies Belgium 53 D10
Sokch'o South Korea 98 C5
Sokhumi Georgia 89 E1
Sokodé Togo 77 G7
Sokoto Nigeria 77 H6
Solapur India 93 C8
Sol, Costa del *coastal region* Spain 56 E8
Solingen Germany 59 B7
Sollentuna Sweden 49 E10
Solomon Islands *country* S.W. Pacific Ocean 101 E5
Solomon Sea *sea* W. Pacific Ocean 100 D5
Solothurn Switzerland 60 B4
Soltau Germany 58 E4
Solway Firth *inlet* England/Scotland, United Kingdom 51 E7
Solwezi Zambia 80 E3
Somalia *country* E. Africa 71 I7, 75 G11
Somalia Tanzania 79 H7
Somali Basin *undersea feature* N.W. Indian Ocean 82 D3
Sombor Serbia & Montenegro 68 E2
Sombrero Channel *channel* Nicobar Islands, India 93 H11
Somerset Island *island* Nunavut, Canada 25 E3
Somerset-West South Africa 80 C9
Somme *river* France 55 F2
Somoto Nicaragua 35 H7
Sonch'on North Korea 98 B4
Sondrio Italy 62 C2
Songea Tanzania 79 I9
Songhua Jiang *river* China 97 J2
Songnam South Korea 98 B5
Songnim North Korea 98 B4
Son La Vietnam 94 C2
Sonneberg Germany 59 F8
Sonoran Desert *desert* Mexico/U.S. 27 F12
Sopka Klyuchevskaya *volcano* Russian Federation 87 K4
Sopot Poland 66 E2
Sopron Hungary 67 D10
Sora Italy 63 E7
Soria Spain 57 F3
Soroca Moldova 65 D10
Sorong Indonesia 95 I7
Sørøya *island* Norway 49 F2
Sorsele Sweden 49 E5
Sosnowiec Poland 67 F7
Sotavento, Ilhas de Cape Verde 76 A5
Sotkamo Finland 49 H6
Sousse Tunisia 73 H3
South Africa *country* S. Africa 71 F12, 80 C8
South America *continent* 38–43
Southampton England, United Kingdom 51 G12
Southampton Island *island* Nunavut, Canada 22 F5, 25 F5
South Andaman *island* Andaman Islands, India 93 H10
South Australia *state* Australia 103 E5
South Australian Basin *undersea feature* S.E. Indian Ocean 83 I6
South Australian Plain *undersea feature* S.E. Indian Ocean 83 I7
South Bend Indiana, U.S. 32 C6
South Carolina *state* U.S. 31 J4
South China Sea *sea* S.E. Asia 85 G7, 95 E4, 97 I9
South Dakota *state* U.S. 29 F4
South Downs *hill range* England, United Kingdom 51 G12
Southeast Indian Ridge *undersea feature* S.E. Indian Ocean 83 F7
Southeast Pacific Basin *undersea feature* S.E. Pacific Ocean 107 H8
South East Point *headland* Victoria, Australia 103 H8
Southend-on-Sea England, United Kingdom 51 H11
Southern Alps *mountain range* New Zealand 105 B10
Southern Bug *river* Ukraine 65 E11
Southern Cook Islands *island group* Cook Islands 101 H6
Southern Cross Western Australia, Australia 102 C6
Southern Ocean *ocean* 45 E13, 82 D9
Southern Uplands *mountain range* Scotland, United Kingdom 51 E7
South Fiji Basin *undersea feature* S.W. Pacific Ocean 106 E6
South Georgia *island* S.W. Atlantic Ocean 45 E11
South Georgia *U.K. dependent territory* S.W. Atlantic Ocean 39 G13
South Indian Basin *undersea feature* S.E. Indian Ocean 83 G8
South Island *island* New Zealand 101 E8, 105 B9
South Korea *country* E. Asia 85 G5, 98 C5
South Orkney Islands *island group* S.E. South America 45 D12
South Platte *river* Colorado/Nebraska, U.S. 29 E6
South Pole *pole* Antarctica 21 C3
South Sandwich Islands *island group* S.E. South America 45 E12
South Saskatchewan *river* Alberta/Saskatchewan, Canada 24 C7
South Taranaki Bight *bay* New Zealand 105 F6
South Uist *island* Scotland, United Kingdom 50 C5
South West Cape *headland* New Zealand 105 B13
Southwest Indian Ridge *undersea feature* S.W. Indian Ocean 82 C7
Southwest Pacific Basin *undersea feature* S. Pacific Ocean 107 F7
Sovetskaya Gavan Russian Federation 87 J6
Soweto South Africa 80 E7
Soya-misaki *headland* Japan 99 H1
Spain *country* S.W. Europe 46 A7, 56 D5
Spanish Town Jamaica 36 D5
Sparks Nevada, U.S. 27 C7
Sparta Greece 69 F8
Spartivento, Capo *headland* Italy 63 B10
Spartivento, Capo *headland* Italy 63 H11
Spencer Iowa, U.S. 29 I5
Spencer Gulf *gulf* South Australia, Australia 103 F7
Spey *river* Scotland, United Kingdom 51 E5
Spiez Switzerland 60 B5
Spijkenisse Netherlands 53 D6
Spitsbergen *island* N.W. Europe 44 G1
Spittal-an der Drau Austria 61 H5
Split Croatia 46 E7, 68 C4
Spokane Washington, U.S. 26 E2
Spoleto Italy 63 E6
Spratly Islands *disputed region* S.E. Asia 95 F5
Spree *river* Germany 59 I6
Springfield Colorado, U.S. 29 F8
Springfield *state capital* Illinois, U.S. 32 B7
Springfield Massachusetts, U.S. 33 I5
Springfield Missouri, U.S. 29 J8
Springfield Oregon, U.S. 26 B4
Squillace, Gulf of *gulf* N.W. Ionian Sea 63 H10
Sri Jayewardenepura Kotte *legislative capital* Sri Lanka 84 D8, 93 D11
Sri Lanka *country* S. Asia 84 D8, 93 E11
Sri Lanka *island* S. Asia 83 F3
Srinagar India 92 C2
Stadtlohn Germany 59 B6
Stakhanov Ukraine 65 I10
Stalowa Wola Poland 67 H7
Stamford Connecticut, U.S. 33 I6
Stanley Falkland Islands 39 E13, 43 G12
Stanley Tasmania, Australia 103 H9
Stanovoy Khrebet *mountain range* Russian Federation 85 G4, 87 H5
Starachowice Poland 67 G6
Stara Zagora Bulgaria 69 H4
Stargard Szczecinski Poland 66 C4
Starograd Gdanski Poland 66 E3
Stavanger Norway 46 D4, 49 A9
Stavropol Russian Federation 47 I6, 86 A5
Steinkjer Norway 49 C6
Stendal Germany 58 F5
Sterling Colorado, U.S. 29 E6
Sterling Illinois, U.S. 32 B5
Sterling Heights Michigan, U.S. 32 E5
Stewart Island *island* New Zealand 105 B13
Steyr Austria 61 I3
Stillwater Minnesota, U.S. 29 I4
Stip Macedonia 69 F5
Stirling Scotland, United Kingdom 51 E6
Stockholm *country capital* Sweden 47 E4, 49 E10
Stockton California, U.S. 27 B8
Stoke-on-Trent England, United Kingdom 51 F9
Stony Tunguska *river* Russian Federation 85 E3, 87 F5
Store Bælt *channel* Baltic Sea/Kattegat 49 B12
Støren Norway 49 C7
Stornoway Scotland, United Kingdom 50 D4
Storsjön *lake* Sweden 49 D7
Storuman Sweden 49 E6
Strakonice Czech Republic 67 B8
Stralsund Germany 58 H2
Stranraer Scotland, United Kingdom 51 E7
Strasbourg France 46 D6, 55 I3
Stratford New Zealand 105 F6
Streaky Bay South Australia, Australia 103 F6
Stromboli *island* Italy 63 G10
Stromness Scotland, United Kingdom 50 F3
Strömstad Sweden 49 C10
Strömsund Sweden 49 E6
Strumica Macedonia 69 F5
Stryy Ukraine 65 B10
Sturt Desert *desert* Queensland/South Australia, Australia 103 G5
Stuttgart Germany 46 D6, 59 D10
Stykkishólmur Iceland 48 B2
Suakin Sudan 75 E6
Subotica Serbia & Montenegro 68 E2
Suceava Romania 69 H1
Sucre *legal capital* Bolivia 9 D7, 40 E7
Sudan *country* N. Africa 71 F6, 75 C7
Sudbury Ontario, Canada 25 G8
Sudd *wetland* Sudan 71 G6, 75 C9
Sudeten *mountain range* Czech Republic/Poland 67 C6
Suez Egypt 70 G3, 74 C3
Suez Canal *canal* Egypt 74 C3
Suhar Oman 89 I6
Suhbaatar Mongolia 97 G2
Suhl Germany 59 E8
Suihua China 97 J2
Suizhou China 97 H6
Sukchon North Korea 98 B4
Sukkur Pakistan 91 F11
Sukumo Japan 98 E8
Sulaiman Range *mountain range* Pakistan 91 F10
Sula Islands *island group* Indonesia 95 H7
Sulawesi *island* Indonesia 85 G9, 95 G8
Sullana Peru 40 B4
Sulmona Italy 63 F7
Sulu Archipelago *island group* Philippines 95 G6
Sulu Sea *sea* Philippines 95 G5
Sulzbach-Rozenberg Germany 59 F9
Sumatra *island* Indonesia 83 G3, 85 F9, 94 C7
Sumba *island* Indonesia 95 G9
Sumbawa *island* Indonesia 95 F9
Sumbawanga Tanzania 79 H8
Sumbe Angola 80 A3
Sumeih Sudan 75 B9
Summel Iraq 89 F3
Sumqayit Azerbaijan 89 G1
Sumy Ukraine 65 G9
Sunch'on South Korea 98 B7
Sunderland England, United Kingdom 51 G7
Sundsvall Sweden 49 E7
Sunnyvale California, U.S. 27 B8
Suomussalmi Finland 49 H5
Superior Wisconsin, U.S. 32 A2
Superior, Lake *lake* Canada/U.S. 23 F8, 25 F8, 32 B2
Sur Oman 89 J6
Surabaya Indonesia 85 F9, 95 E9
Surakarta Indonesia 94 E9
Surat India 84 D7, 93 B7
Surat Thani Thailand 94 B5
Surendranagar India 93 B6
Surgut Russian Federation 86 E5
Surigao Philippines 95 H5
Suriname *country* N. South America 38 E3, 41 F2
Surt Libya 73 I5
Susa Italy 62 A3
Susch Switzerland 60 E5
Sutlej *river* India/Pakistan 91 G10
Suva *country capital* Fiji 101 F6
Suwalki Poland 66 H3
Suwon South Korea 98 B5
Suzhou China 97 I6
Svalbard *Norwegian dependent territory* Arctic Ocean 20 C4
Svartisen *glacier* Norway 48 D4
Sveg Sweden 49 D8
Svenstavik Sweden 49 D7
Svitavy Czech Republic 67 D7
Svitlovodsk Ukraine 65 F10
Svobodnyy Russian Federation 87 I6
Svyetlahorsk Belarus 65 E7
Swakopmund Namibia 80 B6
Swan Islands *island* Honduras 35 I6
Swansea Wales, United Kingdom 51 E11
Swaziland *country* S. Africa 71 G12, 81 F7
Sweden *country* N.W. Europe 47 E3, 49 D8
Swiebodzin Poland 66 C5
Swindon England, United Kingdom 51 G11
Swinoujscie Poland 66 C3
Switzerland *country* C. Europe 46 D6, 60 C5
Sydney New South Wales, Australia 100 D8, 103 I7
Sydney Nova Scotia, Canada 25 J7
Syeverodonetsk Ukraine 65 I10
Syktyvkar Russian Federation 86 C4
Sylhet Bangladesh 93 H5
Sylt *island* Germany 58 C2
Syracuse New York, U.S. 33 H5
Syr Darya *river* C. Asia 84 C5, 91 E6
Syria *country* W. Asia 84 B6, 88 D3
Syrian Desert *desert* W. Asia 88 E4
Szczecin Poland 66 C3
Szczecinek Poland 66 D3
Szeged Hungary 67 F11
Szekesfehervar Hungary 67 E10
Szekszard Hungary 67 E11
Szolnok Hungary 67 G10
Szombathely Hungary 67 D10

T

Tabas Iran 89 I3
Tabor Czech Republic 67 B8
Tabora Tanzania 79 H7
Tabriz Iran 84 B5, 89 F2
Tabuaeran *island* Kiribati 101 H4
Tabuk Saudi Arabia 88 D5
Täby Sweden 49 E9
Tacheng China 96 C2
Tacloban Philippines 95 H4
Tacna Peru 40 D6
Tacoma Washington, U.S. 26 B2
Taco Pozo Argentina 42 E3
Tacuarembó Uruguay 43 G5
T'aebaek-sanmaek *mountain range* North Korea/South Korea 98 C4
Tafi Viejo Argentina 42 D4
Taganrog, Gulf of *gulf* N.E. Sea of Azov 65 I11
Taguatinga Brazil 41 H5
Tagus *river* Portugal/Spain 46 A7, 56 A6
Tahat *mountain* Algeria 73 F7
Tahiti *island* French Polynesia 101 I6
Tahoe, Lake *lake* California/Nevada, U.S. 27 C7
Tahoua Niger 77 H5
Taichung Taiwan 97 J8
Tainan Taiwan 97 J8
Taipei *country capital* Taiwan 85 G6, 97 J7
Taiping Malaysia 94 C6
Taitao Península *peninsula* Chile 43 B10
Taiwan *country* E. Asia 85 G7, 97 J8
Taiwan Strait *strait* China/Taiwan 97 J8
Taiyuan China 85 F7, 97 H5
Ta'izz Yemen 89 F9
Tajikistan *country* C. Asia 84 D5, 91 F8
Tajumulco, Volcán *volcano* Guatemala 35 G7
Tak Thailand 94 B3
Takamatsu Japan 99 E7
Takaoka Japan 99 G6
Takasaki Japan 99 H6
Takayama Japan 99 G6
Takikawa Japan 99 I2
Takla Makan Desert *desert* China 84 D5, 96 B4
Talak *physical region* Niger 77 H5
Talas Kyrgyzstan 91 F6
Talaud Islands *island group* Indonesia 95 H6
Talavera de la Reina Spain 56 D5
Talca Chile 43 C7
Talcahuano Chile 43 B7
Taldyqorghan Kazakhstan 91 H5
Tallahassee *state capital* Florida, U.S. 31 I5
Tallinn *country capital* Estonia 47 F4, 64 C3
Taloqan Afghanistan 91 F8
Talsi Latvia 64 B4
Talwood Queensland, Australia

ULUNDI–WINDWARD ISLANDS .127

of Ireland/United Kingdom 51 C8
Ulundi South Africa 81 F7
Uluru *rocky outcrop* Northern Territory, Australia 103 E5
Uman Ukraine 65 E10
Umeå Sweden 49 F6
Umeälven *river* Sweden 49 E6
Umtata South Africa 81 E8
'Unayzah Saudi Arabia 89 F6
Ungava Bay *bay* Québec, Canada 25 H5
Ungava Peninsula *peninsula* Québec, Canada 23 G6, 25 G5
Ungheni Moldova 65 D11
Uniontown Pennsylvania, U.S. 33 F7
United Arab Emirates *country* S.W. Asia 84 C7, 89 H6
United Kingdom *country* N.W. Europe 46 C4, 51 E7
United States of America *country* N. North America 26–33
Upington South Africa 80 C7
Upper Lough Erne *lake* Republic of Ireland/United Kingdom 51 C8
Uppsala Sweden 49 E9
Upua New Zealand 104 F2
Ural *river* Kazakhstan/Russian Federation 47 J4, 84 B4, 86 C5, 90 B4
Ural Mountains *mountain range* Asia/Europe 47 I1, 84 C3, 86 D4
Urawa Japan 99 H6
Urbino Italy 62 E5
Urengoy Russian Federation 87 E4
Urganch Uzbekistan 91 D7
Uritskiy Kazakhstan 90 E3
Urmia, Lake *lake* Iran 89 F2
Urosevac Serbia & Montenegro 69 E5
Uroteppa Tajikistan 91 F7
Uruguay *country* S. South America 39 E9, 43 G6
Uruguay *river* S. South America 39 E9, 41 G8, 42 G4
Urumqi China 84 E5, 96 D3
Usak Turkey 88 C2
Usedom *island* Germany 58 H3
Ushuaia Argentina 43 D13
Ussuri *river* China/Russian Federation 97 K2
Ussuriysk Russian Federation 87 J7
Ustica *island* Italy 63 E10
Ust-Ilimsk Russian Federation 87 G5
Usti nad Labem Czech Republic 67 B6
Ustka Poland 66 D2
Ust-Kamchatsk Russian Federation 87 K3
Ustrzyki Dolne Poland 67 H8
Ustyurt Plateau *plateau* Kazakhstan/Uzbekistan 91 B6
Usumacinta *river* Guatemala/Mexico 35 G6
Utah *state* U.S. 27 G8
Utica New York, U.S. 33 H5
Utiel Spain 57 G5
Utrecht Netherlands 53 E5
Utsjoki Finland 48 G2
Utsunomiya Japan 99 H6
Uvs Nuur *lake* Mongolia 96 E2
Uyo Nigeria 77 I8
Uzbekistan *country* C. Asia 84 C5, 91 D7
Uzhhorod Ukraine 65 A10

V

Vaal *river* South Africa 71 F12, 80 D7
Vaasa Finland 49 F7
Vac Hungary 67 F10
Vacaville California, U.S. 27 B8
Vadodara India 93 B6
Vadsø Norway 48 H2
Vaduz *country capital* Liechtenstein 46 D6, 60 D5
Vah *river* Slovakia 67 E9
Valdecañas, Embalse de *reservoir* Spain 56 D5
Valdepeñas Spain 57 E6
Valdés, Peninsula *peninsula* Argentina 43 E9
Valdivia Chile 43 C8
Valdosta Georgia, U.S. 31 I5
Valence France 55 H6
Valencia Spain 46 B7, 57 H5
Valencia Venezuela 38 C2, 40 D1
Valencia, Gulf of *gulf* Spain 57 H6
Valenciennes France 55 G1
Valentine Nebraska, U.S. 29 F5
Valera Venezuela 40 D1
Valga Estonia 64 C4
Valladolid Spain 46 B7, 56 D3
Valledupar Venezuela 40 C1
Vallejo California, U.S. 27 B8
Vallenar Chile 42 C4
Valletta *country capital* Malta 46 E9, 63 F13
Valmiera Estonia 64 C4
Valparaíso Chile 43 C6
Valverde del Camino Spain 56 C7
Van Turkey 89 F2
Vanadzor Armenia 89 F1
Vancouver British Columbia, Canada 23 C6, 24 B7
Vancouver Washington, U.S. 26 B3
Vancouver Island *island* British Columbia, Canada 23 C6, 24 A7
Vancouver, Mount *mountain* Yukon Territory, Canada 24 A4
Van Diemen Gulf *gulf* Northern Territory, Australia 103 E1
Vänern *lake* Sweden 46 E4, 49 C10
Vånersborg Sweden 49 C10
Vangaindrano Madagascar 81 J6
Van, Lake *lake* Turkey 89 F2
Vannes France 54 C4
Vanrhynsdorp South Africa 80 C8
Vantaa Finland 49 H9
Vanua Levu *island* Fiji 101 F6
Vanuatu *country* S.W. Pacific Ocean 100 E6
Varanasi India 93 E5
Varangerfjorden *fjord* Norway 48 H2
Varano, Lake *lagoon* Italy 63 G7
Varazdin Croatia 68 C2
Varberg Sweden 49 C11
Varde Denmark 49 A12
Varese Italy 62 B3
Varkaus Finland 49 H7
Varna Bulgaria 69 I4
Vasa *see* Vaasa
Vaslui Romania 69 H2
Västerås Sweden 49 E9
Vasto Italy 63 F6
Vatican City *country* S. Europe 46 D7, 63 E7
Vatican City *country capital* Vatican City 63 E7
Vatnajökull *glacier* Iceland 48 C2
Vättern *lake* Sweden 46 E4, 49 D10
Växjö Sweden 49 D11
Veenendaal Netherlands 53 F6
Vega *island* Norway 49 C5
Vejle Denmark 49 B12
Veles Macedonia 69 F5
Vélez-Málaga Spain 56 E8
Veliko Turnovo Bulgaria 69 H4
Vellore India 93 D9
Velsen-Noord Netherlands 52 E4
Venado Tuerto Argentina 43 F6
Vendas Novas Portugal 56 B6
Venezuela *country* N. South America 38 D2, 40 D2
Venezuela, Gulf of *gulf* Colombia/Venezuela 40 D1
Venice Italy 62 E3
Venice, Gulf of *gulf* N.W. Adriatic Sea 62 E3
Venlo Netherlands 53 G7
Ventspils Estonia 64 B4
Vera Argentina 42 F5
Veracruz Mexico 35 F6
Veraval India 93 A7
Vercelli Italy 62 B3
Verdalsøra Norway 49 C6
Verde, Costa *coastal region* Spain 56 D1
Verden Germany 58 D4
Vereeniging South Africa 81 E7
Verkhoyanskiy Khrebet *mountain range* Russian Federation 87 H4
Vermont *state* U.S. 33 I4
Vernon Texas, U.S. 30 D4
Vernon, Mount Illinois, U.S. 32 B7
Veroia Greece 69 F6
Verona Italy 62 D3
Versailles France 55 F3
Verviers Belgium 53 G10
Vesoul France 55 H4
Vesterålen *island group* Norway 47 F1, 48 D3
Vestfjorden *fjord* Norway 48 D4
Vestmannaeyjar Iceland 48 B3
Vestmann Islands *island group* Iceland 48 B3
Vestvagøy *island* Norway 48 D3
Vesuvius *volcano* Italy 63 F8
Veszprem Hungary 67 E10
Vetlanda Sweden 49 D11
Veurne Belgium 53 A8
Viana do Castelo Portugal 56 B3
Viareggio Italy 62 C5
Viborg Denmark 49 B11
Vibo Valentia Italy 63 H10
Vicenza Italy 62 D3
Vichy France 55 G5
Victoria *river* Northern Territory, Australia 103 E2
Victoria *state* Australia 103 H7
Victoria British Columbia, Canada 24 B7
Victoria Falls *waterfall* Zambia/Zimbabwe 71 F10, 80 E5
Victoria Island *island* Northwest Territories/Nunavut, Canada 22 E4, 24 D3
Victoria, Lake *lake* E. Africa 71 G7, 79 H7
Victoria Land *physical region* Antarctica 21 C4
Victoria River Downs Northern Territory, Australia 103 E2
Vidin Bulgaria 69 F3
Viedma Argentina 43 E8
Vienna *country capital* Austria 46 E6, 61 J3
Vienne *river* France 55 E5
Vientiane *country capital* Laos 85 F7, 94 C3
Vierwaldstätter See *lake* Switzerland 60 C5
Vietnam *country* S.E. Asia 85 F7, 94 D4
Vignemale *mountain* France 54 E8
Vigo Spain 56 B3
Vijayawada India 93 E8
Vik Iceland 48 B3
Vikna *island* Norway 49 C6
Vila do Conde Portugal 56 B4
Vila Nova de Gaia Portugal 56 B4
Vila Real Portugal 56 B4
Vila Real de Santo António Portugal 56 B8
Vilhelmina Sweden 49 E6
Viljandi Estonia 64 C4
Villach Austria 61 H5
Villahermosa Mexico 35 G6
Villa María Argentina 43 E6
Villaputzu Italy 63 B9
Villarrica Paraguay 42 G3
Villarrobledo Spain 57 F6
Villavicencio Colombia 40 C2
Villeurbanne France 55 H5
Vilnius *country capital* Lithuania 47 F5, 65 C6
Vilyuy *river* Russian Federation 85 G3, 87 H4
Viña del Mar Chile 43 C6
Vinaròs Spain 57 H4
Vincent, Gulf St *gulf* South Australia, Australia 103 F7
Vindhya Range *mountain range* India 93 C6
Vinh Vietnam 94 D3
Vinnytsya Ukraine 65 D10
Vinson Massif *mountain* Antarctica 21 B3
Virginia *state* U.S. 33 F8
Virginia Beach Virginia, U.S. 33 H9
Virgin Islands *U.S. dependent territory* E. West Indies 37 I5
Virovitica Croatia 68 D2
Vis *island* Croatia 68 C4
Visakhapatnam India 93 E8
Visby Sweden 49 E11
Viscount Melville Sound *strait* Northwest Territories/Nunavut, Canada 24 D3
Viseu Portugal 56 B4
Visoko Bosnia & Herzegovina 68 D3
Vistula *river* Poland 47 E5, 66 E4, 67 G7
Viterbo Italy 63 D6
Viti Levu *island* Fiji 101 F6
Vitim *river* Russian Federation 87 H6
Vitória Brazil 41 I7
Vitória da Conquista Brazil 41 I6
Vitoria-Gasteiz Spain 57 F2
Vitsyebsk Belarus 47 G4, 65 E6
Vittangi Sweden 48 F4
Vittoria Italy 63 F12
Vjose *river* Greece 69 F6
Vlaardingen Netherlands 53 D6
Vladikavkaz Russian Federation 86 A6
Vladimir Russian Federation 86 B4
Vladivostok Russian Federation 85 H5, 87 J7
Vlieland *island* West Frisian Islands 52 E2
Vlissingen Netherlands 53 C7
Vlore Albania 68 E6
Vltava *river* Czech Republic 67 B7
Vocklabruck Austria 61 H3
Voghera Italy 62 B3
Voinjama Liberia 76 D7
Vojvodina *cultural region* Serbia & Montenegro 68 E2
Volga *river* Russian Federation 47 G4, 86 B5
Volgograd Russian Federation 47 I5, 86 B5
Völkermarkt Austria 61 I5
Vologda Russian Federation 86 C4
Volos Greece 69 F6
Volta, Lake *lake* Ghana 71 C6, 77 G7
Volyn-Podolian Upland *hill range* Ukraine 65 D9
Vorkuta Russian Federation 86 D4
Voronezh Russian Federation 47 H5, 86 B4
Voru Estonia 64 D4
Vosges *mountain range* France 55 I3
Voss Norway 49 A8
Voznesensk Ukraine 65 E11
Vranje Serbia & Montenegro 69 F4
Vratsa Bulgaria 69 G4
Vrbas Serbia & Montenegro 68 E2
Vryburg South Africa 80 D7
Vukovar Croatia 68 D3

W

Waal *river* Netherlands 53 E6
Waalwijk Netherlands 53 E7
Wabash *river* N. U.S. 32 C7
Waco Texas, U.S. 30 E5
Waddan Libya 73 I5
Waddenzee *sea* Netherlands 52 E2
Waddington, Mount *mountain* British Columbia, Canada 24 B7
Wadi Halfa Sudan 75 C5
Wad Medani Sudan 75 D8
Wagga Wagga New South Wales, Australia 103 I7
Wagin Western Australia, Australia 102 C7
Wah Pakistan 91 G9
Waiau *river* New Zealand 105 B12
Waidhofen an der Ybbs Austria 61 I3
Waigeo *island* Indonesia 95 I7
Waikato *river* New Zealand 104 G4
Waikerie South Australia, Australia 103 G7
Waimangaroa New Zealand 105 D8
Waiouru New Zealand 105 G6
Waipara New Zealand 105 E9
Waipu New Zealand 104 F2
Waipukurau New Zealand 105 H6
Wairoa New Zealand 105 H5
Waitakere New Zealand 104 F3
Wakasa-wan *bay* Japan 99 F6
Wakatipu, Lake *lake* New Zealand 105 B11
Wakayama Japan 99 F7
Wake Island *U.S. dependent territory* S.W. Pacific Ocean 101 E2
Wakkanai Japan 99 I1
Walachia *cultural region* Romania 69 G3
Walbrzych Poland 67 D6
Wales *national region* United Kingdom 51 E10
Walgett New South Wales, Australia 103 I6
Wallis & Futuna *French dependent territory* C. Pacific Ocean 101 F5
Walpole Western Australia, Australia 102 C7
Walvis Bay Namibia 71 E11, 80 B6
Walvis Ridge *undersea feature* S.E. Atlantic Ocean 45 G9
Wanaka New Zealand 105 C11
Wanaka, Lake *lake* New Zealand 105 B11
Wandel Sea *sea* Arctic Ocean 20 C4
Wanganui *river* New Zealand 105 G6
Wanganui New Zealand 105 G6
Wanxian China 97 G6
Warangal India 93 D8
Warburg Germany 59 D6
Warnemünde Germany 58 G3
Warrego *seasonal river* New South Wales/Queensland, Australia 103 H5
Warren Michigan, U.S. 32 E5
Warri Nigeria 77 I8
Warsaw *country capital* Poland 47 F5, 66 G5
Warta *river* Poland 66 D4, 67 F6
Warwick Queensland, Australia 103 J6
Washington *state* U.S. 26 C2
Washington, D.C. *country capital* District of Columbia, U.S. 23 G9, 33 G7
Washington, Mount *mountain* New Hampshire, U.S. 33 I4
Wash, The *bay* England, United Kingdom 51 H9
Waterbury Connecticut, U.S. 33 I6
Waterford Republic of Ireland 51 C10
Waterloo Iowa, U.S. 29 J5
Watertown New York, U.S. 33 H4
Watertown South Dakota, U.S. 29 H4
Watford England, United Kingdom 51 H11
Watsa Democratic Republic of the Congo 79 G6
Watson Lake Yukon Territory, Canada 24 B5
Watzmann *mountain* Germany 59 G12
Wau Sudan 75 C10
Wawa Ontario, Canada 25 G8
Weald, The *physical region* England, United Kingdom 51 H11
Weddell Plain *undersea feature* C. Southern Ocean 45 E12
Weddell Sea *sea* S.E. Southern Ocean 45 D13
Wedel Germany 58 E3
Weert Netherlands 53 G8
Wei He *river* China 97 G6
Weinan China 97 H6
Welkom South Africa 80 E7
Wellesley Islands *island group* Queensland, Australia 103 G3
Wellington *country capital* New Zealand 101 F8, 105 F7
Wellington, Isla *island* Chile 39 C12, 43 C11
Wellsford New Zealand 104 F3
Wels Austria 61 H3
Wenzhou China 97 J7
Werra *river* Germany 59 E8
Weser *river* Germany 58 C4
Wessel Islands *island group* Northern Territory, Australia 103 G1
West Cape *headland* New Zealand 105 A12
Western Australia *state* Australia 102 C5
Western Desert *desert* Egypt 74 B4
Western Dvina *river* W. Europe 47 F4, 65 D5
Western Ghats *mountain range* India 84 D7, 93 B7
Western Sahara *disputed region* Morocco 70 A3, 72 B6
Westerschelde *inlet* S. North Sea 53 C7
West Falkland *island* Falkland Islands 39 E13, 43 F12
West Frisian Islands *island group* Netherlands 52 E2
West Indies *island group* Caribbean Sea 23 G11, 36 E2, 45 C6
West Mariana Basin *undersea feature* W. Pacific Ocean 106 C4
West Palm Beach Florida, U.S. 31 J7
Westport New Zealand 105 D8
West Siberian Plain *physical region* Russian Federation 84 D3, 86 D4
West Virginia *state* U.S. 33 E7
Wetar *island* Indonesia 95 H9
Wetzlar Germany 59 C8
Wewak Papua New Guinea 100 C5
Wexford Republic of Ireland 51 D10
Weymouth England, United Kingdom 51 F12
Whakatane New Zealand 104 H4
Whangarei New Zealand 104 F2
Wharton Basin *undersea feature* E. Indian Ocean 83 G5
Wheatland Wyoming, U.S. 28 E5
Wheeler Peak *mountain* New Mexico, U.S. 30 B3
Whitehorse Yukon Territory, Canada 24 B4
White Mountains *mountain range* Maine/New Hampshire, U.S. 33 I4
White Nile *river* Sudan 71 G6, 75 D8
White Sea *sea* Russian Federation 20 D5, 47 G2, 86 C3
White Volta *river* Burkina Faso, Ghana 77 G7
Whitney, Mount *mountain* California, U.S. 23 C8, 27 D9
Whyalla South Australia, Australia 103 G7
Wichita Kansas, U.S. 29 H8
Wichita Falls Texas, U.S. 30 D4
Wick Scotland, United Kingdom 50 F3
Wicklow Mountains *mountain range* Republic of Ireland 51 D9
Wielkopolska *cultural region* Poland 66 E4
Wiener Neustadt Austria 61 J3
Wiesbaden Germany 59 C8
Wight, Isle of *island* England, United Kingdom 51 G12
Wilcannia New South Wales, Australia 103 H6
Wildon Switzerland 61 J5
Wildspitze *mountain* Austria 61 E5
Wilhelmshaven Germany 58 C3
Wilkes Land *physical region* Antarctica 21 D4
Willemstad Netherlands Antilles 37 G8
Willhelm II Land *physical region* Antarctica 21 E3
Williston North Dakota, U.S. 29 E2
Willmar Minnesota, U.S. 29 H4
Wilmington Delaware, U.S. 33 H7
Wilmington North Carolina, U.S. 31 K4
Wilson North Carolina, U.S. 31 J3
Wilson, Mount *mountain* Colorado, U.S. 28 C7
Wiluna Western Australia, Australia 102 C5
Windhoek *country capital* Namibia 71 E11, 80 B6
Windsor Ontario, Canada 25 G9
Windward Islands *island group*